WITHDRAWN
UTSA LIBRARIES

Children Who Fail at School But Succeed at Life

A Norton Professional Book

CHILDREN WHO FAIL AT SCHOOL BUT SUCCEED AT LIFE

Lessons from Lives Well-Lived

MARK KATZ

W.W. Norton & Company
New York • London
Independent Publishers Since 1923

Copyright © 2016 by Mark Katz

Some of the programs described in the book include material from the author's promising practices column, which appears in *Attention* magazine, a publication of CHADD (Children and Adults With Attention Deficit Disorder). The author wishes to personally thank *Attention* magazine for its permission to use this material.

Figure 6.1: Reprinted with permission from: *Best Behavior: Building Positive Behavior Supports in School.* Copyright 2008 by Voyager Sopris Learning, 17855 Dallas Parkway, Suite 400, Dallas, TX 75287. For more on this and other products published by Voyager Sopris Learning, please call 800.547.6747 or visit their website at: www.voyagersopris.com.

Figure 6.2: Reprinted with permission from: *RTI and Behavior: A Guide to Integrating Behavioral and Academic Supports.* Copyright 2008 by LRP Publications, 360 Hiatt Drive, Palm Beach Gardens, FL 33418. All rights reserved. For more information on this or other products published by LRP Publications, please call 1-800-341-7874 or visit our website at: www.shoplrp.com.

All rights reserved
Printed in the United States of America
First Edition

For information about permission to reproduce selections from this book, write to Permissions, W. W. Norton & Company, Inc., 500 Fifth Avenue, New York, NY 10110

For information about special discounts for bulk purchases, please contact W. W. Norton Special Sales at specialsales@wwnorton.com or 800-233-4830

Manufacturing by Maple Press
Production manager: Christine Critelli

ISBN: 978-0-393-71141-7

W. W. Norton & Company, Inc., 500 Fifth Avenue, New York, N.Y. 10110
www.wwnorton.com

W. W. Norton & Company Ltd.,
Castle House, 75/76 Wells Street, London W1T 3QT

1 2 3 4 5 6 7 8 9 0

Library
University of Texas
at San Antonio

To Terri

CONTENTS

Contents

PREFACE

Why is it that some children who fail at school still manage to succeed at life decades later? Do they grow stronger and more resilient as they age? Are they late bloomers who finally bloom? Have they finally resolved underlying emotional or other psychological conflicts? Certainly, in some instances each or all of these reasons apply. But as you are about to learn, some children who fail at school yet succeed at life are also some of the most resilient and resourceful people you'll ever have the pleasure of meeting. And they include, though by no means are limited to, children with attention-deficit hyperactivity disorder (ADHD), children with executive function challenges, children with learning disabilities, children whose differences arise as a result of exposure to trauma, and even children affected by all of these. What's more, they also include children blessed with extremely loving parents, excellent and caring teachers, and access to some of the most experienced health care professionals in their community, all of whom may have exhausted every available resource they know of to help turn these children's lives around.

What, then, could cause otherwise resilient and resourceful children—including those showing various learning and behavioral differences—to fail year after year in school then rebound decades later? In some instances, the answer may well lie in five entirely understandable yet erroneous perceptions regarding the mysterious, troublesome, and often paradoxical patterns of learning and behavior they exhibited throughout their school lives, perceptions on which loving parents and caring teachers based equally understandable interventions that led to disappointing outcomes.

Erroneous Perception #1: That anyone capable of performing exceptionally well on intellectual, creative, or artistic tasks that others find difficult is necessarily capable of performing equally well or better on academic or behavioral tasks that others find easy. It's simply a matter of trying harder, logically speaking.

Erroneous Perception #2: That anyone who knows what they're supposed to do in a given situation can be expected to consistently, predictably, and independently do what they know 100 percent of the time. It's all a matter of willpower, logically speaking.

Erroneous Perception #3: That the true measure of human intelligence is school performance. Those that are able to achieve good grades in school therefore are very smart, and those unable to achieve good grades are not, logically speaking.

Erroneous Perception #4: That resilient people, children included, think and act the same way in places they find threatening and dangerous as they do in places they find warm and friendly. Contextual influences, in other words, count for very little in understanding how we successfully rise above or endure in the face of adversity.

Erroneous Perception #5: Believing as we do in erroneous perception #4, it follows that resilience and success must be one and the same. Those who succeed at school are resilient. Those who fail at school are not, logically speaking.

But if human misunderstanding can prolong a difficult past, those who fail at school yet succeed at life also teach us that human understanding can help us rise above one, human understanding that is, of our context-sensitive ways. With time, we now know that many will find or create social contexts where they feel valued for their contribution. Many will learn to see past and present challenges in a new and more hopeful context, aided in large part by the ability to reframe personal limitations and vulnerabilities within the context of strengths and talents. Many of their loved ones will learn to see these challenges in a new and more hopeful context as well, having overcome previous contextual blind spots. Many will come to realize that people can be smart in many different ways that cannot be measured by how we did in school, a realization based on their ability to see intelligence in context. And many will come to believe that our greatest strength lies between rather than within us—a belief they owe to the ability to see their most valued relationships in a new and different context. As it turns out, when it comes to rising above a difficult past, context counts more than we realize.

So far we have not considered children who fail at school but succeed at life as an important resource for helping others avoid the years of school failure they endured decades ago. Instead, we've focused on the strengths and qualities of those who do well in school in an effort to help those who fail to be more like them. Although this may have been a remedy for some, it hasn't worked for others. In some cases, it's even made matters worse. Children who fail at school but succeed at life provide us new remedies, ones that can potentially prevent serious learning, behavioral, emotional, and later life medical problems; reduce juvenile crime, school dropout, and substance abuse; increase productivity at work and in life; and improve our closest and most important personal and professional relationships.

A word of caution: We know now that five entirely understandable yet erroneous perceptions in the past often led us to entirely understandable yet ineffective interventions, which in turn have led to disappointing results. Before delving into new remedies, therefore, we're learning that it's best to abandon the five erroneous perceptions and be guided instead by five new, more empirically validated ones.

1. It's indeed possible that some people can be capable of doing difficult things easily yet find easy things difficult for reasons that can have nothing to do with laziness or moral character.

Although it's always important to try one's best, the key to success in these simpler areas may not come down to trying harder but to trying differently.

2. It's entirely possible for someone to know what to do yet have difficulty consistently, predictably, and independently doing what they know, in part because they call into play different skills (Barkley, 2010a, b; Goldstein, 2001). Improving the ability to do what one knows, therefore, may require learning an entirely new set of strategies, compensatory or otherwise, related specifically to these functions.

3. There are many different ways of being smart, some of which can't be measured by school performance.

4. Resilient people, school-age children included, sometimes think and act differently in places they find threatening and dangerous as opposed to places they find warm and friendly, particularly when those threatening and dangerous places feel stigmatizing, inescapable, and beyond their ability to control or influence. To really appreciate human resilience, one needs to also appreciate contextual influences, the visible and invisible experiences affecting our lives.

5. These contextual influences can determine whether we endure in the face of adversity or are stretched to our limits of emotional endurance, which helps explain why some of the most resilient people may struggle significantly just to get through a typical day.

To capture the unspoken strength and courage these individuals display, we refer to them in the chapters that follow as portraits of human resilience—in context.

WHY WRITE A BOOK ABOUT CHILDREN WHO FAIL AT SCHOOL BUT SUCCEED AT LIFE?

It's very important that parents of children who are failing at school know that success at life is indeed possible. It's also very important that others know this: teachers and others in the school community, health care providers working with the child and family, and educational and mental health staff who treat these children in intensive treatment programs. Furthermore, it's important that those who continue to struggle into their adult years know this, and the same goes for their spouses, partners, and other loved ones. Most important perhaps, the struggling child needs to know this. Knowing that a number of children who fail at school will eventually succeed at life keeps hope alive. What's more, knowing why they may have failed can help us prevent other children with similar learning and behavioral differences from suffering the same fate. I truly believe this, and many of you will too after reading this book.

It's a pretty bold statement to say that people who fail at school but succeed at life may hold the key to helping us learn how to keep a significant number of children from failing at school in the first place. Actually, that may be an understatement. I believe that in some instances, they also hold the key to helping adults who have not been as fortunate lead equally successful lives as well.

Bold statements, I know. In the chapters that follow, I'll explain how I arrived at these and other conclusions, along with empirical evidence to support them. I begin with a brief introduction. It includes background information that helps explain how I came to write a book about children who fail at school but succeed at life. It also includes an overview of the book, followed by a brief discussion of how I arrived at the title.

To date, not much has been written about children who fail at school but succeed at life. I believe the reason is because we've been focusing on the wrong question. I'll explain in my following introductory remarks.

I hope you enjoy the book.

INTRODUCTION

WHY DO PEOPLE KEEP ASKING
THE WRONG QUESTION?

Two days after the 110-story Twin Towers were destroyed on September 11, 2001, an architectural engineer from the firm that designed them was interviewed on a nationally televised morning news program. The interviewer's first question was one the engineer had been asked in a number of similar interviews over the previous two days, and a question that apparently had been on the minds of many Americans. The question was, "Could the architects have done anything differently to prevent the Twin Towers from collapsing?"

The engineer paused for a moment. He then told the interviewer and the national TV audience about all of the e-mails he had been receiving from his colleagues around the country—other architectural engineers—all of whom were wondering the same thing: Why do people keep asking the wrong question? According to these engineers, the question shouldn't be "Why did the buildings collapse?" The question should be "How did they remain standing?," after being penetrated by jumbo jets going at 500 miles an hour, culminating in massive fires approaching 2000°F! After all, they reasoned, steel begins to melt at 1500°F. How in the world, they wondered, did these structures remain standing as long as they did?

Many Americans felt that if we could only build skyscrapers stronger, then maybe, in the event of another such attack, they wouldn't collapse like the World Trade Center towers did. What so many of us couldn't see at the time was that buildings don't come any stronger than the Twin Towers.

The reason this story fascinated me was because since the publication of my book, *On Playing a Poor Hand Well* (Katz, 1997), I've also been wondering about whether we've been asking the wrong question, not about buildings; but about people, particularly people who succumb to adversity. In that book, I explored two questions in depth. First, why is it that so many people who were exposed to multiple risks and adversities during their childhood years never developed the problems many would have anticipated and were eventually able to go on to lead meaningful and productive lives? Second, why is it that so many people who succumbed to multiple risks and adversities during their childhood years—struggling with different kinds of behavioral, learning, and life adjustment problems as a result—manage to stage a complete turnabout years later, and eventually also go on to lead meaningful and productive lives?

For years now, researchers, educators, policy makers, and others have shown far more interest in the first question than in the second, and, as a result, correspondingly far greater interest in individuals in the first group—the group of individuals who, as children, "beat the odds." They've come to be known in books, journal articles, news reports, and other publications as "resilient" children—children who, despite growing up under adverse conditions, did not develop serious emotional and behavioral problems as a result, and who went on to lead successful lives. Our strong interest in their personal lives and earlier childhood achievements should come as no surprise. Many now believe that these resilient people provide important clues about what it takes to withstand the impact of adverse childhood conditions. And by better understanding the important sources of resilience these individuals demonstrated in their younger years, many believe we could then incorporate similar sources of resilience into the lives of those less fortunate—those exposed to adverse childhood experiences who succumb. In other words, maybe those who beat the odds can teach others how it's done. Maybe. But maybe not.

Is it possible that some individuals who succumbed to early adversity were every bit as resilient as those who endured? Might some have been even more resilient? And is it possible that those who succumbed but then rebounded decades later might have done so for reasons having less to do with resilience than we might think? Up to this point, it's hard to know, because we've been asking the wrong question. The far more important question, the one I believe we should be asking is the second one.

Why, then, do so many people who succumb to childhood risks and adversities—struggling for years with learning, behavioral, emotional, or life adjustment problems—eventually rebound years later, and carve out meaningful and productive lives for themselves? That's the question I've been exploring for the last several years. For answers, I've turned to a group of people who, up until recently, have been largely ignored. They're children who fail at school but succeed at life decades later. In exploring their lives, I've been focusing on three questions in particular: (1) Why did they fail? (2) How did they succeed? (3) What can we learn?

OVERVIEW OF THE BOOK

The book is divided into two parts. Part I explores answers to the first two questions above. Part II explores answers to question three.

Part I: Lessons on Lives Well-Lived

As readers will learn in Part I, for at least some individuals who failed at school but succeed at life, the years of school failure they experienced as well as the various learning, behavioral, emotional, and/or life adjustment problems they exhibited as children, teenagers, and in some instances adults may have stemmed less from a lack of resilience and more as a result of our misunderstanding of the sometimes paradoxically uneven ways they responded to our day-to-day requests and their day-to-day responsibilities. If researchers and other experts in the field are accurate in how they currently view the causes and consequences of their paradoxically uneven ways, we begin to see why the countless hours that family members, teachers, and others spent trying to help turn their troubled childhoods around never yielded the outcomes that were hoped for. It actually wouldn't be until years later that these children, now grown adults, would enjoy access to experiences that eventually allowed them to carve out successful lives, experiences that were made possible by a range of contextual influences unavailable to them decades earlier.

Part II: What Can Be

Today, there's a great deal of interest in the study of human resilience. This has led to an exponential increase in the number of programs designed to foster it. And it seems that many of these programs draw their lessons in resilience from people who beat the odds, people with a track record for productivity and success, even in the face of significant challenge or adversity. At first glance, it makes a lot of sense. If we want people to be more productive—from school-age children to adults in the workplace—we should study how these resilient, successful, and productive people do things, and then teach these things to everyone else. Study the resilient qualities and character traits of good students, for example, or the successful habits of top employees at work. Then, when we figure out how these really productive people think, learn, and act, teach other people to do the same. That way, children with failing grades can start achieving good grades, and unproductive workers can then become productive. It sounds plausible. And for some people, maybe this formula works. But for a lot of others it hasn't, particularly those who were already resilient to begin with.

What if we began drawing more of our lessons on human resilience not from the lives of those who beat the odds but from those who succumbed to risk and adversity—children who endured years of school failure, for example—then rebounded years later? As we'll see in Part II, we may find ourselves coming away with a deeper appreciation of human resilience. Among other things, we'll realize that resilience is not always a matter of overcoming adversity. Sometimes it's learning how to live a meaningful and productive life in spite of it. It turns out that some of the most resilient people have to work very hard just to get through a normal day.

We'll also come away with new and different ideas about how to prevent serious learning, behavioral, emotional, and later life medical problems; how to reduce juvenile crime; how to improve children's emotional self-regulation and self-control skills; how to prevent child maltreatment; and how to improve the quality of our adult lives, including ways to repair and strengthen our closest personal and professional relationships.

To Learn More

On several occasions throughout the book, readers will be directed to the book's web page to learn more about a particular topic of discussion. The web page can be accessed by going to http://www.learningdevelopmentservices.com and then clicking the icon for *Children Who Fail at School But Succeed at Life.*

Visitors to the web page can also learn more about the Resilience through the Lifespan Project. (Instructions are provided to those who wish to participate.) Over the past several years, project participants have had much to say about the five erroneous perceptions discussed already. Many have corroborated the impact these perceptions have had on their lives. Some find that they continue to affect their lives today. Until recently, some still believed these perceptions to be accurate. Many have been helped by knowing they're erroneous.

During the course of this book, readers will be introduced to five individuals, alternately referred to as "portraits of resilience—in context." I've created them as a way to convey, in more personal terms, empirical findings and professional observations from experts encompassing diverse fields of study, including (but not limited to) the study of risk and resilience through the life span, studies on the effects of prolonged stress exposure, and studies from fields such as clinical psychology, social psychology, cognitive neuroscience, and education. I draw as well from my own personal and professional experiences, having spent many years working with and getting to know a significant number of individuals who today enjoy successful lives, despite having succumbed to a range of adverse experiences during their childhood years. Brief background sketches are presented here. The five portraits of resilience speak here on behalf of many others.

> Carl, a 48-year-old small business owner in Southern California. Carl's learning differences led to years of school failure, but these same differences helped catapult him to heights as an adult he never dreamed he would reach.

Javier, a 29-year-old social worker at a small mental health center in Northern California who lived in a number of different foster homes, each new one requiring that he transfer to a new school. The many moves, transitions, and disruptions clearly took their toll on Javier, psychologically, behaviorally, and academically.

Linda, a 35-year-old successful college art instructor whose bouts of clinical depression during her teenage years were believed to be the cause of her struggles in school. Looking back, Linda believes her struggles in school actually caused her clinical depression.

Pam, a 55-year-old mother, grandmother, wife, nurse practitioner, and advocate for those whose lives have been affected by interpersonal violence, including bullying. Unlike many of the other portraits, Pam actually did well in school up until seventh grade, when her life took an unexpected turn for the worse. Two classmates began tormenting her almost daily, under the command of a third classmate, a very popular student who seemed intent on making Pam's life miserable. Pam seriously considered taking her life and wonders whether she would have, had her mother not transferred her to another school.

Bill, a happily married 52-year-old small business owner in San Diego and a "late bloomer" (at least that's what his teachers thought many years ago). As it turned out, Bill never bloomed. After being held back a grade for the second time in three years, he eventually quit going to school. Bill's story also illustrates that sometimes it takes only a single erroneous perception to transform a resilient six-year-old child into a demoralized young adult.

I spend the first three chapters of the book focusing exclusively on Carl's story.

INTENDED AUDIENCES

In arriving at the conclusions and recommendations I share in this book, I drew heavily on the wisdom of many different people from different backgrounds. Some spoke from personal experience, some from professional experience, and others from both perspectives. Despite their diverse backgrounds and varying perspectives, each is actively seeking new ways of helping those with learning, behavioral, and other differences enjoy more rewarding lives. Collectively, they represent the book's intended audiences. These audiences are:

1. Parents of struggling school-age children, including children with ADHD, executive function challenges, and learning disabilities, as well as those suffering the psychological and physiological effects of exposure to prolonged traumatic stress.

2. Teachers, school administrators, resource specialists, school counselors, school psychologists, school nurses, and other members of the education community involved in identifying specific areas of challenge among students experiencing learning, behavioral, emotional, and/or social difficulties and in providing interventions, supports, and accommodations to address these challenges.

3. Health care professionals, including pediatricians and mental health practitioners, who treat conditions that include though are not limited to ADHD, executive function challenges, learning disabilities, and the psychological and physiological effects of exposure to traumatic stress.

4. Educational, mental health, and child care staff working in intensive child and adolescent mental health treatment settings, including day treatment and residential treatment programs.

5. Adults who continue to struggle with attentional, executive function, and/or learning challenges or with persisting psychological and physiological symptoms associated with early exposure to traumatic life events. Neurodevelopmental challenges such as ADHD and learning disabilities can persist well beyond childhood for many. In some cases, they can affect individuals for their entire lives. So can the psychological and physiological effects of early exposure to trauma. This book speaks to the benefits that can be derived when individuals learn to see their persisting challenges in a new light.

6. Spouses and partners of adults with ADHD, executive function challenges, learning disabilities, or challenges stemming from earlier exposure to trauma. The book also speaks to how mar-

riages and significant personal relationships can grow stronger when a spouse or partner's challenges are understood in a new light.

7. Professionals and policy makers with an interest in the ACE (Adverse Childhood Experience) Study, considered by some to be one of the most significant studies to date in the field of health care. ACE Study findings showed a link between exposure to categories of adverse childhood experiences and later life health and mental health problems. *Children Who Fail at School But Succeed at Life* explores how experiences can be woven in and around a school day to neutralize the effects of exposure to multiple adverse experiences, thus decreasing the likelihood of later health and mental health problems.

8. Organizations nationwide working to prevent child abuse and neglect who have adopted the Strengthening Families five protective factor model. Unlike previous approaches to prevention that focused on identifying family risks and deficits, this new model, developed by the Center for the Study of Social Policy in Washington, D.C., focuses on five protective factors, each of which promotes family strengths and family resilience in the face of adversity. The factors have been linked through research to reduced incidents of child abuse and neglect. An increasing number of states are embracing the model.

9. Health care professionals and educators with particular interest in the field of resilience and in strengths-based interventions.

10. Instructors of undergraduate and graduate level courses in psychology, social work, and education, including special education.

ABOUT THE TITLE

Success in life can mean different things to different people. Some equate it with wealth. Others equate it with power. Others equate it with influence. Success in life is relative, defined in part by one's values and other personal, situational, and cultural influences. In the chapters that follow, "success" refers neither to wealth, power, nor influence. Rather, it refers to one's personal perception of their life as meaningful and productive—in short, a perception of a life well-lived.

A number of individuals who view their lives as meaningful

and productive attribute their current quality of life partly to their previous school experiences. Others feel that success came in spite of their school experiences. Of those in this second group, the terms "fail," "failing," or "failure" appear often in their personal narratives of life at school as they remember it. These narratives, in turn, reveal that failure in school can also mean different things to different people. To many, it means failing grades, being retained, or dropping out. To others, it means feeling rejected, shunned, or ridiculed. And to others, it means feeling unworthy, unintelligent, or hopeless about one's future. In the chapters that follow, failure at school encompasses any or all of the above.

Children Who Struggle at School But Succeed at Life was considered at one point as a possible title but quickly dismissed, since the title casts the word "struggle" in a negative light. Struggle is a key ingredient in the lives of those who grow stronger in the face of challenging situations. To struggle and persevere in the face of adversity is a strength to be celebrated, not a weakness to overcome. What's more, a number of people who currently enjoy successful lives despite exposure to adverse childhood experiences continue to struggle in some of the same areas they struggled in decades ago.

This brings us to the matter of human resilience. Resilience appears to be a depletable resource. It turns out that there are limits to emotional endurance for even the most resilient among us. We sometimes fail to appreciate this, in part the result of our contextual blind spots. It's these contextual blind spots—ones we all experience from time to time—that can prevent us from truly appreciating the unique challenges and hardships some individuals must contend with every day. These are the same individuals who, to the outside world, may not be perceived as successful at life. Yet once we gain a greater understanding of their life circumstances, we may come to see them as remarkably resilient. In at least some cases, the same can be said for children who "fail at school."

~

In the chapters that follow, I share why I believe that some children who fail at school eventually succeed decades later at life. I also share how lessons from these lives well-lived can benefit those who still struggle the way they did years ago. I share this information knowing that there are many other reasons some children fail at school, many other ways they eventually succeed at life, and many other things we can learn from their experiences. When it comes to better understanding the lives of children who fail at school but succeed at life, the information here just scratches the surface.

Children Who

Fail at School

But Succeed

at Life

PART I

Lessons from Lives Well-Lived

Question: What could possibly transform a resilient six-year-old child, blessed with loving parents, caring teachers, and access to excellent health care professionals, into a demoralized young adult? As we'll see in Chapter 1, in some cases the answer may lie in five entirely understandable yet erroneous perceptions regarding that child's paradoxically uneven learning and behavioral profile, perceptions that can sometimes lead to equally understandable yet ineffective remedies resulting in disappointing results.

Certainly there are many inaccurate perceptions that can arise when trying to make logical sense of uneven learning and behavioral profiles. But the five I discuss in Chapter 1 seem to carry particularly serious consequences. I explain why this is so in Chapter 2.

In Chapters 1 and 2, I explore reasons an otherwise resilient school-age child failed at school. In Chapter 3, I revisit the child decades later and show how he was eventually able to succeed at life. Readers are introduced to contextual influences that changed the odds.

It was a wise person who once said, "A man with one watch always knows what time it is, but a man with two is never really sure." A lot of people exhibit uneven learning, behavioral, and/or emotional profiles, and for different reasons. Despite the different underlying causes, however, the same five erroneous perceptions can arise. This, in turn, can have the same demoralizing effects on otherwise resilient school-age children. In Chapter 4, readers are introduced to four very different people, who each struggled mightily in school for different reasons. All are currently leading successful lives, thanks largely to similar contextual influences. Their life experiences provide new insights into these challenges, new ways to succeed in spite of them, and a very good reason to believe that better days lie ahead for those who struggle much like they did years ago.

Chapter 1

THE CHILDHOOD YEARS:
WHY DO THEY FAIL?

*What is madness? To have erroneous perceptions
and to reason correctly from them.*

—Voltaire

Imagine for a moment being six years old again. Also imagine being blessed in these three special ways. First, you're a picture of perfect health. You're happy, hopeful, and full of life. Second, you've got the most loving family any child could ever want. Third, you love school and absolutely adore your teacher, who, by the way, absolutely adores you, too. A happy, healthy, resilient child, surrounded at home by loving family members and at school by a kind and compassionate teacher. Could it get any better? You're truly blessed. Then one day you notice a problem at school. Virtually all of your classmates are having a much easier time than you are in doing the things your teacher asks. So you try harder, but things don't seem to be improving. In fact, they're getting worse. Months go by. You fall further and further behind your classmates, and nothing you do seems to be working. Months turn into years. Feeling discouraged, you stop trying your best. You begin to panic at the slightest sign of failure. Eventually, you lose all hope of being successful years down the road. Keep in mind, you're the same child, older but still blessed in the same ways. You're still healthy, at least physically if not emotionally. Your family is as concerned about you as they ever were, and so are your teachers.

What could so alter the life course of a healthy, resilient child, growing up in a loving home, attending schools taught by great teachers? The culprit, at least in some cases, may be five entirely understandable yet erroneous perceptions regarding these mysterious, troublesome, and often paradoxical patterns of learning and behavior you're evidencing, erroneous perceptions on which we may base equally understandable interventions leading to inevitably disappointing outcomes.

- Erroneous Perception #1: That anyone capable of performing exceptionally well on intellectual, creative, or artistic tasks that others find difficult is necessarily capable of performing equally well or better on academic or behavioral tasks that most others find easy. It's all simply a matter of trying harder, logically speaking.
- Erroneous Perception #2: That anyone who knows what they're supposed to do in a given situation can be expected to consistently, predictably, and independently do what they know 100 percent of the time. It's all about willpower, logically speaking.
- Erroneous Perception #3: That the true measure of human intelligence is school performance. Those that are able to achieve good grades in school, therefore, are very smart, and those unable to achieve good grades are not, logically speaking.
- Erroneous Perception #4: That resilient people, school-age children included, think and act the same way in places they find threatening and dangerous as they do in places they find warm and friendly. Contextual influences count very little in understanding how we successfully rise above or endure in the face of adversity.
- Erroneous Perception #5: Believing as we do in erroneous perception #4, it follows that resilience and success must be one and the same. Those who succeed at school are resilient. Those who fail at school are not, logically speaking.

"TO HAVE ERRONEOUS PERCEPTIONS AND TO REASON CORRECTLY FROM THEM"

> **Erroneous Perception #1:** Anyone capable of performing exceptionally well on intellectual, creative, or artistic tasks that most others find difficult, is necessarily capable of performing equally well or better on academic or behavioral tasks that most others find easy. It's all simply a matter of trying harder, logically speaking.

Despite failing at school, Carl is succeeding at life. He has a loving wife, is the father of two healthy and happy grown children, and enjoys the freedom and independence that comes with owning his own website design and Internet marketing business. Life is going well, he says, and has been going well for some time now. But, says Carl, "Life was very difficult growing up."

As best as I can remember, all of my problems at school began in the fourth grade, right after my father lost his job. He changed. He started drinking. When he was sober he was kind and wonderful, a lot of fun to be around. He really cared about us, and he showed it. But when he was drunk he was the nastiest person you ever met. He drank a lot back then, and when he did, he was completely out of control. It scared me to death. He'd scream at me, sometimes even beat me, over the littlest mistakes. Then when he was sober, he'd apologize. I watched my younger brother Steven go through the same thing. The worst of it was knowing what my mother went through. There were nights when me and Steven couldn't sleep, worrying if she was okay or not. When my dad was sober, he was a joy to be around. When he was drunk, he was a monster. My school problems started around the fourth grade, around the time my dad lost his job and started drinking.

Several years have passed since Carl conveyed these thoughts to me. He now realizes that he was right about one thing but wrong about another. His grades did decline significantly in fourth grade, the same year his father lost his job, began drinking, and started acting violently and abusively. But problems at school actually began many years before then. As far back as first grade, in fact, his teacher had personally contacted his parents about her concerns, two of which were particularly worrisome to her. One had to do with problems Carl was having learning to read, the other with problems learning to behave. Regarding his reading problems, Carl came to realize decades later that his first-grade teacher had successfully identified early signs of what has been a lifelong reading disability, a condition that went undiagnosed and untreated during his years in school and continued to affect him through much of his adult life.

From early on in his educational history, Carl's teachers were impressed with his intellectual and creative strengths. But reading was always a struggle. As he is now well aware, it turns out that he's in good company. A number of people with similar reading disabilities also enjoy impressive strengths in areas that most of us would consider to be far more difficult than reading (Gardner, 1993, 1999; Sternberg, 1997). As was the case with Carl, however, their strengths lie in areas that are unrelated to the phonological, auditory analytic, visual memory, or other brain functions necessary to become proficient at reading. It's among the reasons people can sometimes be remarkably skilled at performing intellectual or creative tasks that others find difficult, yet struggle at tasks that others might find simple. As hard as Carl tried to learn to read, without proper help and understanding he would never read as well as most others his age. Unfortunately, virtually everyone believed the reason was that he wasn't trying hard enough—entirely logical, but entirely erroneous.

Reading disabilities come in different forms and in different degrees. Carl evidences features of a particularly common subtype referred to as auditory or dysphonetic dyslexia. Individuals who present with this subtype experience poor phonemic or phonological awareness. Specifically, they have difficulty detecting subtle differences in phonemes. This ability turns out to be an extremely critical function in learning to read and spell in the English language. During his years in school, Carl had great difficulty performing this function and to some degree still struggles with it today. A number of neuroscientists believe that phonological awareness problems may represent the core deficit for many people with dyslexia. Researchers Sally Shaywitz and Bennett Shaywitz (et al., 1998), a pediatric team from Yale University, discovered they can actually pinpoint disruptions in specific neural systems in the brains of persons with this core deficit. Researchers have also discovered that when dyslexic readers learn ways to read more fluently—when their phonological awareness skills improve, for example—they show a corresponding shift in the neural systems used for reading. Carl participated in an intensive reading remediation program as an adult and eventually strengthened the skills necessary to read more fluently. He's now using brain regions similar to those used by lifelong fluent readers.

Although developing better phonological awareness skills put him on the path to literacy, it was only one step in a long process. Carl aslo had to laern to vesaully remumbar the wey wrods louked, somthung yu probalbey are vury guod at wethuot ruelizeng it. Thyt's wy yu're abuel to raed theuse senteuncez puerfeiktly waell. To those who have difficulty remembering the visual configuration of words (remembering what words look like) as well as the contextual meaning of words (what words mean within the context in which they appear), the sentences may make little sense. To read fluently and comprehend what we read, we rely on several different skills, not just those allowing us to appreciate subtle differences in phonemes. Struggling readers can experience weaknesses in any or all of these skills. On his journey to become a fluent reader, Carl also had to become proficient in other skills, including those calling into play specific visual memory and other functions, simple skills for most but not for all.

Today, Carl is a successful small business owner, despite his poor school history. Studies show that a surprisingly large number of small business owners struggled in school, with many also experiencing reading disabilities. In a survey of 139 business owners, 35 percent identified themselves as dyslexic (Bowers, 2007). The study's author, Julie Logan, attributes their success to the "extraordinarily creative ways they've learned to maneuver around problems." In another study that explored the lives of 5,000 self-made British millionaires, researchers reported that a majority performed badly at school and continued to perform poorly on aptitude tests administered during their adult years (Dowell, 2003). Virgin Airlines founder and English billionaire Sir Richard Branson, perhaps one of the world's best-known reading-disabled adults, believes that being dyslexic has always allowed him to see the bigger picture. It also required that he get good at delegating, which, as we'll see, Carl eventually became very good at as well.

> **Erroneous Perception #2:** Anyone who knows what they're supposed to do in a given situation can be expected to consistently, predictably, and independently do what they know 100 percent of the time. It's all about willpower, logically speaking.

Carl possesses a range of very impressive intellectual and creative strengths. It's quite a paradox when you stop to think about it. From as far back as he can remember, he always excelled at things intellectually complex or at things requiring creative, "out-of-the-box" solutions, yet he always struggled when it came to tasks involving reading, a skill that for most of us was simpler to master. But as paradoxical as this seems, at least Carl's reading problem was predictable. You could see it whenever he was required to read anything more than a paragraph in length. From early on in his school history until completing an intensive reading remediation program, Carl never had a great reading day. Such is the general nature of reading disabilities. Such may not be the nature of some fairly common childhood behavioral difficulties. Carl's early school behavior problems are a great illustration of this.

CHILDREN WHO KNOW WHAT TO DO BUT HAVE DIFFICULTY CONSISTENTLY DOING WHAT THEY KNOW

Based on what we can glean from comments on report cards and progress reports, Carl's first-grade teacher painted a portrait of a six-year-old novelty seeker, a child in constant motion, in and out of his chair, twirling his pencil, never sitting still for very long, and very easily bored. A child who also, according to his teacher, didn't follow instructions or do what he was told. His behavior didn't seem malicious, just inexplicable. After all, Carl knew what to do. He just had problems doing it. His second- and third-grade teachers noticed these same problems. In fourth grade, when the amount of homework began to increase, Carl sometimes worked for hours to complete assignments most other children could complete in minutes. Worse, he often forgot to turn them in the next morning.

In those early grade school years, Carl can recall his teachers reminding him constantly about how he was supposed to behave: "Sit still," "keep quiet," "pay attention," "stop rocking in your chair," "follow my instructions," "stop talking to your neighbor," "turn in your work," "use your planner," on and on. They reminded him day after day, year after year. In return, Carl always obliged, but only for a while. No matter how many reminders or reprimands were given, no matter how many negative consequences or time-outs he received, Carl seemed unable to control himself in class the way other children did, despite knowing what was expected of him and despite being able to do what was expected of him when asked. Certainly this was confusing to his teachers. On occasion, it also made them angry. "I've seen him control himself when he wants to." "He needs to make better choices." "He needs to care more." "If he would just stay focused!" "He's wasting my time and the time I could be spending with other children."

Carl didn't start failing until fourth grade. But when you look at his teachers' comments before then, failure in the fourth grade seemed almost inevitable. As Carl eventually realized, events occurring at home, though traumatic in nature, may have exacerbated problems at school, but they didn't cause them.

With the benefit of hindsight, we now know that the behavioral characteristics Carl's teachers found so frustrating were the result of challenges he experienced in areas associated with executive functioning. He actually struggled with executive function challenges throughout his school years and beyond. It wasn't until later in life that he finally learned how to effectively navigate around them.

Executive function: what is it? Why is it important? Why were Carl's executive function challenges the source of so much contusion and misunderstanding?

Executive function is an umbrella term encompassing a family of mental processes we call on throughout the day to reach our goals, solve problems, and get along with others. It serves a managerial role, ensuring that these mental processes work in harmony (Katz, 2014b). Although experts in the field have not yet arrived at universal consensus on the number of mental processes under the executive function umbrella, many agree that they include self-control, emotional self-regulation, organization, time management, planning, mental flexibility, the ability to sustain motivation, self-monitoring, and working memory (or the ability to keep information in mind long enough to reach a goal or solve a problem). Though we often see these mental processes discussed separately, it's important to remember that they work in harmony. In fact, our ability to successfully coordinate these processes is what allows us to plan, organize, manage, and emotionally regulate our lives. Experts in the field have used different metaphors to describe executive function and its role in coordinating a variety of mental processes. Among the more common metaphors: our brain's orchestra conductor, air traffic control system, and chief executive officer.

Why is executive function important? We rely on executive function skills to help us start things, finish things, organize and plan things, and stay focused. We call on them when having to focus our attention and sustain that focus on things we're attending to. We rely on them to move forward on a goal and help us organize and prioritize our efforts in pursuit of that goal. We call on them to manage frustration, control emotions, and sustain motivation. And we call on them to hold information in mind while working toward a goal without getting derailed.

EXECUTIVE FUNCTION CHALLENGES:
FIVE REASONS LEARNING AND BEHAVIORAL
PROFILES APPEAR SO CONFUSING

Back to our earlier question: why were Carl's executive function challenges the source of so much confusion and misunderstanding? There were at least five reasons. First and foremost, children with executive function challenges (as well as adults) can know what to do yet be inconsistent and unpredictable in doing what they know (Barkley, 2010a, b; Goldstein, 2001). Their problem is often one of performance or execution. What this means is that teachers will observe these children doing what they're supposed to do— sometimes. Carl remained in his seat sometimes. He followed his teacher's instructions sometimes. He brought the right books home from school sometimes. He turned his homework in sometimes.

Carl's teachers spent years instructing him on the use of different strategies and tools in an effort to help him be more organized, less forgetful, and in better control of his behavior and emotions. He heard every word they said. It was obvious to his teachers that he knew what to do. And anyone who knows what to do should be able to do what they know, if they really care. Logically speaking, that's accurate. But it's not necessarily true for children with weak executive function skills. According to experts in the field, strengthening executive function skills requires that children learn more than specific strategies or helpful tools. They also need to learn how to effectively execute these strategies and use these tools. What Carl's teachers didn't realize was that helping him perform a host of day-to-day tasks went beyond teaching him what to do. It also required teaching him to do what he knows—in other words, teaching him to execute. This would involve opportunities to practice successfully executing these skills in actual situations where they're required. Experts sometimes refer to these situations as the "point of performance" (Barkley, 2013).

A second source of confusion: children (and adults) with weak executive function skills sometimes exhibit exceptional strengths in intellectual, creative, or other areas. As a result, they may excel at doing tasks most would consider difficult and complex yet struggle at tasks most would consider simple, if not automatic (like remembering to turn in their homework). Executive function challenges, therefore, not only contribute to our second erroneous perception. They contribute to our first one as well.

Several years ago, I had the opportunity to assist in a comprehensive evaluation of Carl's learning strengths and challenges. On measures of abstract reasoning and other complex intellectual abilities, he scored at the ninety-eighth percentile in relation to others his age. On the other hand, he showed up on the wrong day for his first day of testing, thought of calling in advance but couldn't find the slip of paper where he wrote down the phone number, and didn't think of delegating the task to his secretary, who would have gladly called to check on the correct date. Among other abilities, these tasks all call into play executive function skills. Conventional measures of intellectual functioning were not designed to assess executive function (Hale and Fiorello, 2004). It's entirely possible for individuals (children and adults) to score well on measures that call into play intellectual skills yet experience problems in handling real-life tasks that call into play executive function skills. Carl is a good example.

During his years in school (and for that matter, throughout much of his life), people attributed Carl's challenges to a lack of willpower. Why else would someone as intellectually gifted have so much difficulty doing what he knows how to do? Remember, it's not like he *can't* do it. People have actually seen him effectively execute, just not consistently. I witnessed this myself. Carl showed up on time and on the right day for his second and third testing sessions (although he was a little late for the fourth one). Yale University psychologist Thomas Brown studies the impact of problems associated with executive functioning on different aspects of people's lives and has become acutely aware of the difficulty many of them experience in reaching their goals, despite very much wanting to. Brown also works extensively with individuals like Carl, who, despite problems in execution, enjoy superior intellectual abilities (Brown, 2014). The very notion that someone can be gifted intellectually yet struggle at consistently executing relatively simple behaviors represents a paradox to many, but such is the case with people exhibiting this profile. Unfortunately, left untreated, they suffer at work, school, and life in general. Brown illustrated this in a study he conducted with 103 individuals presenting with this profile, all of whom were seeking treatment. Intellectually, they were in the top ninth percentile in relation to others their age. Yet they were unable to succeed at work or school, a result of problems associated with executive functioning (Brown and Quinlan, 1999).

A third source of confusion: children (and adults) with executive function challenges typically do far better (and sometimes very well) in situations they find interesting and stimulating. Where they struggle is in sustaining their interest, even on tasks they know are important. For children (and adults) with executive function challenges, interest will sometimes trump importance (Katz, 2014b).

If anything sounds willful, it's this. We all get bored at times with tasks we have to complete. But we still have to get them done. There's no excuse. Yet it seems that when people with executive function challenges get bored, it significantly affects their ability to finish what they start.

A fourth source of confusion: when they finally do successfully complete a particularly lengthy, uninteresting assignment, they may now be so mentally exhausted that they're less able to complete their next assignment. It can look as though they're not trying or that they don't care. After all, if they were able to complete the last assignment successfully, why can't they complete the current one, especially if it's no more difficult than the one they just finished? They can. First though, they may have to refuel their "emotional self-regulation fuel tank."

Self-regulation, it turns out, is a depletable resource. The more we use it to successfully complete a current task, the less of it we have available for the next one (Barkley, 2010b; Baumeister and Tierney, 2011; Baumeister, Vohs, and Tice, 2007). It's like fuel in a car's tank. Those who struggle to regulate their emotions and control their behavior use more fuel than others to get through daily tasks. As a result, they're at greater risk of running on empty if they don't continually refuel (take breaks, move about, exercise, etc.).

When Carl returned home from a normal school day, his emotional self-regulation fuel tank was on empty. He was in no mood for homework or for any activity requiring sustained periods of concentration, emotional self-regulation, or self-control. This is one of the reasons doing homework turned into a battleground. He now knows that the solution would have been to simply engage in relaxing activities that could have helped him feel replenished first, before engaging in new activities requiring sustained mental effort.

A fifth source of confusion: when children (and adults) with executive function challenges are examined by health care professionals who specialize in treating these difficulties, many will meet diagnostic criteria for attention deficit hyperactivity disorder (ADHD; see American Psychiatric Association, 2013). Yet their teachers at school and their family members at home will observe them paying attention just fine when they're doing things they're interested in. The diagnosis of ADHD therefore can result in further confusion, since it may not speak to the areas of greatest challenge. Carl serves as a good example. He was initially diagnosed with ADHD in fifth grade by his pediatrician, then again in seventh grade by a psychologist in his community. He clearly met criteria for the disorder. Yet he paid attention well when he was interested in what he was doing. Rather than leading to greater understanding of his challenges, the diagnosis seemed to create only greater confusion. (We revisit the matter of Carl's diagnosis of ADHD in Chapter 3, including how he eventually came to understand the condition in an entirely new light.)

It should also be noted that although delays in areas involving executive function are frequently associated with ADHD, researchers have identified executive function challenges among children and adults struggling with a range of other conditions as well, any or all of which can lead to similarly uneven learning and behavioral profiles and similar erroneous perceptions. We revisit this issue in part II of this book.

In grades five, six, and seven, Carl took medication to help manage his ADHD symptoms, which did improve his ability to focus in class. But it didn't seem to help as much with other mental processes under the executive function umbrella. Fifteen-minute homework assignments still took hours to complete, and he would still frequently forget to turn homework assignments in the next day. He also continued to misplace important papers, and continued to have difficulty using day planners, calendars, or other tools to help keep track of important due dates. Carl's struggles in this regard seemed to particularly center around tasks involving organization, time management, and planning, or what psychologist Howard Abikoff refers to as OTMP. This is not entirely unexpected, according to Abikoff. He and colleagues conducted a study that explored the effects of medication on the OTMP skills of children with ADHD. Although results showed that medication significantly improved functioning in several areas, 61 percent of children with ADHD continued to evidence problems in areas involving OTMP (Abikoff et al., 2009; Gallagher, Abikoff, and Spira, 2014).

In retrospect, Carl struggled mightily with a range of mental processes associated with executive function. But one in particular—working memory—seemed to be weakest. This helps explain the problems he had in following his teachers' instructions, as well as problems in handling several other school-related tasks.

Working memory is our ability to keep information in mind long enough to reach a goal or solve a problem. When the demands of a task, academic or otherwise, exceed what we can fit into this mental workspace, we don't have the information we need to successfully complete the task. We rely on working memory more than we realize. We rely on it when we mentally rehearse tasks that have to be accomplished at work, when reading an e-mail and simultaneously forming a response in our mind, and when we read a complex sentence or hear a complex speech and try to decipher its meaning. Whenever we need to keep information, simple or complex, in mind long enough to reach a goal or solve a problem, we use our working memory (Katz, 2014b).

Working memory has its limits. We can only hold a limited amount of information in mind at any one given time. What's more, people vary in terms of their working memory capacity, and studies show that those with higher working memory capacity enjoy certain advantages, among them the ability to sustain their attention, screen out distractions, and remember what they have to concentrate on. Those with lower working memory capacity can find themselves at a significant disadvantage in situations that call on these functions (Klingberg, 2009; Lavie, de Fockert, and Viding, 2004; Vogel, McCollough, and Machizawa, 2005). Year after year, Carl's teachers would note problems that he was having in listening to instructions and retaining things he was told moments before. These difficulties were related to his weaknesses in working memory, weaknesses he still experiences. Working memory challenges also affect reading. Persons with working memory challenges often complain that by the time they've finished reading a paragraph in a book they've already forgotten the first couple of sentences. Carl remembers having the very same problem.

It's possible that Carl's working memory problems also contributed to his self-control problems. Working memory is what allows us to keep in mind the consequences of acting on impulse (Brown, 2014). For school-age children, it's keeping in mind the teacher's warning not to blurt answers out in class, not interrupt others when they're speaking, and not leave one's seat without permission. When emotionally excited, some children with weak working memory skills have difficulty keeping in mind the consequences of their actions. This seemed to be the case with Carl. During his earlier school years, he recalls a number of occasions when the emotional excitement of the moment took over and he responded on impulse, oblivious to the consequences of his actions. When he calmed down he would regret what he did, since under these calmer, non–emotionally charged conditions, he knew he shouldn't have responded that way. Under calmer conditions, he had no difficulty keeping the consequences of his actions in his mental workspace. (In part II of the book we briefly revisit the relationship between self-control and working memory.)

As with other mental processes under the executive function umbrella, weak working memory skills can also result in confusing patterns of performance. During the course of his assessment, Carl performed well within the average range on measures of working memory. Yet he clearly evidences working memory problems in real life. Adding to the confusion, his working memory challenges can fluctuate. In situations he finds interesting and stimulating, for example, his challenges can be far less of an issue. Recall that even as a struggling school-age child, it wasn't as though he never followed his teachers' instructions. It was just that it was far more difficult for him to consistently do so than it was for other children, especially when it required that he carry out more than one step at a time.

The good news is that people with executive function challenges can learn to successfully execute daily tasks and responsibilities consistently and predictably, including those that are important but uninteresting. They can also learn to do so regardless of whether they meet diagnostic criteria for ADHD or other conditions, including those resulting from or exacerbated by exposure to extreme stress. But that's a conversation reserved for later chapters. The current topic is the impact of entirely understandable yet erroneous perceptions on otherwise resilient school-age children. The confusion resulting from executive function challenges can contribute significantly to these erroneous perceptions.

ERRONEOUS PERCEPTIONS CAN LEAD TO INEFFECTIVE REMEDIES

Carl could focus for hours on projects he was interested in, but only minutes on those he was not. He could figure out creative solutions to complex problems but fail to carry out a simple request. He was able to give a lecture on how to be organized yet wasn't able to find his day planner. He struggled for hours to complete a fifteen-minute homework assignment then forgot to turn it in the next day. He could seem so responsible and thoughtful one moment yet so irresponsible and thoughtless the next. If you happened to be on the other end of a relationship with Carl during these earlier school years, you knew firsthand just how confusing and at times infuriating his behavior could be.

When listening to Carl describe his childhood struggles, it's clear that his parents tried everything they could think of to help him succeed at school and resolve the emotional and behavioral struggles observed in later grades. The same could be said for many of his teachers. But as can be the case when well-intentioned efforts are based on erroneous perceptions, the approaches we think are most likely to work may not work at all. Alan Deutschman (2005, 2007) has studied this matter closely, with widely divergent groups of people. Included among them were heart patients facing a life-or-death choice: change their existing behavioral lifestyle or die from heart disease. While a number of patients did in fact choose to change, for some, behavioral changes were short-lived, and they soon reverted back to their previous unhealthy behavioral ways. Neither facts nor fear were sufficient motivation to convince them to change.

Deutschman found that we often rely on three entirely logical yet often unsuccessful solutions to inspire change in others who we believe need to change but are unwilling or unmotivated to do so. Facts and fear are two of them. The third is force. Deutschman's findings are relevant here because Carl's parents often relied on these same three remedies as well in order to convince him to change his ways.

Facts: "If you just try harder, Carl, I know you'll do better."
"Anyone as intelligent as you should be getting much better grades."
"You have so much potential. Please start working up to your potential."

Fear: "You're destroying your future."
"How do you ever expect to handle a real job someday if you can't even handle a simple responsibility like turning in your homework?"

Force: "Until you improve your grades, you're grounded."
"You told me you finished your work at school today. You lied. Forget about seeing your friends this weekend, or next weekend, or the weekend after that."

Desperate to help Carl any way they could, in his eighth-grade year his parents settled on a remedy involving all three methods. They placed him in a private residential school where he remained for a year. The hope was that the placement would remedy his persisting school-related difficulties.

It seems that entirely understandable yet erroneous perceptions about the paradoxically uneven ways of those we care the most about can sometimes lead us to entirely understandable yet ineffective remedies. Included among these ineffective remedies are facts, fear, and force. In Carl's case, things didn't improve, and he eventually spent a year at a residential school. In effect, he lost his home as a result of his persisting problems at school.

Deutschman's findings are revisited in part II, focusing not on how people resist change but on how they arrive at meaningful and lasting change, particularly when changing their behavioral ways had previously been so difficult.

In retrospect, it appears that Carl came to see his school failures as inevitable. Others, he believed, had it within their power to do better, even excel, but not him. Yet he could learn to live with this. What was far more difficult to live with was a third entirely logical yet erroneous perception. This one was personal, and it was humiliating.

> **Erroneous Perception #3:** The true measure of human intelligence is school performance. Those that are able to achieve good grades in school, therefore, are very smart, and those unable to achieve good grades are not, logically speaking.

Though rarely spoken aloud by teachers or parents, this was a misperception that permeated the school culture, and shared by the vast majority of other school-age children that Carl interacted with every day. He estimates that by about age 10, if not sooner, he came to believe that intelligence and school performance were one and the same. Those who did well in school were smart. Those who did poorly were not. The term he most often used to describe how he saw himself in relation to others was "stupid." "I felt so stupid." "I hated others thinking of me as stupid." "He never said so, but I was sure my father thought I was stupid." "Kids would tease me, call me stupid." "Sure I skipped school. You would, too. You learn early on it's better to be bad than stupid."

This misperception seems to take a great toll on the human spirit. Listening to Carl talk about it, one can easily understand why. Other day-to-day setbacks may have felt frustrating, but to be viewed publicly as stupid in relation others felt humiliating. What's more, it felt inescapable, and this combination in some cases can produce feelings of rage and despair. It's a combination that also helps explain why the fourth entirely erroneous perception may have been the one that eventually brought Carl face to face with his personal limits of emotional endurance.

> **Erroneous Perception #4:** Resilient people, school-age children included, think and act the same way in places they find threatening and dangerous as they do in places they find warm and friendly. This is even the case when those threatening and dangerous places also feel stigmatizing, inescapable, and beyond their ability to control or influence.

Late one evening, when his parents were asleep, Carl, then age 16, contemplated suicide. His younger brother, Steven, knowing that Carl had not been himself, decided to stop by his room to say goodnight. In the process, he may have saved his life. Carl reached a point where he felt no longer able to cope with a life he perceived as both unbearable and inescapable.

INESCAPABLY STRESSFUL CONDITIONS BEYOND OUR ABILITY TO CONTROL OR INFLUENCE

Suffering is half pain and half being alone with the pain.
—Edwin Shneidman

It's one thing to feel humiliated. It's quite another to feel trapped at the same time. Experiences that we perceive as intensely stressful carry a far greater risk to our health and well-being when they occur repeatedly, under conditions we believe to be inescapable and beyond our ability to control or alter. Researchers who study the human stress response are well aware of this. In the face of great danger, we rely on our natural physiological resources and hormonal responses to organize an effective response. When we experience ourselves as physically helpless, we no longer have access to these resources and responses. According to some experts in the field, this perception of powerlessness in the face of intense stress distinguishes traumatically stressful experiences from less harmful ones (van der Kolk, 2006).

When posttraumatic stress disorder (PTSD) was established as a diagnostic classification in 1980, it allowed us to begin to appreciate that overwhelming emotional experiences can produce serious psychological injuries in otherwise healthy people. Researchers now know that for many people suffering the effects of traumatic stress exposure, PTSD as it was described in 1980 has missed the mark. Nowhere has this been more evident than in the lives of those exposed as children to intensely stressful experiences that were prolonged, inescapable, and uncontrollable.

Psychologist Martin Seligman and his colleagues started suspecting these harmful effects as far back as the 1960s as a result of their early studies of learned helplessness in animals. Their experiments began by restraining a dog in a device known as a Pavlovian harness. While restrained, the dog would hear a tone, followed by a mild electrical shock. As soon as the dog heard the tone, it knew a shock wasn't far behind. But it was restrained and thus had no means of escape. The experience was repeated over and over; tone, shock, tone, shock. The dog was then placed in a shuttle box made of two chambers separated by a barrier low enough in height so that it could easily leap from one chamber to the other. The floor of one of the two chambers was wired to emit a shock, thereby replicating the Pavlovian harness experience. Researchers placed the dog on the side of the box that produced the shock, but 10 seconds before emitting the shock, they provided the dog with a signal in the form of a dimming light. If the dog simply learned to leap the barrier as soon as it saw the signal, the shock was prevented. Dogs not exposed to inescapable shock usually learned to escape to the other side quickly after only a single shock. They learned to escape even faster on successive trials, eventually nonchalantly jumping over to the other side as soon as they saw the signal. But dogs initially exposed to inescapable shock ran around frantically, then gave up a few seconds later. Surprisingly, they let themselves be shocked rather than try to escape (Overmier and Seligman, 1967; Seligman, 1992). (To read more, log on to the web page.)

In Seligman's early experiments, dogs exposed to single sessions of inescapable stress, though rendered helpless initially, eventually learned to escape if researchers waited 72 hours before putting the dog in the shuttle box a second time. Time restored the dog's sense of personal control. But when researchers exposed dogs to four separate sessions in the Pavlovian harness within the course of a week—four exposures to uncontrollable and inescapable stress—dogs remained helpless weeks later. The consequences of prolonged, inescapable, and uncontrollable stress were chronic, not temporary (Seligman, 1992; Seligman & Maier, 1967).

Early inescapable stress experiments with animals in time led to a better understanding of one pathway to a sense of helplessness, hopelessness, and despair in humans. It's a pathway paved by uncontrollable experiences of failure and defeat, where no matter how hard one repeatedly tries, one never achieves the goal. This path appears to be most easily established when uncontrollable experiences of failure and defeat start early, during our childhood years (Seligman, 1998a).

We have no way of confirming whether the emotionally stressful school-related experiences that Carl endured met criteria that researchers are now using to establish whether a stressor is traumatic. What we do know is that these stressful experiences were ongoing, inescapable, and beyond his ability to control or alter. We also know that school wasn't the only persisting source of stress. Life at home was difficult to bear as well.

One other particularly significant event occurred prior to Carl finally coming face to face with his personal limits of emotional endurance—an event that was overlooked at the time, since it didn't seem out of the ordinary. In retrospect, it may have been his emotional tipping point. Before starting 10th grade, Carl and his family moved to a new community, hundreds of miles away from where he had grown up. As a result of the move, he lost contact with his two closest friends. The three had grown up together, and according to Carl, they were inseparable. He recalls hardly a day going by when they didn't either see or speak to one another. Though Carl's school difficulties persisted year after year, they never affected the strong bond he enjoyed with his two closest friends.

Carl's friends were quick to come to his defense when others at school were causing him harm. This was often all it took to convince others to leave him alone. At his new school, he made new friends, but not the type who were willing to accept the risks associated with speaking out on behalf of a friend in danger. Carl's struggles at his new school were as much a source of shame and humiliation as they were in his old school. The difference was that in his old school he had two friends he could always count on. They stayed his friends, no matter what others thought or said. Not only did they provide him a sense of acceptance and belonging, they served as an important buffer, one that helped soften the effects of the stigma associated with his differences. In his new school, he was on his own.

No one really knew how distraught Carl felt at the time he contemplated suicide. He had been distressed before and never thought of taking his life. What was different this time was that he felt *alone*.

STIGMATIZING AND INESCAPABLY STRESSFUL CONDITIONS

Stress of the inescapable and uncontrollable kind can cause serious harm to otherwise resilient individuals. These harmful effects are magnified when conditions also feel stigmatizing. Such was the case for Carl in the years after he lost contact with his two friends. His friends seemed to buffer him somewhat from these harmful effects. When he moved away, he lost that important buffer. Stigma became another source of ongoing, inescapable stress beyond his ability to control or alter.

Very few at the time seemed to perceive stigma as a serious source of stress in the lives of children experiencing its effects. We now know that it is. Thanks to the National Stigma Study—Children, we also know how prevalent these views are even today, especially for children who experience behavioral challenges similar to the ones that Carl experienced (Pescosolido, 2010).

As is often the case for children with these profiles, the stigma Carl endured eventually led to self-stigma, that internal acceptance of the stigmatizing views others have of them as true. It came as no surprise that in time Carl succumbed to his own erroneous perception, one that originated at school, eventually extended to other life areas, and probably helps explain his road to demoralization: the perception that trying harder does not equate with doing better. What's so unfortunate about this perception, and so potentially harmful, is that it prevents us from accessing the experiences we find in the lives of those who endure and/or overcome exposure to a range of childhood risks and adversities. I refer to experiences leading to strong self-efficacy beliefs, also called a strong sense of *mastery*, a term I use throughout the rest of the book. (To learn more about self-efficacy theory, log on to the web page.)

The term "mastery" grew out of decades of research on the effects of inescapable stress. These studies show that one relatively simple belief—that we exert personal control over the potentially distressing events and experiences in our lives—can help us endure a variety of different stressful conditions, including those representing defeats and failures. Research also shows that a sense of mastery is learned. It's not a personality trait we're born with, not something we can bestow on a person, and it's not a given. Rather, mastery is something we earn (Seligman, 1992). While the road to mastery is paved with success experiences, researchers point out it's also paved with an abundant supply of failures and defeats. That's because a sense of mastery requires, above all, learning how to overcome life's inevitable failures and defeats successfully. The earlier in life we learn this—the earlier we come to believe that our actions control our destiny—the better we immunize ourselves from potential adversities and hardships down the road (Seligman, 1998a).

Carl attended school at a time when it was commonly believed that all learning, behavioral, and emotional challenges were willful in nature (Hinshaw and Stier, 2008) and that those struggling with these challenges simply had to try harder. In fact, many were already trying hard, yet still failing. Loving parents and caring teachers notwithstanding, they had little access to those day-to-day experiences we all need if we're to believe we can achieve our goals by trying our best, never giving up, and treating our mistakes, failures, and setbacks as learning experiences. For Carl, that illusive sense of mastery came decades later, when adult life experiences taught him that one's actions really can influence one's destiny.

Carl and his brother Steven were exposed to years of violent and abusive behavior at home. Those who knew Steven back then considered him to be a very resilient young man, capable of rising above a traumatic home life, and his excellent grades in school served as proof. Carl, on the other hand, was considered emotionally troubled, and his failing grades served as proof. No one back then thought that otherwise resilient children might think and act very differently based on contextual influences, influences that in Carl's case were inescapably stressful, stigmatizing, and beyond his ability to control or alter. Ignoring the potential impact of these contextual influences, they fell prey to our fifth entirely understandable yet erroneous perception.

> **Erroneous Perception #5:** Resilience and success must be one and the same. Those who succeed at school are resilient. Those who fail at school are not, logically speaking.

In reality, we know that resilience can only be understood within the context of one's unique life experiences. These contextual influences, in turn, can determine whether we endure in the face of adversity or are stretched to our emotional limits.

Back to our earlier question: what could so alter the life course of a healthy, resilient child, growing up with loving parents, and attending schools taught by great teachers? The culprit, at least in some instances, may be the five erroneous perceptions regarding the child's mysterious, troublesome, and often paradoxical patterns of learning and behavior, perceptions that can potentially guide caring and concerned people to ineffective remedies resulting in disappointing outcomes. Furthermore, these perceptions affect us at a time in our lives when our otherwise strong human connections can no longer buffer us, a time in our lives when we feel alone with our pain.

SUMMARY

- Otherwise resilient individuals sometimes learn and behave in paradoxically uneven ways.
- During their school-age years, their uneven learning and behavioral ways can occasionally lead to significant school-related challenges.

- Unfortunately, a child's paradoxically uneven ways can lead parents, teachers, and health care professionals to logical yet flawed perceptions regarding the root cause of these challenges. These erroneous perceptions appear capable of stretching even the most resilient among us beyond the limits of our emotional endurance.

- One common erroneous perception attributes the root cause of the child's challenges to a lack of effort. This frequently occurs when a child performs far better on tasks that most others find difficult than on tasks that most others find simple. We see this type of unevenness among those with learning differences, including though by no means limited to dyslexia, as was the case with Carl.

- We also see this unevenness among those with challenges in areas of executive function. Although they may perform very well on more difficult intellectual or creative tasks, they can perform poorly or inconsistently in areas under the executive function umbrella: emotional self-regulation and self-control, organization, planning, time management, and working memory.

- In the absence of cues, prompts, reminders, or other strategies and accommodations, executive function challenges often result in inconsistent and unpredictable learning and behavior profiles, which is why they often give rise to our second and equally common erroneous perception: anyone who knows what they're supposed to do in a given situation can be expected to consistently, predictably, and independently do what they know 100 percent of the time. It's all a matter of willpower, logically speaking.

- Although delays in areas involving executive function are frequently associated with ADHD, researchers have identified executive function challenges among children and adults struggling with a range of other conditions as well, any or all of which can lead to similarly uneven learning and behavioral profiles.

- Executive function challenges, particularly those associated with problems in emotional self-regulation and self-control, can have far-reaching implications in a person's life.

- A third often unspoken erroneous perception attributes challenges to a lack of intelligence, an assumption that a child often internalizes at a young age and continues to believe for years to come.
- A fourth erroneous assumption helps explain the rapid rise and slow demise of the first three: the incorrect assumption that resilient people think and act the same way in places they find threatening and dangerous as they do in places they find warm and friendly; contextual influences, in other words, count very little when understanding how we successfully rise above or endure in the face adversity. In fact, contextual influences matter a great deal.
- A fifth mistaken perception is that resilience and success must be one and the same. Those who succeed at school are resilient. Those who fail at school are not, logically speaking.
- Any one of these entirely understandable yet erroneous perceptions can lead to apparently logical yet ineffective remedies, which in turn often lead to disappointing results.
- Remedies are drawn from what appear to be three reasonable agents of change: facts, fear, and force. Unfortunately, they can at times make matters worse rather than better.

Chapter 2

≈≋≈

HUMAN RESILIENCE AND THE LIMITS OF EMOTIONAL ENDURANCE

WHY DO THEY FAIL? CONTINUED

We form many perceptions about the behavior and intentions of others, especially those we care the most about. For those struggling to overcome the effects of a range of adverse childhood experiences, the five erroneous perceptions discussed in Chapter 1 seem to carry unintended consequences far more serious than many others. Why might this be the case? One reason is that they prevent access to the conditions and experiences that outweigh the effects of exposure to multiple risks and adversities. Researchers who study resilience through the life span refer to these conditions and experiences as protective processes. Steven enjoyed uninterrupted access to them, but his older brother, Carl, did not. Later in the chapter, I explain how our five erroneous perceptions prevented access to these processes. This serves as a good segue into the discussion that immediately follows, where we revisit a question I posed in the introduction: Is it possible that some individuals who succumb to early adversity were just as resilient as those who endured? I believe the answer is yes. For supporting evidence, we'll look at recent advances in our understanding of human resilience and the limits of emotional endurance.

First I briefly review findings from the Kauai Longitudinal Study, perhaps the most important prospective longitudinal study of human resilience to date. The protective processes I'll be reviewing shortly were identified in this landmark investigation. The study traces the developmental trajectories of two groups of resilient individuals, each exposed to a range of adverse childhood experiences. One group "beat the odds," never succumbing to the learning, behavioral, emotional, or life adjustment problems expected, given their early risk exposure. In contrast, those in other group did succumb, but surprisingly rebounded decades later, eventually leading meaningful and productive lives, much like those in the first group. In many respects, Carl's journey from years of school failure to eventual life success bears a striking resemblance to those in this second group, whereas Steven's journey bears an equally striking resemblance to those in the first.

THE KAUAI LONGITUDINAL STUDY

In 1955, principal investigators Emmy Werner and Ruth Smith (2001) began following the developmental trajectories of several hundred children born on the island of Kauai, Hawaii, a number of whom were exposed to four or more risk factors associated with negative life outcomes. Risk factors included (but were not limited to) significant perinatal stress, chronic poverty, parental alcoholism or mental illness, and exposure to chronic family discord. Two-thirds of these children succumbed to serious learning, behavioral, or emotional problems by age 10, and/or mental health problems, delinquent behavior, or teenage pregnancy by age 18. One out of three, however, beat the odds. They were free of serious emotional, behavioral, and learning problems; adapted well to day-to-day demands and responsibilities; and enjoyed uninterrupted years of school success. When reassessed at age 31 to 32, the vast majority were still adjusting well. Surprisingly, though, of the original two-thirds who succumbed, most were *also* now adapting well. When study participants from both groups were reassessed at age 40, researchers found similar results. Roughly one in three who beat the odds were still adapting well, and of the two-thirds that originally succumbed—including youth with identified mental health problems, youth in trouble with the law, unwed teen mothers, and children and youth who experienced significant school-related problems (similar to Carl's)—most were adapting well to adult life

(Werner, 2005; Werner and Smith, 2001). Findings from the Kauai Longitudinal Study have since been replicated by a number of other longitudinal studies in the United States, Great Britain, Germany, and Australia (Werner, 2005).

INDIVIDUALS WHO BEAT THE ODDS AND THOSE WHO SUCCUMBED

Might children who succumbed and then rebounded decades later been exposed to additional risks and adversities less known to researchers, health care professionals, and educators in years past, but well known to them today? The answer is yes, and Carl is a very good illustration. He went to school at a time when most believed that children who had the intellectual capability to do well at school could do so if they simply put in the effort. The fact that neurodevelopmental differences could prevent otherwise resilient school-age children from performing up to expectations was not well known. With the advantage of hindsight, we know that Carl was exposed to a greater number of risks than his brother was—risks of the neurodevelopmental kind. We also know that they deprived him of access to an extremely important buffer: school. Steven loved school. In fact, the first day of first grade was a turning point in his life. From that point on he enjoyed countless meaningful and rewarding successes. He enjoyed them every day, five days a week, for 12 years. These continued through four years of college and two years of graduate school. These experiences taught Steven a lot about himself, not the least of which was that if he tried hard, never gave up, and treated mistakes as learning experiences, he could achieve his goals. School was where he learned that his actions controlled his destiny. He did not learn this at home, since no matter what he did or how hard he tried, he had no control over his father's violent and abusive episodes. For Steven, home remained a source of prolonged, inescapable stress, and he could do nothing to change this. Home was also a source of prolonged, inescapable stress for Carl, and he, too, could do nothing to change this. But for Carl, so was school, and he could do nothing to change that either. And knowing what we now know about his particular learning and behavioral profile, no amount of resilience would have helped him read more fluently or regulate his behavior more effectively.

Still, this added degree of risk exposure by itself wasn't what led to Carl's years of school failure. That was the result of an added degree of risk exposure in the absence of protective processes that could have outweighed them. Let me expand upon the meaning of the term *protective processes*.

PROTECTIVE PROCESSES

Researchers who study resilience through the life span use the term "protective processes" when describing the mechanisms that neutralize or outweigh the potentially harmful effects of risk exposure (Luthar, Cicchetti, and Becker, 2000; Masten and Reed, 2005; Rutter, 1990; Wright, Masten, and Narayan, 2013). Researchers have grown increasingly interested in studying these processes, particularly in the lives of children exposed to multiple risks. Protective processes are not the equivalent of programs or practices, nor are they the equivalent of strategies or techniques, such as those employed in the context of treatment. On the other hand, researchers who study these mechanisms note that any number of different programs, practices, strategies, or techniques can foster protective processes that neutralize the effects of risks and that underlie change (Prochaska, Norcross, and DiClemente, 2002). Based on findings from the Kauai Longitudinal Study, Emmy Werner and colleagues identified the following four processes (Rutter, 1990; Werner and Smith, 2001):

1. Experiences and conditions that reduce the impact of prevailing risks by either (a) enabling the person to learn to see adversities in a new light, and/or (b) providing a protective shield or buffer that reduces exposure to the potentially damaging effects of the prevailing risks. This would speak directly to the role of contextual influences. Some social climates, for example, buffer us from risk exposure, whereas others might increase our exposure.
2. Experiences that prevent negative life events from spiraling out of control. The likelihood of this occurring increases as risk exposure increases. Those caught in this downward spiral benefit from a safety net that short-circuits their downward spiral, thereby allowing them to regain a sense of control and stability in their lives.

3. Experiences and conditions that help foster a sense of mastery or self-efficacy (the perception that one will successfully achieve the goals they set by virtue of their actions).

4. Experiences and conditions that open the door to turning points and second chance opportunities.

Other researchers in the field are engaged in the study of protective processes as well, among them Ann Masten and James Prochaska. In a review of the research literature on resilience in the context of adversity, Masten identified three protective processes: (1) those that build and foster a sense of self-efficacy (as noted by Rutter, 1990, and Werner and Smith, 2001); (2) those that foster and sustain attachments between children, their caregivers, and/or other nurturing and supportive positive role models; and (3) those that encourage and support friendships with other children (Masten, 2014; Masten and Reed, 2005). In a large-scale investigation of underlying processes that helped people overcome problems without the benefit of professional intervention, Prochaska and colleagues identified internal and external processes. Internal change processes included greater insight into how problematic behaviors seriously affected one's life and one's decision to commit to making personal changes. External change processes included environmental modifications that reduced exposure to stimuli likely to trigger problems and the presence of helping relationships that provided much needed support as one successfully moved through stages of change. Study participants included individuals who overcame weight problems, problems with substance abuse, addiction to nicotine, and other difficulties. Results showed that people who successfully overcame problematic behaviors, regardless of their nature, typically drew on very similar processes (Prochaska, Norcross, and DiClemente, 2002).

A closer examination of the protective processes identified by Masten, Prochaska, and others reveals considerable overlap with the four processes identified by Werner and colleagues. For this reason, they are relied on extensively in this and other chapters when discussing the role of protective processes in overcoming exposure to adverse childhood experiences.

Now let me explain why I believe the five erroneous perceptions offset these critical protective processes. I'll begin the discussion by focusing specifically on two of the protective processes listed above:

the ability to see adversities in a new light (meaning) and the belief that if we try hard, don't give up, and learn from our mistakes, we will achieve what we set out to achieve, or simply stated, the belief that our actions determine our outcomes (mastery). In the research literature on risk, resilience, and recovery through the life span, protective processes are often discussed and even studied separately. But they can overlap in important ways, as is the case with meaning and mastery.

Martin Seligman and colleagues conducted a series of landmark studies that helped us see how these processes work hand in hand (1992; 1998a, 2002). In these studies, researchers identified three different and measurable ways we can choose to view adverse life experiences and the resulting impact these choices have on the quality of our lives. Those who choose to view adverse experiences as (1) permanent (believing there to be no end in sight to the difficulties we now confront), (2) pervasive (believing that difficulties are wide ranging, affecting many life areas), and (3) personal (believing that difficulties are the result of something inherently wrong with us) are shown to be at significantly greater risk for depression, a sense of helplessness and hopelessness, and a number of other psychological and health-related problems down the road. On the other hand, those who learn to view adversity as temporary, limited in scope, and not the result of something inherently wrong with them seem to grow stronger and are better able to bear up under future adversities. Seligman and colleagues went on to use these and related findings to create programs and practices designed to foster resilience through the lifespan (Seligman, 2002, 2011).

Perceiving life's adversities as permanent, pervasive, and personal (meaning) increases the likelihood of psychological and physical problems down the road. On the other hand, perceiving life's adversities as temporary and limited (meaning) fosters hope and strengthens our will to fight on in spite of difficulties (mastery). Seligman and colleagues have repeatedly demonstrated how this mind-set, referred to as our "explanatory style," affects us in virtually all life areas. In a study of productivity in the workplace, insurance salesmen scoring high on a measure of explanatory style outsold coworkers scoring lower (Seligman, 1992; Seligman and Schulman, 1986). In a study involving first-year college students, explanatory style was a better predictor of success by the end of their first semester than was SAT scores. Those with high explanatory style scores were also less likely to get depressed after receiving an unexpectedly poor grade (Kamen and Seligman, 1986; Seligman, 1992). In a study of later life health outcomes among male World War II veterans, explanatory style at age 25 predicted health status at 60. Men with more optimistic views at age 25 were healthier at age 60, and those with more pessimistic views were coming down with common diseases of middle age sooner. In fact, these differences in health status were visible at age 45.

Seligman has long maintained that we have a choice in how to interpret the good and bad events occurring in our lives. He has shown through repeated studies how this choice can profoundly affect our health, psychological well-being, and productivity. He also believes our culture today places less weight on personal choice than in times past, and more weight on environmental explanations for human behavior, including misbehavior (Seligman, 2011). He analyzed headlines from the *New York Times* going back 60 years and found a growing trend toward victimization, with a correspondingly decreasing trend toward personal choice. Seligman sees a relationship between this cultural trend and research that shows a rise in the national rate of clinical depression (Seligman, 1998b).

So here, then, is the question. Is it possible that otherwise resilient individuals—in this instance, six-year-old children who do not wish to see themselves as victims and work as hard as they can to reach their goals—could still grow increasingly demoralized over time, despite having access to loving parents, caring teachers, and professionals willing to do everything in their power to help?

Seligman actually raised the possibility years ago when he identified three factors beyond a child's control that influence the meaning he or she attaches to adverse life events: (1) the degree to which optimistic and hopeful explanations are attached to these events; (2) the degree to which personal failures are met with criticisms that communicate a sense of permanence and pervasiveness surrounding these failures; and (3) whether early crises, losses, and traumatic experiences are successfully endured, or whether the child is left believing that bad things never change (Seligman, 1998a).

It would appear, then, that conditions beyond the control of school-age children can significantly influence the meaning they attach to adverse experiences, the nature of which can determine whether they learn to see these adverse experiences as permanent, pervasive, and personal or as temporary, limited, and not the result of an inherent flaw or shortcoming. If this is the case, it can also be said that factors beyond their control can potentially determine whether they grow stronger in the face of adversity or, conversely, demoralized or depressed. Here is where the five erroneous perceptions enter the picture.

Mistaken perception #1 states that anyone capable of performing exceptionally well on intellectual, creative, or artistic tasks that others find difficult is necessarily capable of performing equally well or better on academic or behavioral tasks that others find easy. Developing a sense of mastery requires that we work very hard, not give up, and learn from our mistakes so that we arrive at a mind-set where we come to believe we will achieve our goals. Through our lived experience, we learn that our actions determine our outcomes. What if trying hard, not giving up, and being willing to learn from our mistakes doesn't result in success? In time, a struggling child can come to a different conclusion about the value of their effort. Remember, we're asked to do these tasks virtually every day, year after year.

The second misperception is that anyone who knows what they're supposed to do a given situation can be expected to do what they know 100 percent of the time. What's so insidious about this misperception is how easily it can convince us of the accuracy of the first one. It can be hard to find a logical explanation for why anyone would know what to do, want to do it, then fail to do it, particularly when we've seen them do it successfully before. It's not simply the lack of execution that's confusing, it's that execution occurs successfully only some of the time. Knowing what to do but being inconsistent and unpredictable in doing it appears entirely willful. It's a challenge to convince anyone otherwise.

To succeed in school (and in life), we need to be able to work hard in the face of challenging situations and learn from mistakes. But we also need to recognize that our actions matter. These two misperceptions rob at least some struggling children of this learning opportunity.

Erroneous perceptions #1 and #2, it seems, can potentially convince otherwise resilient children that their challenges are permanent and, depending on the impact on other aspects of their lives, pervasive as well. Erroneous perception #3 makes it personal: the true measure of human intelligence is school performance. Of the first 10 participants I interviewed as part of the Resilience through the Lifespan Project, all believed throughout their school lives that those who did well in school were smart and those who did poorly were not. When asked about how they viewed themselves in relation to others back then, almost all used the word "stupid." "I felt so stupid." Many seemed tormented by the thought, and many were tormented by the thought of others viewing them this way. "I hated school. Everyone there looked at me like I was stupid." Having no awareness of their strengths and talents and the important role these would ultimately play in helping them achieve success years down the road, all seemed convinced that working hard, not giving up, and learning from mistakes, although admirable qualities, did not make one smarter.

Learning to see adversities in a new light would prove difficult for Carl, given erroneous perceptions one, two, and three. Erroneous perception #4 (resilient people think and act the same way in places they find threatening and dangerous as they do in places they find warm and friendly) served to create a context in which he remained exposed to experiences that were stressful, inescapable, and stigmatizing.

Even under these conditions, however, people can gather strength from knowing others are viewing them as resilient in the face of challenge. This was not the case in Carl's situation, the result of the last erroneous perception: resilience and success are one and the same.

These five misperceptions, I believe, override two important protective processes observed in the lives of those who manage to carve out meaningful and successful lives in spite of exposure to multiple childhood risks and adversities: the ability to see adversities in a new light (meaning), and the experiences we require to learn that our actions can alter our destiny (mastery).

Furthermore, I believe these erroneous perceptions also override two other protective processes: experiences or conditions that shield us from the potentially damaging effects of risk exposure, and the availability of a safety net, one that can potentially prevent negative life events from spiraling out of control. Let me explain why I believe this to be the case.

If we currently enjoy meaningful and productive lives, we also believe that we matter and have something important to contribute. We arrived at these beliefs as a result of our choices. We chose what to do for a living, where to do it, and possibly around whom. We chose to stay at some jobs and not at others. We chose where to live and where to leave. In each of these instances, the role of context loomed large. We took advantage of the opportunity to change and/or alter the context within which our life experiences were unfolding. As adults, we have the opportunity to prevent bad experiences from becoming permanently damaging. We leave, replace, seek out, and/or change our social climates to increase the likelihood that the bad things affecting our lives are temporary and limited. During our earlier years, the context within which we were required to function was mostly beyond our ability to control or influence. If we were strong academically and enjoyed a friendly, easy-going temperament, school probably worked to our advantage. We enjoyed many rewarding and successful experiences. Carl's brother, Steven, can relate to this. He loved school and school loved him. For Carl, it was a different story.

Still, I believe Carl would have fared better even under difficult conditions had he not lost access to another important protective process, a safety net, which came in the form of two close childhood friends. These friendships seemed to neutralize (at least partly) the impact of frustrating and humiliating school experiences. Back then, there was a stigma associated with Carl's challenges. But it wasn't until he no longer had access to his two friends (when his family moved) that these perceptions became internalized. For those struggling with learning, behavioral, emotional, or physical challenges, researchers now believe the negative effects of stigma can outweigh the negative effects of the actual challenges (Hinshaw, 2007; Hinshaw and Stier, 2008).

Research shows that close friends can serve as an important buffer in times of stress. Recall the last of three protective processes that Masten identified in her review of the research literature on resilience in the context of adversity (processes that encourage and support friendships with other children). Carl lost access to an important source of protection when he lost contact with his two closest friends.

I have already showed how misperceptions can override protective processes. Now I circle back to a question I initially raised in the introduction: is it possible that some individuals who succumb to early adversity were every bit as resilient as those who endured? I believe it is, for these reasons. First, we've underestimated our inherent resilient nature. According to leading experts in the field, we're actually more resilient than we realize, especially during our childhood years. Second, we now know that for even the most resilient among us, children included, there are limits to emotional endurance. Researchers who study dose effects, for example, have shown that as risk exposure increases, our capacity to endure in the face of these risks decreases, if, that is, protective processes capable of neutralizing these risks are unavailable to us. Third, we have more influence than we realize in determining who ultimately accesses these protective processes and who does not. This is especially so for school-age children. As we've already shown, for example, the meaning we attach to the adversities others endure (our perceptions) often determines the meaning they attach to these same adversities (their perceptions).

WE'RE MORE RESILIENT THAN WE REALIZE, ESPECIALLY DURING THE CHILDHOOD YEARS

Soon after the terrorist attacks of September 11, 2001, Bessel van der Kolk (2002), one of the world's leading authorities on the physical and psychological effects of traumatic stress exposure, was in New York to help victims cope with the aftermath. Among the people he reached out to help was a five-year-old child who witnessed the collapse of the World Trade Center towers in its entirety from a window in a nearby building. The child also witnessed people jumping out of windows of the collapsing buildings. To better understand what the experience felt like, van der Kolk asked the child if he could draw everything he had seen. He later displayed a copy of the drawing to a small number of attendees at a workshop he was conducting in 2002, nine months after the events of 9/11. The following is my best attempt to describe the drawing.

In the center of the page are two tower-like structures drawn with long, wavy lines. Crashing into one of the structures is the child's version of a jumbo jet, with big floppy wings. Falling from the top of the structures are stick figures, representing people jumping from the upper floors. At ground level, adjacent to the two structures, is a drawing of a big brown circle. Everything in the drawing makes sense except for the brown circle. It seems meaningless. But actually, it may represent one of human nature's greatest gifts. The problem is that we might have to be five years old to appreciate it. The big brown circle is "a trampoline," says the child, matter-of-factly. "It's there so that when the people jumping from the windows land on it, they bounce back up."

While young children are no doubt defenseless in the face of certain physical and other threats, they are also resilient by nature. In fact, say researchers, it's very hard to find hopelessness in five-year-olds. For children under age eight, scores on measures of hopelessness were equivalent to scores typically achieved by highly hopeful and optimistic adults. Scores obtained by depressed children resembled those obtained by average (nondepressed) adults (Seligman, 1998a). Young children have the ability to take tragic events and distort their perceptions in ways that culminate in hopeful endings. According to Seligman, nature has bestowed on young children a deep reservoir of hopeful thoughts and feelings as a way of equipping them to psychologically endure difficulties.

What's more, say researchers, we may have seriously underestimated the resilient nature in all of us. Research shows that our ability to overcome a hurtful past and the potential damaging effects of exposure to a variety of adverse experiences occurs much more often than most people realize or even believe possible (Werner and Smith 2001). For those who do ultimately succumb to childhood adversities, research also suggests that many will rebound years later. Consider results from the landmark Kauai Longitudinal Study, showing that most of those who succumbed to multiple risk exposures are now leading meaningful and productive lives. And included among these now successful individuals are those who struggled in school (Werner and Smith, 2001).

Human resilience turns out to be much more ordinary than extraordinary (Masten, 2001, 2014). Rather than drawing on rare and special qualities, people seem to possess a surprising degree of resilience to begin with. But we also now know that resilience alone may not be enough to withstand the cumulative impact of the risks and adversities affecting our lives.

THERE ARE LIMITS TO EMOTIONAL ENDURANCE

Researchers who study risk, resilience, and recovery through the life span know that as risk exposure increases, so does our vulnerability to negative life outcomes, often exponentially, if these risks exist in the absence of protective processes that can neutralize or outweigh their impact. British psychiatrist Michael Rutter (1979b) demonstrated this in a study he conducted that explored the effects of exposure to six potential risk factors resulting from family adversity. Children exposed to a single risk factor fared as well as children who were not exposed to any, whereas exposure to two risks increased the likelihood of potential problems 4-fold, and exposure to four risks increased the likelihood of potential problems 10-fold.

More recently, results of the Adverse Childhood Experiences Study showed a strong graded relationship between the number of categories of adverse childhood experiences endured up through age 18, and a variety of later life health and social problems (Dube et al., 2003; Felitti et al., 1998; www.acestudy.org). Those growing up exposed to four or more categories, for example, showed a 4- to 12-fold corresponding increase in their risk for alcoholism, drug abuse, depression, and suicide attempts, and a 2- to 4-fold increase in smoking. Regarding suicide attempts, of those reporting no exposure to categories up through age 18, the prevalence of self-reported attempts was 1.1 percent. For respondents reporting exposure to seven or more categories, the prevalence rose to 35.2 percent (Chapman, Dube, and Anda, 2007). There was also a 2- to 4-fold increase in their rate of sexually transmitted diseases, and a 2- to 4-fold increase in poor self-rated health. Those exposed to four or more categories also showed a 1.4- to 1.6-fold increase in physical inactivity and severe obesity. But one of the most startling findings was the relationship between exposure to adverse childhood experiences up through age 18 and the presence of life-threatening diseases later in life. Those exposed to four or more categories were significantly more likely to be suffering from diseases representing some of the leading causes of death among American adults today, diseases like ischemic heart disease, cancer, chronic lung disease, skeletal fractures, and liver disease. (To learn more about the ACE Study, including mechanisms that help explain pathways to biomedical disease, log on to the web page.)

Certain risk combinations may pose more serious problems than others. Studies conducted by psychiatrist Dorothy Lewis, for example, found higher rates of criminal activity among youth experiencing neurological vulnerability co-occurring with severe abuse (Gladwell, 1997; Lewis, 1998). (We revisit Lewis's research in Chapter 9).

Should risk exposure affect a child's emotional self-regulation and self-control skills, serious later life problems become more likely. According to findings from the Dunedin Study, for example, self-control skills in childhood can predict physical health and illness, criminal offending, addiction, heavy smoking, personal finances, saving for retirement, dropping out of high school, and unplanned single parenting (Moffitt, 2012; Moffitt et al., 2011). (We revisit Dunedin Study findings in Chapter 7).

At least some of those who succumb to the impact of stressful life experiences, including struggling school-age children, may not necessarily be less resilient than those who endure but may have had to contend with greater levels of stress in the absence of protective mechanisms. Researchers studying these dose effects find that it can actually help explain why some people suffer more emotional, behavioral, and physiological symptoms in response to traumatic stress than do others. In one study of Vietnam War combat veterans, for example, researchers found that 31 percent of those suffering from PTSD also had histories of severe physical and/or sexual abuse in childhood, while only 7 percent of non-PTSD veterans had similar histories (Bremner et al., 1993). In another study, sexually assaulted women with histories of child sexual abuse were more likely to develop PTSD than were women with no similar histories (Bremner, 2001).

In the absence of protective processes that can buffer the impact of risk, those of us growing up exposed to such conditions are increasingly likely to suffer a range of negative life outcomes down the road. What's more, multiple risks not only co-occur but persist. Children exposed to multiple risks early in life may be exposed to these same risks many years later. These include stresses that are environmental in nature as well as those associated with more neurodevelopmental influences. For example, a six-year-old child exposed to traumatically stressful experiences at home and who also begins school with neurodevelopmental challenges affecting learning and behavior may very well be affected by the same environmental and neurodevelopmental risks 10 years later. At age 16, life experiences at home may still be traumatically stressful, and life at school may remain a source of ongoing failure and frustration. Although this is not entirely descriptive of Carl's childhood experiences, some aspects do apply. Many of the sources of stress present in his life during earlier grades were present during later grades as well.

If multiple risk exposure persists, then vulnerability persists. If vulnerability persists, those exposed will require access to protective processes capable of neutralizing the potentially harmful effects of long-term risk exposure. Research shows that these protective processes do exist. But in Carl's case, they were inaccessible, the result of five entirely understandable yet erroneous perceptions.

This brings us to the third point: The meaning we attach to the adversities of others (our perceptions) can influence the meaning they attach to these same adversities (their perceptions).

WE SEE OURSELVES THROUGH THE EYES OF OTHERS

In a study dating back to the 1960s, Robert Rosenthal and colleagues instructed each of 12 experimenters to teach five rats to run a maze. Before beginning, half of the experimenters were told their rats were bred for "maze brightness" and half for "maze dullness." Results revealed that those supposedly raised for maze brightness performed significantly better. In actuality, rats were not raised in any particular way. Yet experimenters perceiving this to be so obtained results in the direction they expected. In a second similar experiment, this one using a Skinner box (a chamber containing a bar or key that a rat can press to obtain a reward) half of the experimenters were led to believe that rats were raised to be "Skinner box bright," half were told they were bred to be "Skinner box dull." Rats in the Skinner box bright experiments performed better. Again, simply perceiving how rats would be expected to perform led to results in the expected direction (Rosenthal, 2002).

If experimenter perception could influence the rate at which rats learn, Rosenthal wondered, could teacher perceptions influence the rate at which children learn? To answer the question, he and colleague Lenore Jacobson administered a nonverbal IQ test to all children at a San Francisco elementary school. Teachers were led to believe the test measured intellectual "blooming" or "spurting" (it did not). All teachers in grades one through six, 18 total, were given the names of children who were predicted to show dramatic intellectual growth based on their test results. Roughly 20 percent of children were identified as potential "spurters." In reality, their scores were no different than the remaining 80 percent. When retested one year later, children who were expected to do better scored significantly higher, with the greatest gains being observed in grades one and two (Rosenthal and Jacobson, 1992). Results represent what has come to be known as the "Pygmalion effect," according to which our perception of how we believe others will perform can create a self-fulfilling prophecy, potentially increasing the likelihood that they will perform much as we expect them to. The effect has been documented not only between teachers and students but also between employers and employees.

The capabilities we perceive in others can influence the capabilities they perceive in themselves. The same can be said about our perception of the adversities of others. Cultures throughout the world are well aware of this. From Red Cross disaster relief efforts, to nationwide fund-raisers, to tribal morning ceremonies, to religious and spiritual leaders putting events into a larger meaningful context, cultures throughout the world realize that validation and support hasten the healing process, while its absence compromises it (McFarlane and van der Kolk, 1996; van der Kolk, 2001).

All individuals have opinions of themselves, says social psychologist William Swann (1996), and these self-views are not formed in a vacuum. Rather, they are shaped, at least partly by the way people were treated by others. The link between how others come to view us and how we ultimately come to view ourselves appears particularly strong during our childhood years. For children who struggle in school year after year, it's no surprise that many come to doubt their ability to succeed. Unfortunately, studies have also shown that these self-views are not easy to alter. Once people establish a view of who they are in relation to others and to the world, they often "act the part" (Swann, 1996).

Research shows that we are more resilient than we realize. Research also shows that there are limits to emotional endurance for even the most resilient among us. Furthermore, you and I may have more influence than we realize in determining who among us endures in the face of adversity and who succumbs. Why is this so? Because the meaning we attach to the adversities others endure can determine the meaning they attach to these same adversities. And that meaning, in turn, will likely determine whether they see themselves as resilient and courageous in the face of life's challenges, or as helpless and hopeless. If we get it wrong, they get it wrong. And if they get it wrong, we may have taken away one of the most important ingredients we know of for rising above a difficult past: the ability to see adversities in a new light.

SUMMARY

- Researchers who study resilience through the lifespan have identified a series of protective processes in the lives of individuals who are currently enjoying lives well-lived, despite previous exposure to multiple childhood risks and adversities. As children, these protective processes appeared to outweigh the effects of earlier adverse childhood experiences. As a result, they never developed the learning, behavioral, and/ or emotional problems many would have anticipated. In the resilience literature, they have come to be known as children who "beat the odds." To many, they serve as our examples of resilient lives.

- Other children, however, were not as fortunate. As might have been anticipated, they succumbed to these conditions, with many also experiencing significant school-related problems.

- But contrary to what many of us may think, at least some children who succumbed to adverse childhood experiences may not have been less resilient than those who beat the odds. Instead, their challenges were misunderstood, and for good reason. They performed in very uneven ways. This led to a series of erroneous perceptions regarding contributing causes. These inaccurate perceptions, in turn, offset the same protective processes that helped other at risk children to beat the odds.

- Erroneous perceptions seemed to also lead to ineffective remedies for improving emotional self-regulation and self-control skills, which in and of themselves have been linked to a range of negative later life outcomes.

- Advances in our understanding of human resilience and the limits of emotional endurance corroborate three other important lessons: We are more resilient than we realize, especially during our childhood years; there are limits to emotional endurance for even the most resilient among us; and we have more influence that we may realize in determining who "beats the odds" and who succumbs. A lot will depend upon the meaning we attach to the adversities they endure, especially during their childhood years.

Chapter 3

THE ADULT YEARS:
HOW DO THEY SUCCEED?

STILL STANDING

Carl is currently doing very well. As noted earlier, he has a loving wife, is the father of two healthy and happy grown children, and enjoys the freedom and independence that comes from owning his own website design and Internet marketing business. And although it's been a bumpy road, there are several lessons to be learned from his decades-long journey from troubled childhood to successful adulthood. First, it's indeed possible that some people can be capable of doing difficult things easily yet find easy things difficult for reasons that can have nothing to do with laziness or their strength of character. And while it's important to always try your best, the key to success in these simpler areas may not come down to trying harder, but rather trying differently. Second, it's entirely possible for someone to know what to do yet have difficulty consistently, predictably, and independently doing what they know, in part because they call into play different skills. Improving the ability to do what one knows, therefore, may sometimes require a new set of strategies, compensatory or otherwise, related specifically to these functions. Third, some of the smartest, wisest, and most successful people did not appear very smart, wise, or successful in school. There are many different ways of being smart, and these ways are more likely to be captured through our life experiences rather than our school experiences. Fourth, resilient people, school-age children included, will think and act differently in places they find threatening and dangerous as opposed to warm and friendly, especially when those threatening and dangerous places also feel stigmatizing, inescapable, and beyond their ability to control or alter. And fifth, it's these contextual influences that can determine whether we endure in the face of adversity or are stretched to our limits of emotional endurance, which helps to explain why some of the most resilient people may struggle significantly just to get through a typical day.

It turns out that the difference between success and failure in life and in school can sometimes have a great deal to do with context.

A REVEALING PORTRAIT OF HUMAN RESILIENCE—IN CONTEXT

Humans are very context-sensitive beings, say neuroscientists. This helps us flexibly change our behavior to adapt to different situations. We act, think, and feel one way in situations that frighten us, and another way in situations that welcome us. Rather than seeing this as a weakness, liability, or character flaw, neuroscientists see it as one of our greatest strengths (Quartz and Sejnowski, 2002). Carl is a good example. Today, he enjoys a rewarding and successful life, thanks in part to a well-honed ability to find, create, alter, and adapt to social contexts where he feels valued and recognized for the things he loves doing and does well. Central to this has been his ability to find a profession that highlights his personal strengths and talents. Just as important are his ongoing efforts to learn about and successfully employ an assortment of tools and strategies to navigate around his persisting challenges. It's been a successful formula that has allowed him to continually raise his professional expectations, while simultaneously leveling his professional playing field. In time, Carl also came to value the benefits of a fresh start. A change of scenery, it turns out, can go a long way in reducing failure experiences and replacing them with personally meaningful and rewarding ones. It wasn't until his third job that he began enjoying success at work. Similarly, it wasn't until attending a third different college that he began enjoying success at school. Choosing to start anew, however, should not be confused with having to start anew, as when Carl's family moved to a new community. While both can potentially result in a fresh new start, in Carl's case, the latter proved to be a riskier proposition.

As context-sensitive beings, we have other advantages—emotional, psychological, and spiritual ones. Just as we have the ability to seek out new social horizons, for example, our context-sensitive ways provide the opportunity to seek new emotional, psychological, and spiritual horizons. As social psychologist Ellen Langer (1989) reminds us, we have the capacity to view events, experiences, and conditions in our lives in a new and different context. This includes how we choose to view our personal successes and failures as well as our differences. We see this at work in Carl's long and winding road to a sense of mastery. Despite his persisting challenges, today he believes that working hard, not giving up, and treating mistakes as learning experiences can lead to rewarding and successful outcomes. He arrived at this mind-set by virtue of succeeding at things he loves doing and does well in the company of people he views as important in his life and who feel the same about him. And with a sense of mastery comes an ability to see challenges in a new light. Today, Carl understands his challenges in ways he was unable to before. Unlike in years past, he now views them in the context of his many strengths. Today, he also has a very different view of human intelligence. He knows that people can be smart in different ways, and these ways cannot be measured by school success. What it means to be smart can vary significantly—when viewed in its proper context.

For those who struggle with learning, behavioral, emotional, or other life challenges, associated stigma can be more painful to bear than the challenges themselves. So it was with Carl during his earlier years, but not so today. Previously, Carl defined himself in relation to others and the world through the lens of one or two negative labels. Today, he defines himself through many positive ones, each representing an important role or responsibility he maintains. He sees himself as a successful business owner, loving husband, loving parent, mentor to others in the community—all positive labels. Furthermore, the labels that were viewed as stigmatizing are now viewed as legitimizing. Once again, the role of context looms large here, as labels that represent areas of persisting challenge are viewed in the context of the many more labels representing strengths, talents, and valued roles and responsibilities. In fact, Carl's journey teaches us that one cure for overcoming the emotional pain associated with a stigmatizing label may actually be more labels—positive ones representing important roles and responsibilities.

Carl seemed to stumble on other cures as well. One of these came in the form of what appears to be a new mind-set about the very definition of one's abilities, including human intelligence. As a struggling student, he used to perceive his abilities in general and human intelligence in particular as fixed and intractable. He now thinks of them as malleable. It's a mind-set we find among those who believe that with the right amount of determination we grow stronger and smarter. It's a new perspective that not only takes the danger out of difference but also fosters a sense of mastery and allows us to see abilities in general, and intelligence in particular, in a new light.

In recent years, Carl arrived at yet another way to overcome the emotional pain associated with a stigmatizing label: view the label in historical context. He has worked hard to stay abreast of advances in our understanding of human differences. Doing so has allowed him to better understand why once harmful labels can transform into legitimizing ones. It's an understanding derived from an ability to see learning, behavioral, emotional, and mental health challenges in historical context.

Context looms large as well in terms of how Carl views his closest and most important relationships. In times past, his challenges and differences drove a wedge between he and those he cared the most about. This is no longer the case. Today, those he feels closest to value his unique qualities and view his imperfections within the context of these qualities. He himself has learned to view others he cares about through much the same lens.

In relation to all of those inescapably stressful experiences in times past, Carl's life has improved dramatically. He is truly a portrait of human resilience—in context.

The sections that follow delve more deeply into the contextual influences contributing to Carl's successful journey from troubled childhood to successful adulthood. Contextual influences are divided into three sections (see page 50): "Social Context" explores contextual influences contributing to Carl's socially valued roles and responsibilities, and to his eventual arrival at a place in life where he feels recognized for his contribution. "Life Experiences—in Context" explores contextual influences contributing to his ability to see strengths, challenges, and adverse life experiences in a new light. "Relationships—in Context" highlights the role that his closest personal and professional relationships played in his journey from school failure to life success.

CONTEXTUAL INFLUENCES = CONTEXTUALLY EXPRESSED PROTECTIVE PROCESSES

The contextual influences discussed throughout the book all link directly to the four protective processes identified by Werner and colleagues in the Kauai Longitudinal Study. Recall from Chapter 2 that the researchers identified the following four protective processes in the lives of resilient individuals who currently lead meaningful and productive lives, despite exposure to multiple risks and adverse experiences during childhood (Rutter, 1990; Werner and Smith, 2001):

1. Experiences and conditions that reduce the impact of prevailing risks by either (a) learning to see adversities in a new light, or (b) providing a protective shield or buffer that reduces exposure to their potentially damaging effects. This speaks directly to the role of contextual influences. Some social climates, for example, serve to buffer us from risk exposure, whereas others might increase our exposure.

2. Experiences preventing negative life events from spiraling out of control. The likelihood of this occurring increases as risk exposure increases. Those caught in this downward spiral benefit from a safety net that provides experiences that short-circuit their downward spiral, thereby allowing them to regain a sense of control and stability in their lives.

3. Experiences and conditions that help foster a sense of mastery or self-efficacy (the perception that one will successfully achieve the goals they set by virtue of their actions).

Social Context

Social context: The ability to successfully seek out, change, and/or accommodate to social contexts where we enjoy socially valued roles and responsibilities, and the opportunity to contribute significantly.

1. The Opportunity to Do What We Love to Do and Also Do Well: The Transforming Power of Meaningful Work
2. Raising the Bar and Leveling the Playing Field
3. A Change of Scenery: The Value of a Fresh Start

Life Experiences—In Context

Life experiences—in context: Learning to see strengths, challenges, and adverse life experiences in a new light.

4. Personal Pathways to a Sense of Mastery
5. Learning to See Human Intelligence in a New Light
6. When Difference No Longer Signals Danger
    6a. More Labels, Not Less
    6b. Learning to See Abilities as Malleable, Not Fixed
    6c. Learning to See Challenges in Historical Context
7. Translating the Pain of Our Past Into Meaningful Action on Behalf of Others

Relationships—In Context

Relationships—in context: While resilience is typically viewed through the lens of individual journeys, research suggests that our greatest source of strength may actually be each other.

8. Beating the Odds, Thanks to Those Who Changed the Odds
    8a. Safety Nets
    8b. Connecting to Those Who Legitimize Rather Than Stigmatize
9. Growing Closer and Stronger as a Result of Difficult or Traumatic Life Events
    9a. Relationships as Malleable, Not Fixed
10. Our Greatest Source of Strength – Each Other: A Closer Look at Turning Points

4. Experiences and conditions that open the door to turning points and second-chance opportunities.

The terms "contextual influences" and "protective processes" as defined here serve the same functions. They both neutralize or outweigh the potentially harmful effects of multiple risk exposure. These include risks associated with neurodevelopmentally based challenges or risks associated with environmental influences.

The term "contextual influences" however, draws us directly to our context-sensitive ways, especially our gift for contextual thinking. This gift allows us to attach new meaning to events and experiences in our lives and in the lives of others. We would not be able to recognize erroneous perceptions as erroneous if not for our ability to think contextually. If it's true that human understanding indeed plays an important the role in rising above a difficult past, this results from our ability to think contextually.

The term "contextual influences" also allows for the opportunity to extend our discussion to the many different life areas, life events, and life experiences that can override the effects of the challenges we might face. There are many different contexts within which protective processes can express themselves, and the term "contextual influences" provides the opportunity to begin exploring them. Contextual influences as discussed here can best be defined as contextually expressed protective processes.

The challenge is to ensure that readers see the direct correspondence between contextual influences on one hand and protective processes as they appear in the research literature on resilience on the other. (To learn more about how contextual influences link directly to protective processes, log on to the web page.)

Here and in the remaining chapters, the term "contextual influences" appears repeatedly. It is an abbreviation of "contextually expressed protective processes."

Contextual influences contributing to Carl's successful journey appear to have contributed to many other successful journeys as well. Similar influences can be observed in the lives of others who failed at school but succeeded at life, including those growing up under different conditions, exposed to different risks. Perhaps this should not come as a surprise, since contextual influences link directly to protective processes. The next chapter delves more deeply into the generalizability of contextual influences to the lives of others who rebounded from a troubled past.

These influences, if accessed early, can potentially improve the lives of struggling children and their families. Part II of the book discusses how contextual influences can be woven in and around a typical school day to achieve these positive outcomes.

Contextual influences at times share many properties. Consider, for example, a sense of mastery and a growth mind-set. Those who enjoy a sense of mastery believe that if they work hard, don't give up, and learn from their mistakes, their actions will determine their outcomes. Those with a growth mind-set enjoy similar beliefs. They also believe that human intelligence and other abilities are malleable and will grow stronger if we're willing to stretch ourselves beyond our comfort zone. I discuss a sense of mastery and a growth mind-set separately, but in reality they overlap considerably.

It should also be noted that for Carl, as well as others we'll be meeting in the chapters that follow, a sense of mastery and a growth mind-set are inferred by virtue of how they approach difficult tasks, work toward achieving difficult goals, and navigate personal challenges. It's not uncommon for persons to enjoy both a sense of mastery and a growth mind-set yet not be aware that they do.

Contextual influences are divided into three sections for discussion purposes. In reality, contextual influences pave the way for other influences. For example, meaningful and rewarding social and work-related experiences can lead to new ways of viewing life experiences. The reverse is true as well. Learning new ways to view life experiences can lead to meaningful and rewarding social or work-related experiences. Either or both can improve the quality of our relationships. Conversely, improved personal and professional relationships can change the way we view our experiences at work and in life. Contextual influences thus have a positive snowball or cascade effect. The same is true for protective processes.

Finally, those who enjoy lives well-lived despite experiencing years of school failure may never have thought of viewing challenges in historical context, may continue to view certain abilities as fixed rather than malleable, and may avoid situations they find to be stigmatizing rather than legitimizing. Yet their lives are meaningful and productive. Lives can improve for the better, even in the absence of these and other contextual influences.

SOCIAL CONTEXT

1. The Opportunity to Do What We Love and Do Well: The Transforming Power of Meaningful Work

Carl runs his own small business designing websites and coaching business owners on how to increase their online presence to attract customers. Some of his workday is spent traveling from one client's office to another. He loves his job, and his clients love him. Knowing Carl's profile of strengths and challenges, it's really no surprise that he excels at what he does. To design websites well draws on a variety of visual spatial and related skills, including the ability to think creatively. Carl has always been strong in visual spatial areas (despite earlier difficulties remembering the visual configuration of words) and has always been a creative thinker. He is also very warm and friendly, so meeting and chatting with clients comes naturally to him. Given his warm and engaging manner, people enjoy meeting him as well.

If Carl's teachers from years past could see him today, what they would be most surprised about is how motivated he is to produce good work and be recognized for a job well done. His spirit and enthusiasm appear in sharp contrast to how he approached the job of student, particularly in later grades, when he came to believe that doing well in school was beyond his reach.

To Carl, work represents more than a job. It's closer to a calling. Work is where he first experienced the personal sense of accomplishment we derive when given the opportunity to do what we love doing in the company of others who treat what we do as important. Today, Carl believes that he has many important things to contribute to this world, and he learned to feel this way largely through his work.

The meaning we attach to our role in the workplace usually falls into one of three categories, writes psychologist Amy Wrzesniewski: a job, a career, or a calling. Those who see work as a job treat it as a way to earn what they need to fulfill more personally meaningful needs. Career advancement means little. Those who see work as a career choice strive to advance and enjoy the greater prestige, power, esteem, and social standing that comes with advancement. For those who see work as a calling, work serves an even more meaningful purpose (Wrzesniewski et al., 1997). In many respects, this seems closest to defining Carl's relationship to his line of work. In his mind, work serves a greater good.

Wrzesniewski finds that those who treat work as a calling may or may not hold highly visible or high-profile positions. In a study involving administrative assistants working in a university setting, she observed some who treated their work as a job, some who treated it as a stage in their career, and some who treated it as a calling.

2. Raising the Bar and Leveling the Playing Field

Carl has carved out a very successful career, but he's still disorganized, doesn't manage time well, and forgets things like returning phone calls or checking his voicemail regularly. As was the case decades ago, he still knows what to do, but struggles to do what he knows consistently, predictably, and independently. But unlike decades ago, today he has a solution. Her name is Kathy.

Kathy is Carl's office assistant. Although her job description doesn't quite say it this way, she assists Carl in areas that draw heavily on executive function. Every weekday morning, she has the day's to-do list prepared, and she walks Carl through each important task. "It's 9:00 am, Carl, you need to call Mr. Smith." At 9:00 am promptly Carl calls Mr. Smith, and Kathy promptly checks off the first task on the list. "It's 10:00 am, time to call Mr. Jones." Check; "It's 11:00 am, time to visit Mr. Green." Check. "Carl, it's 4:00 pm, you're running late, won't be home exactly when you said, better call your wife." Check. Carl appears to the outside world as organized, efficient, responsible, and reliable. After decades of struggle, he figured out how to effectively execute a number of important day-to-day functions necessary to get things done: hire someone like Kathy.

Experts in the field, among them Sam Goldstein (2001), find that people with executive function weaknesses often respond well to reminders, cues, and prompts. If you cue the skill, they typically execute it. The key is to set up a system of effective reminders or cues throughout the day. It doesn't necessarily have to be a person. When Kathy isn't around, Carl will send himself text messages to remind him of things that need to get done. He checks his text messages constantly. Every time he does, it's another reminder.

Working Memory Is to School Success as Transactive Memory Is to Life Success

If you ask Carl to rate his memory ability in relation to others, he would say it's pretty poor, not for recalling important life experiences but for the mundane, day-to-day things. If you ask a neuropsychologist to rate Carl's memory ability in relation to others, she might comment on his rather poor working memory and spotty memory retrieval skills. What Carl doesn't realize is that he is quite skilled at a certain aspect of human memory: transactive memory (Gladwell, 2000; Wegner, Erber, and Raymond, 1991). When we think of memory, we imagine it as an internal process, as information stored in our minds that we retrieve when needed. But a lot of what we need to know is external, stored in the minds of the people we know. When we need the information, we go to them to get it. We seek out business associates for specific information pertaining to our business, tax advisers for information pertaining to our taxes, our attorney for legal matters, a personal physician for a health question. Transactive memory is not about what we can remember, but what people within our social circle can remember. Some individuals are good at creating social circles composed of people with diverse strengths and talents with ready access to a treasure trove of stored information. When they need access to specific knowledge they don't have or information they can't recall, they know whom to ask. Viewed within the context of transactive memory functions, these people have very good memory skills. Carl knows a lot of people who know a lot of things, and he knows whom to go to when he needs help to achieve a goal or solve a problem.

Transactive memory is also being studied in relation to new technologies (Sparrow, Liu, and Wegner, 2011). Take the Internet, for example. If there's information we need but that we lack knowledge of, or that we know but can't remember, we search for it online. Knowing how to use new tools and technologies allows those with poor memories to actually have superior memories. Carl is a master at using these tools and technologies.

Tools make us better problem solvers (Quartz and Sejnowski, 2002). We're constantly inventing new ones: smart phones, calculators, word processors, voice-to-text software programs, and so on. In the real world, when it comes to successfully getting things done, we rely a great deal on tools and other people. It some respects, this calls into question how well the tests we took in school truly measured our ability to reach goals and solve problems in the real world. In reality, we use external memory systems—transactive memory—to achieve goals and solve problems. On school tests, that would be considered cheating.

Reaching goals and solving problems depends not only on the tools, knowledge, and skills we possess personally but on those we possess collectively. While Carl's working memory skills remain rather weak, his transactive memory skills are excellent. It's among the reasons he has succeeded so well at life, despite struggling at school.

Carl's Strategies for Successfully Completing Important but Uninteresting Tasks

It took him decades, but Carl finally mastered strategies that help him successfully complete boring but important day-to-day tasks and responsibilities. Surprisingly, the things that are helpful are things you might think would make matters worse. He likes to work at his desk standing up, rather than sitting down, because he can focus better when standing and moving about. When attending professional development workshops, he finds it helpful to play a game on his cell phone or doodle on a notepad when listening to lengthy presentations. He listens better when he's doing something with his hands. When reading proposals or other lengthy texts, he concentrates better when he chews gum. He'll also take the reading material to a favorite coffee house near his office. He says the background noise helps him stay focused. Through trial and error, Carl has figured out what a number of experts in the field have been saying for years. People who have difficulty completing important but uninteresting tasks are often better able to complete these tasks when providing added stimulation through a different sense modality (Rotz and Wright, 2005). This is exactly what Carl was doing. Working on material at his desk was largely a visual task. Standing up and moving around was more motoric. Listening to a lengthy lecture involved auditory input. Playing a game or doodling involved tactile-kinesthetic and motoric input. Reading lengthy material is largely a visual task. Chewing gum provided tactile-kinesthetic input. Listening to calming, familiar background sounds at the coffee house provided auditory input.

Carl's Strategies for Refueling

Carl also figured out ways to effectively refuel his emotional self-regulation fuel tank. This occurred in response to a major health crisis (which we later discuss at greater length). Briefly, a few years back, Carl suffered a heart attack which necessitated emergency bypass surgery. To decrease the likelihood of a future heart attack, his doctor insisted he significantly change his behavior. He would have to lose weight, exercise regularly, and start eating healthier foods. It turns out that many of his new routines also proved to be effective strategies for replenishing his self-regulation fuel tank when it began to empty out. Today, Carl frequently takes walks after lengthy meetings. He takes longer lunch breaks, sometimes followed by leisurely walks through a park. He exercises several days a week with a close friend and has joined a program that helps him monitor and maintain his healthier habits. He also pays far more attention to his stress level and will take short, relaxing breaks when it increases. This is quite a departure from how he had been refueling before his heart attack. In years past, he would snack impulsively on various junk foods and spend hours engaged in sedentary activities, like surfing the Internet before going to bed, which often prevented him from getting a good night's sleep. He didn't know it at the time, but Carl's old strategies for refueling eventually contributed to his subsequent health problems.

Over time, Carl eventually created a work-related environment that matched his personal strengths and challenges. He also learned how to effectively modify his work environment in ways that provided him the tools, technologies, and resources to level the professional playing field. What's more, he did so while continuing to raise his personal and professional expectations.

3. A Change of Scenery: The Value of a Fresh Start

The road from challenged childhood to successful adulthood can take many unexpected twists and turns. Before starting his business, Carl sold computers for three different companies. In the first job, his supervisor was a stickler for detail—not a good fit for Carl. In the second, employees were required to do quite a bit of paperwork; again, this was not a good fit. The third company valued out-of-the-box thinkers. Carl was one of their top salespeople. Different contexts, different outcomes.

It's true for work settings and also for school settings, college included. Carl successfully completed his bachelor's degree in business administration, but it required attending three different colleges. He dropped out of the first two schools. Years later, he enrolled in a third one that provided a structure that matched his particular profile of strengths and challenges. Among the advantages, it allowed him to take one class at a time. While the classes were more intensive in nature, he didn't mind, since he found it easier to focus on one subject rather than many. He also accessed the school's resources for students with disabilities and arranged for accommodations that proved very helpful, including extra time on exams, copies of lecture notes, and academic coaching. The school was also much smaller than the first two, and much more personal. Carl was able to meet and get to know his professors, some of whom he is still in contact with.

Over the course of his adult life, Carl has been able to find, create, and on occasion adapt to settings and situations that provide him with opportunities to do what he loves. Furthermore, this ultimately occurred in the company of others who value and recognize the important things he has to contribute. In combination, this helped propel him to a level of success that would probably come as a surprise to those who knew him as a struggling child decades ago. Social context plays a huge role in helping explain Carl's ability to rise above earlier adversities. It helps explain why his intellectual and creative strengths carry importance and why less importance is placed on simpler things that seemed to matter so much in school. It also explains why he's able to freely use tools, technologies, and other strategies, in contrast to previous work and school settings where these efforts were frowned on.

Carl's context-sensitive ways have served him well. Don't forget, though, he is resilient by nature, and always has been. These resilient qualities are what he relied on to find, create, and adapt to contexts in ways that eventually propelled him to new heights.

LIFE EXPERIENCES—IN CONTEXT

"When we are no longer able to change a situation, we are challenged to change ourselves."
—*Viktor Frankl,* Man's Search for Meaning

As context-sensitive beings, we have a choice as to the meaning we attach to life events, conditions, and experiences. Viktor Frankl (1963) wrote extensively about this choice, one that he felt we always have at our disposal, no matter how dire things might appear. To illustrate the point, he often referred to personal experiences while imprisoned in a Nazi concentration camp during World War II. Frankl believed the choice we have in this regard is what allows us to endure personal suffering with courage and dignity.

4. Personal Pathways to a Sense of Mastery

For Carl, the chance to succeed in areas he views as important, in the company of those who value his contribution, helped foster a sense of mastery. Interestingly, though, he was well on the road to mastery before gaining insight into the nature of his challenges and the resulting erroneous perceptions that wreaked havoc on his school life. Many of us assume that behavioral change happened in reverse order: first we learn to view our challenges in a new light (new meaning) and then we're willing to work hard, not give up, and learn from our mistakes (new mastery). Carl shows us that new mastery can also lead to new meaning. Our actions, in other words, can also affect our beliefs (Deutschman, 2007; Myers, 2000). Carl eventually learned to see his challenges in new ways *after* learning to achieve in new ways.

Successful Actions That Lead to New Beliefs:
The Mastery to Meaning Connection

When Carl was in high school, school staff members spent countless hours trying to repair his damaged self-esteem. It was an entirely understandable goal in light of his low self-regard. But efforts to improve his self-esteem were not likely to foster a sense of mastery. The reason is that mastery and self-esteem are not one and the same. On the road to mastery, our actions matter the most.

Mastery occurs as a result of hard work and continually accomplishing things one sets out to accomplish. It also requires the ability to view failures and setbacks as learning experiences.

Furthermore, mastery relates directly to improved performance. This is not necessarily the case with high self-esteem. Social psychologist Roy Baumeister cites two studies to illustrate. In the first study, researchers found that grades in 10th grade predicted self-esteem in 12th grade, but self-esteem in 10th grade failed to predict grades in 12th grade. Students with higher self-esteem did in fact earn better grades, but better grades predicted higher self-esteem, not the reverse (Baumeister and Tierney 2011). Perhaps even more revealing is the second study, conducted by Donald Forsyth at Virginia Commonwealth University. Students obtaining a grade of C or lower on Forsyth's midterm exam were randomly assigned to two groups; one received weekly self-esteem-enhancing messages, another (the control group) received neutral messages. Surprisingly, students receiving weekly self-esteem boosters received lower grades on their final exam than did the control group. In fact, grades were even lower than those they earned on their midterms (Baumeister and Tierney, 2011; Forsyth et al., 2007). According to Baumeister, it's possible to learn how to feel better about doing worse. Mastery is about doing better on the things we set out to accomplish. Self-esteem is about feeling better about ourselves. Both are important, but they're different.

Through his repeated accomplishments at work, Carl eventually believed that his actions controlled his outcomes (mastery). In time, successful actions contributed to new beliefs, as he also learned to see his challenges in a new light (new meaning). This was accompanied by a new and far more positive view of himself in relation to others and the world in general (self-esteem).

5. Learning to See Human Intelligence in a New Light

When it comes to designing state-of-the-art websites for businesses wishing to increase their visibility on the Internet, Carl is an expert. He sees himself as an expert in this area, and others do as well. Although he has never said so in words, it nonetheless appears that he has arrived at a conclusion similarly reached by a number or educators, neuroscientists, and prevention specialists. The question we should be asking, they believe, is not how smart we are, but how are we smart?

How Are We Smart?

According to Harvard University neuropsychologist Howard Gardner, it's a myth to think that something as complex as human intelligence can be measured by a single test score. An increasing number of educators, health care professionals, and others agree with him. In reality, there are multiple areas of intellectual strength and talent, each valued differently by different cultures. In Gardner's theory of multiple intelligences (MI theory), eight different areas of intellectual capacity are described: spatial, musical, bodily kinesthetic, interpersonal, intrapersonal, naturalistic, linguistic, and logical-mathematical (ABC News, 1993; Gardner, 1993; Shearer, 2004).

Those strong in spatial intelligence excel in visual spatial thinking and creating mental images in their minds. A number of people who rebounded from a difficult past have gravitated toward jobs and careers allowing them to express their visual spatial gifts. Some, like Carl, went into web design. Others became artists and fashion designers. Some enjoy hobbies like photography and video production. Each draws heavily on visual spatial strengths to succeed. When we inquire about how they perform on these tasks, all feel very skilled. Based on MI theory, they're more than skilled—they're gifted.

Some who rebounded from a troubled past are succeeding in various health care and mental health professions like nursing, social work, couples and family therapy, and clinical psychology, fields where their intrapersonal intelligence serves them well. Those strong in this domain are often skilled in monitoring and managing emotions. Many are strong in interpersonal intelligence, which is apparent in how aware and sensitive they are to other people's perspectives, moods, and feelings. Gardner also finds these intelligences in those succeeding in business, sales, and teaching. Carl is skilled in connecting emotionally with other people. Proponents of MI theory might describe Carl as gifted in this area.

Persons strong in musical intelligence often experience a deep appreciation of music and show unique sensitivity to pitch, rhythm, and timbre. Some are very skilled at singing, playing a musical instrument, or composing. Many are very good at memorizing songs, even if they aren't very good at memorizing other things. Some remember being able to study better in school when listening to music. Among those who did poorly in school but succeed at life, some played a musical instrument, either professionally or simply for personal enjoyment. Music also seems to play an important calming influence in their lives.

Among those evidencing high bodily kinesthetic intelligence, some have successfully completed marathons, some have studied dance, many are athletic and physically active. Those strong in this domain demonstrate precision, control, and agility in their body movements. Those strong in naturalistic intelligence enjoy exploring nature. Many enjoy gardening, fishing, hiking, and other outdoor activities. Others like working with animals. All share an interest in, understanding of, and caring for natural and living things.

Of Gardner's eight intelligences, the two that are particularly highlighted in school are linguistic, which draws on reading, writing, and speaking skills, and logical-mathematical, which draws on calculation skills, logical reasoning, and problem solving. Looking back at his school life, it's quite possible that Carl enjoyed strengths in at least four, five, or even six of Gardner's eight areas of intelligence, in contrast to specific challenges within areas calling into play only two. Unfortunately, these two were the areas most often associated with school success.

"Successful Intelligence"

Carl is very smart in other ways as well. Consider, for example, how effective he is at solving problems and navigating challenges as they occur in the real world. Psychologist Robert Sternberg (2003) refers to this as successful intelligence. Sternberg studies diverse intellectual strengths and how they allow us to achieve in some domains more so than in others. Those high in academic intelligence possess the range of skills required to succeed at school. Those high in successful intelligence can succeed at life. Moreover, successful intelligence accounts for our ability to view life success contextually, based on our own personal notions of success. People tend to have similar notions of what it takes to be successful at school, but most would agree that there are countless pathways to a successful life. Most would also agree that we each can choose our own path, based on our strengths, passions, interests, and values. The successfully intelligent among us do this well. Furthermore, they know how to act on their environment in ways that maximize their opportunities for success. It may require trying to change conditions to match more closely with personal strengths. It may require seeking entirely different environments that provide new and better opportunities for success. Or it may require adapting to current conditions in more effective ways. Being successfully intelligent also requires capitalizing on strengths while correcting or compensating for weaknesses. The successfully intelligent among us, Carl included, know how to raise the bar (capitalize on strengths) and level their playing field (correct or compensate for weaknesses).

6. When Difference No Longer Signals Danger

Throughout his years in school, and for many years after, Carl associated difference with danger. His learning and behavioral differences represented sources of shame and embarrassment, and he worked hard to divert others' attention away from these differences. Certainly he wanted to do better in school, academically and behaviorally. But to do better he needed help, and seeking help was something he never really considered, since doing so would draw more attention to his difficulties. Today, he sees his differences in an entirely new light. He perceives his many strengths in a new way as well. He now thinks of his persisting differences in the context of his strengths. For Carl, and a number of people who rebounded from a troubled past, these accomplishments represent important steps on the road to improved well-being. We explore each in greater depth in the pages that follow.

We begin our discussion by describing a surprising solution for alleviating the suffering of those affected by a label they perceive as stigmatizing: more labels. I then discuss the benefits derived when those struggling with learning, behavioral, and/or emotional challenges learn to perceive abilities as malleable rather than fixed. Finally, I discuss the benefits derived from learning to see challenges in a historical context instead of social or psychological.

6a. More Labels, Not Fewer

In recent years, a number of well-known people—from CEOs, to politicians, to actors, to artists, to athletes—have come forward to share details of the disabilities or mental health conditions they endured in years past. They do so knowing that there still exists a public stigma associated with the diagnostic labels related to these hardships. Yet this stigma hasn't silenced them. If anything, it's among the reasons they choose to speak up. They're telling their stories so that others who are going through what they went through never lose hope and not let shame or embarrassment prevent them from seeking help or finding support. How do some people successfully rise above the stigma associated with various labels? Answer: more labels.

Carl is currently seen as a hard worker who handles his career responsibilities with skill and confidence. He treats daily challenges and/or mistakes as learning experiences, much as people do when they believe their actions control their outcomes. Unlike the years of shame and embarrassment he harbored as a result of his struggles at school, now he feels valued and recognized for the many important skills he possesses.

Carl enjoys a loving relationship with his wife, who values him and accepts him, challenges and all. He is the father of two grown children, and he worked hard over the years to provide for their needs. In his limited free time, he serves as a board member for a local nonprofit organization dedicated to helping children and families affected by challenges similar to those he experienced decades earlier.

When asked to describe himself today, somewhere in the description will be references to his many roles—husband, father, business owner, community board member, to name a few. All are labels—labels that draw attention to his strengths, accomplishments, and important responsibilities. Carl still experiences challenges, also captured through labels. But they are far fewer in number than the other labels, which define much of his life. Today, the labels representing challenges are viewed within the context of strengths.

For those suffering the effects of stigma associated with a label, the answer to overcoming these effects may be more labels. According to social psychologist Ellen Langer (1989), when people view others through different and varied labels rather than one or two global ones, they become more discriminating in their thinking about others. They can see many facets of a person, his or her strengths as well as his or her challenges. Those impacted by a specific disability or challenge are no longer defined by its label. When people become more discriminating, in other words, they're less likely to discriminate. What's especially encouraging about this is that with a little practice, we can learn to think in more discriminating ways. Even more encouraging, we're capable of learning this at a young age. Langer illustrated this in a study she conducted with elementary school children. Results showed that they were able to discriminate between activities that children with disabilities could perform successfully versus ones that put them at a disadvantage. Once they learned to be more discriminating in this way, they learned that a person's disability is related entirely to context. Langer found that children learned to be more discriminating without prejudice (Langer, 1989; Langer and Chanowitz, 1988). (To learn more about the study, log on to the web page.)

Although some adults who rebounded from a troubled past continue to harbor feelings of shame about their struggles, many are also working to change laws, enhance systems of care, and educate others about their kinds of challenges. They're comfortable with labels attached to their struggles, and they work hard to make sure others affected by similar challenges learn to be comfortable with them as well. In light of Langer's research, it's quite possible that their strength in this regard comes from their many rewarding self-defining labels—parent, spouse, partner, successful professional, responsible employee, advocate, civic leader, mentor—rather than one or two associated with their specific challenges. In the final analysis, stigma may not be the result of labels in general, but just one or two global ones, in the absence of others that draw attention to our personal strengths and the important contributions we make.

As noted earlier, contextual influences can have a cascading effect. Carl knows how to seek out, modify, or adapt to situations that highlight his strengths. He also sustains relationships with others who value him as a person. In combination, these contextual influences, both social and relational, played a part in helping him assume a number of personally meaningful roles and responsibilities. These, in turn, helped him learn to view strengths, challenges, and life experiences in a different and more hopeful context.

Self-Views in Context

Research shows that how we see ourselves in relation to others, including how we value or devalue our abilities, can vary from situation to situation (Marsh and Craven, 2002a, b). In some situations, such as those that highlight what we do well, we can look and feel confident and self-assured. In other situations, like those that shine a spotlight on our weaknesses, anxiety can increase and self-confidence can fade, as can our motivation to try our best. We can feel confident and self-assured in one situation, but quite the opposite in another. It's all a matter of context.

It's not unusual to think of a poor self-concept as a constant—that if we devalue our abilities, we do so all of the time, and in all situations. Researchers are saying this may not be the case. We can value our artistic abilities, for example, and devalue our athletic abilities. Or value our athletic abilities but devalue singing and dancing. Or value our artistic, athletic, singing, and dancing abilities, but devalue academic abilities. In other words, self-perceptions can vary from situation to situation and from one life area to another. Today, Carl spends a great deal of his day doing what he does very well in settings where others know and value this. It's no surprise that this is reflected in his current self-views. It's also another illustration of how contextual influences work hand in hand.

6b. Learning to See Abilities as Malleable

When it comes to his day-to-day work responsibilities, Carl believes that trying hard, not giving up, and learning from his mistakes will lead to success on the job. This was not something he believed when it came to success at school many years ago. Stanford University psychology professor Carol Dweck (2006) would likely say that Carl now views his work-related skills as malleable. As a child, on the other hand, he viewed the skills required to succeed in school as fixed. Can learning to see our abilities as malleable help explain why some people rebound from a range of adverse childhood experiences, including years of school failure? I believe it can.

According to Dweck, most people define intelligence in one of two ways: as something that exists in a fixed amount, or as something malleable. Those with "fixed" mind-sets see mistakes as a reflection of how smart they are. As a result, they give up much too soon at things they fear they might fail at, and often refuse to persist once mistakes occur, all in the name of feeling and looking smart. On the other hand, those who believe that intelligence is malleable view their potential as unlimited, depending on how hard they choose to work and how much they choose to learn. People with these malleable or "growth" mind-sets see mistakes, failures, and setbacks not as experiences to fear but as something to learn from and grow. Surprisingly, those who achieve excellent grades in school may not necessarily view intelligence as malleable. In fact, according to Dweck, if grades become our measure of how intelligent we are, the opposite can occur. Good grades can lead to a fixed mind-set. That's because intelligence is no longer about learning new things but about getting good grades. What happens when school becomes so challenging that you begin to struggle academically? If you associate struggling with a lack of intelligence, you might stop trying as hard, or even stop trying completely. After all, you don't want anyone to question your intelligence. You think you're smart, other people think you're smart, and that's the way you want to keep it. Dweck sometimes observes this dynamic among students in middle school who feel challenged in ways they didn't before. When success doesn't come as easy as it did in earlier grades, some are no longer willing to work as hard (Hopkins, 2000). There's too much at stake, identity wise. Dweck observed this dynamic in a study she and colleagues conducted with a group of Ivy League university students, all pre-med majors enrolled in their first semester of chemistry. Those with fixed views of intelligence began losing interest when the coursework became too difficult, despite believing that success in chemistry would determine who would ultimately succeed in medical school. In some instances, students with fixed mind-sets even changed their major. Those with growth mind-sets worked harder (Dweck, 2006).

Carl excels at his job. Although he doesn't use terms like "fixed" or "malleable," by simply watching him at work there can be little doubt that he has a malleable view of the abilities required to perform his responsibilities. He works hard, enjoys engaging in challenging tasks, and learns from his mistakes.

As a struggling child, Carl had a fixed view of his abilities. Surprisingly though, his fixed mind-set probably developed less as a result of how he viewed his challenges, and more as a result of how he viewed his intellectual strengths. Carl can recall countless times that teachers and others at school told him how smart he was. The problem is that this may have led to a fixed mind-set. According to Dweck, teaching students that their abilities are malleable starts by celebrating, valuing, and reinforcing effort, struggle, and hard work. Celebrating intelligence, on the other hand, teaches students to view their abilities as fixed.

Dweck demonstrated this in a study she and colleagues conducted with fifth-graders. Students were first presented with a set of challenging problems they were capable of completing successfully if they tried hard. As expected, they tried hard and completed them successfully. Students were then praised in three different ways. One group was praised for their intelligence, a second group for their effort, and a third group, serving as controls, for their accomplishment. Next, researchers offered the students a choice. They could work on either a new and challenging task that would be difficult but would provide the opportunity to learn something new, or they could work on a more familiar task, one they were much more likely to be successful at. Ninety percent of the students praised for their efforts chose the challenging task. Ninety percent were willing to risk failing in order to learn something new. Most children praised for their intelligence, on the other hand, opted for the safer task. (To read more about this study, log on to the web page.)

Carl's growth mind-set applies not only to this discussion but to several other topics in this section as well. Learning to see abilities as malleable provides a number of potential benefits: (1) fostering a sense of mastery; 2) redefining what it means to be intelligent; and (3) taking the danger out of difference.

6c. Learning to See Challenges in Historical Context

Labels can serve to legitimize, or they can stigmatize, depending on the meaning we attach to them. Unfortunately, there remains a stubbornly persistent stigma associated with the labels and diagnostic categories we use to describe a number of learning, behavioral, emotional, and/or mental health challenges, and this has caused many people to feel shame and embarrassment. How can we remove this unnecessary burden from their lives, so they may finally learn to see themselves as the resilient people they are? Mental health providers whom Carl has consulted have helped him come to one possible solution: learn to view these labels and diagnostic categories in a different context—not social, psychological, or relational, but historical.

Carl has learned to do this and has derived a number of benefits as a result. He realizes how much more is known today about his particular challenges than was known in years past. Perhaps even more important, he realizes how much more there still is to learn. In contrast to how he felt decades ago, his challenges no longer signal threat and danger but an opportunity to learn and grow from advances in fields such as education, psychology, and health care. Carl has become a student in the study of differences. He stays abreast of new research findings, new evidence-based practices, even alternative treatments, for which benefits are more anecdotal. He speaks to experts, attends conferences, and learns from others with similar challenges. He is well aware that new advances, insights, and tools are arriving in the future. He is aware of this by virtue of his ability to view life's challenges and the labels we use to refer to them—learning, behavioral, emotional, mental health, and otherwise—in a historical context. This has helped him greatly in his efforts to rise above challenges associated with a condition he has struggled with since childhood: attention deficit/hyperactivity disorder (ADHD).

Carl's Understanding of ADHD, Then and Now

As a struggling student up through today, Carl's difficulties were consistent with existing diagnostic criteria for ADHD. Perhaps few diagnostic classifications raise more suspicions in our culture these days. For years, Carl maintained those suspicions as well. He didn't see the condition as real, and for good reason: it didn't make logical sense. He paid attention just fine, sometimes. He really paid attention well when he was doing something that interested him. Sure, he would start projects and not finish them, but that was because he got bored, and getting bored is entirely normal. Everyone gets bored with what they're doing from time to time, and when they do, they might stop what they're doing so they can do something more interesting. What Carl couldn't understand was how entirely normal behaviors that everyone exhibits could ever be called a disorder. Logically speaking, it was hard to argue with him. It was an entirely understandable perception, according to experts in the field, entirely understandable yet erroneous. Let me explain why.

True, people with ADHD and people without it each experience similarly normal behaviors, but they experience these normal behaviors to very different degrees. Anyone who exhibits a normal behavior to an extreme may also find it difficult to navigate through a typical day. Many of us lose our keys from time to time, but not every day. We are late to a meeting once in a while, but not all the time. Entirely normal behaviors can be experienced to different degrees, and lives can be affected as a result. To illustrate, consider the following study conducted by Russell Barkley. He and colleagues asked 146 adults diagnosed with ADHD whether they experienced conventionally agreed-on ADHD symptoms "often." They also asked the same question to 109 non-ADHD adults drawn from the general population. What they found was that the vast majority of people in the general population do not report experiencing any of the ADHD symptoms often. For example, to the item, "Difficulty sustaining attention," only 3 percent of the non-ADHD normative sample endorsed "often," compared to 97 percent of the adult ADHD sample. To the item, "Easily distracted by extraneous stimuli," it was 2 percent compared with 97 percent, and to the item, "Feels restless," it was 4 percent compared with 79 percent. Barkley then gave the groups a list of 10 different life domains, and asked them to indicate what domains they feel they are impaired in by virtue of ADHD symptoms. The differences were striking. Persons with ADHD reported being impaired significantly more than those without ADHD in all 10 domains. Here are some examples: in "Work or occupation," 75 percent of adults reported being impaired compared to 2 percent of non-ADHD adults. In "Educational activities," it was 89 percent versus 1 percent, and in "Daily responsibilities," 86 percent versus 1 percent again (Barkley, 2010a, 2011a, c).

To meet full diagnostic criteria for ADHD, several other criteria must be met. It's not simply the presence and impact of behavioral characteristics consistent with the disorder. (To learn more about current diagnostic criteria, log on to the web page.) The point to remember here—one that took Carl a long time to realize—is that entirely normal behaviors can sometimes be exhibited to a far more significant degree than they're exhibited by the vast majority of individuals of the same age in the general population. And whenever this occurs, it also increases the likelihood that the quality of one's life will be significantly impacted as well.

Perhaps even more important to our discussion here is that most people assume by virtue of its name that ADHD is essentially a problem in paying attention. Certainly, this is what Carl always assumed. It's one of the main reasons he hadn't believed ADHD applied to him. He paid attention just fine as long as he was doing something that interested him. Research shows that this happens to be true for most people with ADHD. The label itself can be misleading. According to Barkley, ADHD may be more a disorder of intention rather attention. Individuals can usually pay attention when they're interested in what they're doing and may truly intend to achieve the goals they originally set out to achieve. A major reason for this, Barkley believes, is that ADHD is not so much a skill deficit per se but a problem in performance or execution. Experts have established a close relationship between the behavioral characteristics consistent with ADHD and challenges in executive functioning. We rely on executive function skills to perform a number of daily tasks, everything from planning, organizing, and prioritizing activities to regulating our emotions, to monitoring our behavior, to keeping information in mind long enough so that we can use it to solve a problem or continue to pursue a particular goal.

A lot of us underestimate the potential implications of ADHD throughout the life span. Carl certainly did. These behavioral challenges contributed significantly to his problems in school. What's more, his father and his son evidence the same behavioral challenges. Research shows that most people who meet diagnostic criteria for ADHD show a strong genetic component—it runs in families. It's no coincidence that Carl, his father, and his son have been affected by the same behavioral challenges. Had we known years ago what we know now, it's possible that Carl's father would never have lost his job, Carl would never have failed in school, and his parents would not have had nightly homework battles with him. Learning to attach new meaning to life's challenges, whatever they may be, can be a major victory in the battle to overcome these challenges. Viewing ADHD as simply a problem in paying attention, or sitting still, or remembering where we put our keys, can prevent those struggling with its symptoms from achieving this important victory.

Carl has a very different understanding of ADHD today. What he found particularly helpful in learning to see its characteristics in a new light were five erroneous perceptions outlined in Chapter 1.

Carl realizes those perceptions are understandable and, with closer examination, mistaken. What he hadn't realized though was that the first two describe behavioral profiles often observed among those with ADHD. This is the case for children and adults. Arriving at this realization was important to Carl, since it provided him an alternative explanation for an ADHD behavioral profile, one that no longer attributes it solely to willfulness, laziness, a character flaw, or a lack of resilience. By acknowledging erroneous perceptions three, four, and five he was also now better able to appreciate the potential emotional consequences of others attributing an ADHD profile to a lack of intelligence, resilience, or will, particularly during our school-age years when we have less opportunity to seek out a new school environment, or alter or control the one we're in.

These erroneous perceptions helped enlighten Carl about how those with ADHD can present themselves to the world and how the world sometimes responds back.

Today, Carl is aware that ADHD characteristics can sometimes translate into paradoxically uneven learning and behavioral profiles. He's also aware that ADHD represents normal behaviors that everyone exhibits, and normal behaviors can manifest themselves far more intensely in some people. When they do, he's also aware that they can significantly affect the quality of their lives. Carl knows ADHD isn't the best label to describe the condition he's struggled with most of his life, but he knows that when it comes to evolving fields of study, this is to be expected. He knows this as a result of his ability to view ADHD in historical context.

Carl's Understanding of Learning Disabilities, Then and Now

The erroneous perceptions also helped enlighten Carl to how other challenges can contribute to uneven profiles as well, among them reading disabilities much like his own. For example, when it came to executing certain skills associated with the reading process, some days were better than others. Take, for example, his ability to recall the correct pronunciation of a difficult word on a page. Some days he could pronounce the word correctly, on other days he couldn't. These problems in recall were even more apparent when it came to spelling. Carl remembers how frustrated he felt when not being able to recall the correct spelling of a word on a test when he practiced the correct spelling the night before. Educator Rick Lavoie (2007) refers to these problems in recall as "performance inconsistency," and he observes the pattern among students with specific reading and other learning disabilities. He uses the example of three clocks all running at different speeds. At some point, all three clocks will give us the same time. In other words, inconsistently performing clocks will match up on occasion. The same applies to people with reading or other learning disabilities. The difference is that when people perform inconsistently, it's human nature to think it's intentional. "I saw you do it. I know you can do it. Just do it." But it may not be intentional at all. Growing up, Carl had no idea that otherwise resilient children could perform so inconsistently and unpredictably on tasks that most others could perform effortlessly. He certainly had no idea that children with profiles like his could conceivably excel at far more difficult and complex intellectual and creative tasks. Unable to see his challenges in a new light, he eventually became demoralized and came to believe that trying harder did not result in doing better. Carl has benefited significantly simply by being able to view reading and other learning disabilities in historical context. (To read more on this topic, log on to the web page.)

Carl's Understanding of Interpersonal Trauma, Then and Now

Carl currently serves as a board member for a nonprofit organization that provides mental health and educational services to children, youth, and families struggling with mental health and other life challenges. Through his work, he has learned a great deal about how interpersonal trauma—trauma occurring within the context of human relationships, particularly relationships children depend on to feel safe and protected—can contribute to a range of learning, behavioral, and other challenges. He's learned, for example, about neuroimaging studies conducted on those suffering the effects of traumatic stress exposure that showed decreased activation in brain regions associated with executive functioning (van der Kolk, 2006). Recall that Carl was exposed to years of verbal and physical abuse as a child, and witnessed his mother being abused as well. In the next chapter, we delve more deeply into the potential effects of interpersonal trauma on the learning process. On some occasions, it's possible that Carl struggled in his ability to execute important school-related skills not only because of neurodevelopmentally based executive function delays, or a neurodevelopmentally based reading disability, but because of normal biological reactions to abnormally stressful life experiences.

The ACE Study, Then and Now

Carl suffered a heart attack a few years ago and would have died had he not undergone emergency surgery. His experience is discussed at greater length in a later section of this chapter and again in Chapter 8. Soon after this emergency, he learned about the ACE Study, and more specifically, his elevated ACE score. He had not heard of the study before, and how its results are helping improve later life health outcomes among those exposed to interpersonal trauma in childhood. The ACE Study identifies 10 categories of stressful or traumatic childhood experiences (see web page). Each has been shown through prior research to have significant adverse health or social implications. Each has also been the focus of public and private prevention efforts designed to reduce its frequency and consequences (Anda, 2011). Carl had an ACE score of 7. Based on ACE Study results, a score of 7 placed him at increased risk for later life health problems, including heart disease. Had he known about this study years ago, it might have motivated him to take better care of his health.

From a historical perspective, when it comes to understanding the effects of interpersonal trauma, we've only scratched the surface. Researchers continue to uncover new findings related to its behavioral, psychological, and physiological effects, including the effects of exposure to spousal abuse, physical abuse, and verbal abuse (Felitti et al., 1998), experiences Carl relates to firsthand. Their findings remind us of the different pathways leading to learning and behavioral unevenness. Unlike earlier times though, experts in the field are beginning to work alongside teachers and other school staff to create "trauma-informed" learning environments that are more understanding of and accommodating to children who may be responding to the demands of school in uneven ways. Importantly, these environments also provide children an abundant supply of success experiences that can lead to a sense of mastery. This includes opportunities to translate mistakes into learning experiences. Experts remind us that overcoming a traumatic past is as much about new mastery as new meaning. Overcoming its effects requires that we believe that we have the power to change conditions in our lives (Fisher, 2000).

7. Translating the Pain of Our Past into Meaningful Action on Behalf of Others

"In our sleep, pain which cannot forget falls drop by drop
upon the heart until, in our own despair, against our will,
comes wisdom through the awful grace of God."

—*Aeschylus*

Through his volunteer work as a board member at a local non-profit organization serving children and families, Carl is currently among those involved in this important work. The organization is dedicated to helping schools access the tools and resources they need to serve children and families affected by a range of challenges, including those resulting from interpersonal trauma. As with many others who rebounded from a troubled childhood, Carl is translating the pain of his past into meaningful action on behalf of others.

When Carl finally learned to embrace his strengths, see his challenges in a new light, and master a variety of tools, technologies, and strategies to level his playing field, it motivated him to help others who struggle the way he did. In addition to his volunteer hours at the local group, he lends this organization (and others with a similar mission) his expertise in web design and computer technologies. His efforts in this regard exemplify another contributing influence in his journey from troubled childhood to successful adulthood: the ability to translate the pain of the past into constructive action in the present to improve the lives of others in the future.

Helping Others Learn to See Challenges in a New Light

Today, Carl is playing an important role in helping others learn to see their challenges in a new light. By doing so, he may be helping himself. According to Stephen Post, research shows that giving back to others protects overall health twice as much as aspirin protects against heart disease (Post and Neimark, 2007). This has not gone entirely unnoticed by doctors. In one California HMO, Medicare patients receive written prescriptions recommending that they volunteer their time to help others.

The term "required helpfulness," coined over a half century ago, seemed to convey similar sentiments, albeit in a different context. The phrase emerged from observations of citizens in Great Britain immediately following the bombing of London during World War II. Doctors observed fewer than expected adverse psychological reactions among those looking after others and trying to keep them safe. According to one observer, persons in poor mental health prior to the bombing actually fared better if engaged in a personally satisfying job that others perceived as socially necessary (Rachman, 1979).

More recently, others have referred to "the activism cure" to capture the benefits derived from helping others in meaningful ways (Maran, 2009). In many respects, this term captures Carl's efforts. It's quite possible that his activism on behalf of others may have helped him further reframe and strengthen his view of himself. Consider, for example, a study conducted by Paul Gerber and colleagues that identified four stages of the reframing process among vocationally successful individuals with various learning challenges—recognition, acceptance, understanding, and action. In the recognition stage, subjects realized they do things differently as a result of their disability. In the acceptance stage, disabilities were accepted as real. In the understanding stage, weaknesses were understood in the context of strengths. In the action stage, subjects realized they had to learn to do things in new, different, and creative ways to reach their goals (Gerber, 2001; Gerber, Ginsberg, and Reiff, 1990). In transforming personal pain into meaningful action to help others, Carl has arrived at the action stage, taking it to another level, one in which he works to help people with similar challenges arrive at their action stage as well. (To read about other studies showing the benefits derived from helping others, log on to the web page.)

RELATIONSHIPS—IN CONTEXT

We're a culture that loves stories of resilient individuals who beat the odds, individuals who encountered a variety of hardships during their childhood years, and who, through hard work and a "never give up" attitude, eventually pulled themselves up by their own bootstraps. Yet when we dig deeper into the lives of people who eventually beat the odds, Carl included, we seem to invariably find human relationships that helped change the odds.

8. Beating the Odds, Thanks to Those Who Changed the Odds

Four years ago, Carl suffered a heart attack. It happened while he was having dinner with a friend. He was rushed to the hospital, where the emergency medical care saved his life. He ended up having bypass surgery to prevent another heart attack. Six months later, another unexpected health crisis occurred, this time involving his wife. During a routine medical exam, she was diagnosed with breast cancer. She, too, was fortunate: The early diagnosis allowed her to begin treatment before the cancer spread. She responded very well, and remains cancer free.

There are limits to emotional endurance, even for the most resilient among us. Carl can recall different times over the course of his life when he approached these limits. The first time was at age sixteen, when he contemplated suicide. The last time occurred after his wife's diagnosis.

The bypass surgery went well, and his doctor predicted a full recovery but also the likelihood of additional health problems down the road if Carl chose not to change his behavioral lifestyle. These lifestyle changes would have to include new eating habits and regular exercise. Fearing the potential deadly consequences of his previously unhealthy lifestyle, he heeded his doctor's advice. Surprisingly, however, his behavioral changes were short-lived, and within two months he reverted to his old behavioral ways.

If Carl was to change his behavior successfully, he needed the help and support of those closest to him. And the help and support came swiftly. His closest friend began exercising with him three or four days a week. Kathy and others at the office replaced the assorted pastries available during their morning meetings with fresh fruit. Office staff began taking walks after lunch, accompanied by Carl whenever time allowed. Family, friends, and employees realized that he needed their help and support in developing and sustaining new routines, which they provided in abundant supply.

Six months after his surgery, Carl was feeling much better physically and emotionally. He was exercising regularly, eating well, and losing weight. He had successfully changed his previously unhealthy habits thanks to the help and support of those closest to him. Then came the news of his wife's diagnosis. At first, both were in shock. Carl knew, though, they would not have to go it alone. The help and support from loved ones actually went beyond what he anticipated. Parents, extended family members, friends, employees—all pitched in. They called continuously, sent surprise gifts, dropped off some of the family's favorite meals, cooked dinners, and did whatever they could to let Carl and his wife know that they would get through this, that their family and friends would always be there for them, and that however difficult things may feel, they were not alone.

8a. Safety Nets

Safety nets are relationships that serve as buffers in the face of difficult life experiences. They come in different forms. Some are composed largely of family members, friends, and/or others we may look to for support and guidance. Some include professional resources—physicians, mental health professionals, teachers, and others. Safety nets are often unnoticed when lives are going well. We rely on them a great deal, however, during periods of stress and/or emotional upheaval. Fortunately for Carl, his safety net was strong and readily available when he needed it most.

8b. Connecting with Those Who Legitimize Rather Than Stigmatize

At age sixteen, when Carl contemplated suicide, he felt misunderstood, hopeless about his future, and powerless to do anything about it. What he recalls most about that time was how lonely he felt. If you recall, when his family moved to a new community, he no longer saw his two closest friends since early childhood. They served as a safety net, one that buffered him from frustrating and sometimes humiliating school experiences.

At that time, Carl was also struggling with challenges that were confusing and difficult to understand. As a result of a few misperceptions, those closest to him were as confused about his difficulties as he was. A few years ago, however, no one had difficulty understanding the challenges confronting him. Those closest to Carl were quick to lend a hand, and those closest to his wife were eager to do the same. Human understanding played a pivotal role in Carl's ability to get through a very difficult period in his life (the same holds true for his wife). Those who made up their safety net clearly understood the emotional toll brought on by these health-related crises. As a result, they acted quickly to lend their support and validate the courage each had shown in the face of these challenging conditions.

9. Growing Closer and Stronger as a Result of Difficult or Traumatic Life Events

A few years have passed since his wife's cancer diagnosis, and looking back, Carl feels a stronger connection with his family than ever before. He feels closer to his friends and employees, and holds a deeper appreciation of life in general. He no longer takes what he has for granted. While he also feels more vulnerable, knowing that tragedy can strike with no warning, overall he believes the events of the past few years have changed him in positive ways. These changes are particularly evident in the greater closeness he feels to the important people in his life.

9a. Relationships as Malleable, Not Fixed

Relationships are malleable. But it takes a malleable mind-set to appreciate this. Just as mind-sets vary in terms of how people view intelligence, they also vary in terms of how people view relationships. According to Carol Dweck, people with growth or malleable views know that relationships grow stronger with effort and work.

Those with fixed views, on the other hand, discount the role of effort in helping strengthen relationships. And according to Dweck, a no-effort relationship is a doomed one.

As a struggling child, erroneous perceptions associated with Carl's challenges led to apparently logical but ineffective remedies. When positive outcomes didn't materialize, hurt and angry feelings grew more intense. These were normal human reactions to clearly frustrating and confusing times. But hurt and angry feelings were interpreted through the lens of a fixed mind-set. Carl, his parents, and others close to him came to feel discounted and disconnected as a result. Events over the past few years, however, were seen with far greater clarity and understanding. While hurt, anger, and other normal human emotions emerged here as well, they were interpreted through a more malleable mindset. Misperception, blame, and escalating grievances gave way to compassion, forgiveness, letting go of hurt and angry feelings, and moving on.

Safety Nets at Risk: The Impact of "Compassion Fatigue"

As is the case with otherwise resilient individuals, resilient relationships seem to have limits of endurance. Safety nets can tear apart. Malleable minds can grow fixed and weary. Positive life trajectories can reverse course. Carl realized this while caring for his wife as she went through her cancer treatment. Weeks into her treatment, he felt emotionally and physically exhausted. He was learning firsthand what those attending to loved ones who are suffering know very well: compassion is a depletable resource.

Carl was suffering from "compassion fatigue" (Figley, 1995). Frank Ochberg, an authority on the subject, refers to it as a state of emotional fatigue: "We aren't sick, but we aren't ourselves"; "we hurt too much because we're empathic, and it wears us down" (Ochberg, 2001; Ochberg et al., 2006). Although the phenomenon has been studied most among those caring for someone suffering from the effects of traumatic stress exposure, compassion fatigue casts a much wider net. We find it in adult children caring for aging parents, in parents raising an extremely hard-to-manage child, and in families caring for a loved one with a severe physical or psychiatric illness. We also find it in spouses, partners, and extended family members; in teachers, therapists, and other health care providers; and in police officers, firefighters, and emergency room workers. In fact, we find it in any relationship where there exists a feeling of compassion for the suffering of another person, ongoing exposure to their suffering, and a sense of responsibility for helping.

The Role of Human Understanding in Preventing Compassion Fatigue, the Role of Human Misunderstanding in Increasing It

Erroneous perceptions, it turns out, can contribute significantly to the onset of compassion fatigue. Recall how hard Carl's parents tried to help him do better in school. Each attempt usually ended in disappointment. As Carl grew demoralized, they eventually grew depleted, a sign of compassion fatigue. They had little understanding of the true nature of their son's challenges. More recently, they had a very clear understanding of the challenges he faced, and so did others in Carl's circle of support. Together, they had a shared mission: helping Carl and his wife regain their health. This mission led to a sense of support and understanding, which, in turn, prevented compassion fatigue from taking hold.

Shared support and understanding can also reverse compassion fatigue, as Carl learned after his wife's diagnosis. With the help of family members, friends, and employees at work, he reestablished a sense of balance in his life, reengaged in activities that helped him relax, and spent time each day with those who believed that better days are in store.

10. Our Greatest Source of Strength—Each Other: A Closer Look at Turning Points

Predicting with absolute certainty what will become of us in the future based on what may have happened to us in the past is simply impossible. One reason is that lives can change in very significant ways in response to unpredictable and unanticipated experiences. Experts who study resilience through the life span refer to these experiences as "turning points." Turning points can change the course of our lives in ways we could not have predicted from earlier life events and experiences (Laub and Sampson, 2006).

Turning points are sometimes discussed in the context of two other frequently used terms in the prevention literature: (1) "trajectories," or the long-term patterns of behavior we exhibit throughout our lives, also sometimes described as pathways or lines of development; and (2) "transitions," the shorter-term events and experiences embedded in trajectories. Examples of trajectories include a person's work life or a person's long-term marriage. Getting a new job or getting married are examples of transitions. Turning points are those transitional events leading to significant changes in a person's life course trajectory. While turning points represent transitional events, transitional events are not necessarily turning points.

The Study of Life's Turning Points

Results of the Kauai Longitudinal Study revealed that more than half of those who succumbed to multiple risk exposure by age 18 were adapting well at ages 31 and 32, and still adapting well when reassessed at age 40. Most were in stable marriages and holding down stable jobs. Most were seen as responsible members of their communities, and many were able to identify specific turning point experiences and second chance opportunities (Werner and Smith, 2001). For some, it was going back to school, particularly for teen mothers and teenagers who were in trouble with the law. Going back to school provided the educational, vocational, and social skills they needed to succeed in a competitive job market. It also helped lift them out of poverty. For some, the turning point was enlisting in the armed services. In both cases, experiences resulted in greater self-pride and a stronger belief in their ability to succeed. Benefits were also observed in their children's lives years later. As parents, they watched over their children's educational experiences very closely.

For some, getting married was a turning point. A number of people spoke about how they came to rely on the ongoing emotional support, trust, and friendship of a stable partner. For some, this came in a second marriage. Others mentioned their conversion to a religious faith as an important turning point. They included persons who grew up in an abusive home of an alcoholic parent, and those who struggled with mental health and substance abuse problems during their earlier years. For others, their lives changed after surviving a life-threatening illness or accident. The experience opened their eyes to possibilities they hadn't considered before. After recovering, they seized these opportunities, and their lives changed for the better. Some experienced much the same effect when someone close to them endured a life-threatening illness, accident, or event.

Turning points have also been the focus of another landmark prospective longitudinal study, the longest known study of criminal behavior over the life span. Conducted by principal investigators John Laub and Robert Sampson (2006), the study documents turning points in the lives of previously incarcerated teens with lengthy criminal histories who eventually went on to lead crime-free lives. (To learn more, log on to the web page.)

Carl's Turning Points

Carl remembers his first class on website design as a turning point. Another was the job he had as a computer salesperson at a company that valued his out-of-the-box approach. It was his first successful job experience. Deciding to improve his reading abilities was another turning point. So was starting his own company.

When asked about the role that personal relationships played in his turning points, Carl seemed close to tears. He spoke at length about his wife and what their marriage has meant to him. "She stuck with me through some very tough times." He then began talking about his children, the joy they bring to his life, and how they are always in his thoughts. He recalled his close relationship with his brother: "I don't think I could have ever made it without Steven." He recalled how he and Steven looked after one another as children. He expressed similar sentiments toward his mother, recalling how she always believed in him when others seemed to give up hope. Next, he spoke at length about Kathy, his assistant, the person he counts on in so many ways. He mentioned his cardiologist, who helped him regain his health following a heart attack and continues to advise him on how to prevent health-related problems down the road. He spoke about his wife's physician who helped support the family through cancer treatment.

Viewed within the context of relationships, Carl also began seeing his original responses to the first question in a new light. He recalled the connection he developed with the instructor who taught the class in website design. He looked up to the teacher, who also ran a small business. He feels that in some respects, he followed in his footsteps. When it came to his first successful job experience, Carl felt he had the company's business manager and his immediate supervisor to thank. Both valued his creative ways and his sense of humor. "They really enjoyed working with me and saw me as an asset to the company." One of Carl's clients is an educator who specializes in helping people with learning challenges. She helped Carl understand that many people experience reading challenges similar to his, and that reading abilities can improve at any age, given appropriate intervention. She gave him the courage to enroll in a program that eventually helped him read and write more fluently.

Our Greatest Source of Strength: Each Other

"If you want to go fast go alone. If you want to go far, go together."   *—African proverb*

Carl was asked two questions about turning point experiences, the second one focusing on turning points in the context of his relationships. His responses were strikingly different, not only in content but on a visceral level as well. Carl was not on the verge of tears when talking about turning points in general. He appeared about to cry when talking about them in the context of his most important relationships.

As noted in the introduction to this section, when we dig deeper into the lives of people who eventually beat the odds, we seem to invariably find human relationships that helped change the odds. Some mention their parents, grandparents, or other family members who never lost hope in them and always provided support and encouragement. Some mention a teacher or a coach who helped them believe in themselves. Some mention a doctor, therapist, or other health care professional who helped them overcome a medical or personal problem. Others identify an intimate relationship that resulted in a renewed sense of hope. Others identify long-term close personal friendships. Although the people they identify may vary, the underlying message is clear: life's turning points often occur within the context of human relationships. Carl's story seems to resemble that of many others who rebounded from a difficult past. They are the first to tell you they did not achieve their accomplishments alone. They had a great deal of help along the way.

Researchers who study life's trajectories are well aware of the important role that personal relationships and social supports play in helping us overcome a hurtful past. In her study of adults who overcame the effects of child abuse, Hanita Zimrin (1986) cited the important role that a caring relationship played in their lives. Most of these resilient individuals mentioned a supportive adult whom they had access to, such as a teacher or another person who inspired confidence in them. Werner and Smith (1992, 2001) found that resilient children growing up in homes where their parents experienced chronic psychiatric problems often were able to detach themselves from the discord at home by spending time with caring adults outside of the immediate family. And in their study of teenagers who coped successfully with a parent's affective illness, William Beardslee and Donna Podorefsky (1988) found that they benefited a great deal from the close relationships formed with other family members and friends.

In their study of individuals with learning disabilities who were adapting well as adults, Werner and Smith found that supportive relationships played an important role in their earlier lives. Grandparents, elder mentors, youth leaders, or members of the person's church acted as a kind of gatekeeper to the future. These were trusted individuals who in turn fostered trust and faith in others (Werner, 1993; Werner and Smith, 2001). In their study of factors that distinguished between successful and unsuccessful adults with learning disabilities, Nancy Spekman and colleagues observed that successful learning disabled adults often identified significant individuals in their lives who encouraged and guided them. Often, these individuals were family members. Sometimes, however, the significant relationship they identified was with a teacher, a tutor, or a therapist (Spekman, Goldberg, and Herman, 1992). In her search for possible sources of resilience among young adults with ADHD, Lily Hechtman (1991) noted the important role that a caring relationship played in their lives; that is, someone who always believed in them, whether it be a parent, teacher, or coach.

At any point during the life span, according to Michael Rutter (1990), an intimate relationship can positively affect how we view ourselves and in the way we're viewed by others. Today, resilience is viewed through the lens of individual journeys, one life at a time. But in time we may come to realize that our greatest source of resilience could ultimately be each other.

SUMMARY

- Our context-sensitive ways allow us to act, think, and feel differently in various situations. Neuroscientists see this as one of our greatest strengths.
- Contextual influences—externally, internally, and relationally—link directly to protective processes discussed in Chapter 2. When studied contextually, they allow us to explore the many different ways protective processes can buffer us from the effects of risk exposure. This also draws attention to our capacity for contextual thinking. It's this capacity that allows us to attach new meaning to life's challenges.

Chapter 4

~

PORTRAITS OF RESILIENCE— IN CONTEXT

HOW DO THEY SUCCEED? CONTINUED

Carl's uneven profile is hardly unique. It turns out that many of us exhibit uneven learning, behavioral, and/or emotional profiles. What's more, we can exhibit them for different reasons. To illustrate this point, let me introduce you to four more individuals, each of whom struggled in school for different reasons. All are now leading meaningful and productive lives.

In the discussion that follows, we explore the reasons underlying their similarly uneven ways, how their confusing behavior contributed to misperceptions, and common contextual influences contributing to their successful journey from troubled childhood to successful adulthood.

JAVIER

Javier is a 29-year-old social worker at a small mental health center in Northern California. He spends some of his free time mentoring children and youth currently residing in foster care. He and his wife have been married for five years. They have one child, a daughter, age three.

Javier has overcome a very difficult past. His birth mother suffered from severe mental illness and a long-standing problem with substance abuse. Javier lived with her until age four, at which time she relinquished custody. He spent the next 14 years in foster care. During his first five years in foster placement, he recalls living in six different homes. Then, at the age of 10, the first of several turning point experiences occurred in his life. He was placed with a foster family that he grew to love deeply, and the feeling was mutual. His foster parents and two brothers loved him as well and accepted him into their family.

Considering that he successfully completed college and graduate school, earning a bachelor's degree in psychology and a master's degree in social work, people are often surprised to learn that until college, Javier struggled in school. By the age of 10, he had already attended at least six different schools. (He lost count and wasn't sure of the exact number.) He recalls school being very difficult for him, and he can't remember feeling successful at any of the different ones that he attended. In fourth grade, a year prior to arriving at his permanent foster home, he was assessed by school professionals for the first time. The assessment revealed weaknesses in reading comprehension; weaknesses in organizing, planning, and completing assignments; poor self-control skills; difficulties concentrating; and problems focusing his attention on schoolwork.

Carl and Javier seemed to have very similar learning and behavioral profiles. Both performed very well on difficult intellectual and other problem-solving tasks, yet experienced weaknesses in reading comprehension skills and various mental processes under the executive function umbrella, particularly those associated with emotional self-regulation and self-control. They serve as good examples of how people can have similar learning and behavioral profiles for different reasons. Before the first day of kindergarten and for several years thereafter, Carl grew up in a loving home with loving parents who provided him with an array of enriched early childhood learning experiences. Javier's earlier childhood experiences could not have been more different. Before his first day of kindergarten, he had already been neglected for years. For several years thereafter, he remained without permanent caregivers who could provide loving relationships in a permanent home. Carl's struggles in school were related largely to multiple neurodevelopmental risk exposure, compounded perhaps in later grades by environmental risks as well. Javier's struggles in school were related to multiple environmental risks. Each struggled mightily in very similar areas but for different reasons.

The sections that follow explore the impact of multiple environmental risk exposure on Javier's functioning at school. We begin by revisiting the topic of interpersonal trauma, focusing particular attention on how it can affect a range of learning and behavioral functions. We then explore how poverty during the first several years of life can affect children's later reading skills.

ACE SCORES AND THE EFFECTS OF INTERPERSONAL TRAUMA, REVISITED

In addition to having similar learning and behavioral profiles, Carl and Javier had similar ACE scores. Carl's ACE score was 7, which was high and placed him at risk for later life medical problems. Javier's ACE score was also 7, placing him at risk as well. But while their ACE scores were the same, the actual experiences they endured were very different. Javier was exposed to multiple adversities, even before birth. Carl was not. Javier also experienced neglect, which can potentially have a far greater impact on our eventual life course than other experiences. Also, after being removed from his mother's care (yet another traumatic event in his life), Javier lived in many different homes, resulting in many stressful disruptions. In Javier's case, the nature and degree of these traumatically stressful life experiences seemed to significantly affect functions we rely on to succeed in school. This is not surprising, according to experts. Researchers now know that exposure to extremely stressful experiences can alter the learning and behavioral profiles of otherwise resilient children.

THE IMPACT OF THREAT AND DANGER ON THE LEARNING PROCESS

Under conditions of extreme and constant threat, our nervous system can be in what amounts to a state of alarm (Perry, 2002), a state that appears to capture many of the symptoms and behavioral reactions that Javier recalls experiencing as a child. Skills we perform effortlessly under calm conditions can be difficult to perform in an alarm state. The ability to process information can be compromised, as might the ability to control or regulate behavior. We may be able to remember solutions to problems one minute but not the next, remember a math formula this morning but not this afternoon, recall an instruction given to us today but not tomorrow, only to remember it again the day after. Focusing on our goals, concentrating our attention on the steps needed to reach these goals, and guiding our behavior in the desired direction can be very difficult functions to perform when our nervous system is in a state of alarm.

It's likely that Javier struggled in his ability to consistently execute specific skills during these earlier school years not because of preexisting neurodevelopmental delays but because of normal biological reactions to abnormally stressful life experiences.

Exposure to prolonged interpersonal trauma can sometimes significantly affect mental processes under our executive function umbrella. This may also help explain two other struggles Javier experienced in school, both of which Carl experienced as well: he had great difficulty completing important but uninteresting tasks. And he worked much harder than others to regulate his emotions and control his behavior, thus depleting his emotional self-regulation fuel tank on a regular basis. Bessel van der Kolk (2000), who specializes in treating adults exposed to prolonged traumatic stress in childhood, including interpersonal trauma, reports similar characteristics in some of his patients. He notes, for example, that it's quite common for patients to complain about how quickly they become bored. They also often struggle in sustaining attention and in areas involving emotional self-regulation.

In the year following Javier's initial school assessment, his behavioral difficulties grew increasingly serious. He began receiving special education services for what school officials described as a severe emotional and behavioral disturbance that was affecting his ability to succeed academically. Javier's behavior seemed uncontrollable at times. Angry, impulsive outbursts were on the increase, as were power struggles with those in authority, including teachers, counselors, and administrators. He was also having difficulty completing his work, listening to his teachers, and getting along with some of the other students. School reports described his difficulties as longstanding in nature and significantly interfering with his ability to learn. In retrospect, is it possible that Javier's "severe emotional and behavioral disturbance" wasn't an emotional and behavioral disturbance in the conventional sense, at least not in terms of how schools in the past traditionally defined this, but rather the behavioral, emotional, and physiological consequences of life in an alarm state? According to experts in the field of traumatic stress, it's very possible indeed.

PHYSIOLOGICAL FALSE ALARMS: PERCEIVING THREAT AND DANGER WHERE THEY DON'T EXIST

> *"The cost of treating a stick as a snake is less, in the long run, than the cost of treating a snake as a stick."*
>
> —*Joseph Ledoux*

Looking back, Javier views his impulsive outbursts and hair-trigger emotional reactions in school more as physiological false alarms rather deliberate attempts to harm others. His nervous system seemed in a constant state of hyper-alert, always on the lookout for danger signals, so much so that he sometimes read danger where it didn't exist. His false alarm reactions might also help explain some of the power struggles he experienced with teachers, counselors, administrators, and others in positions of authority, who were simply trying to help. When Javier misbehaved, these were the people who held him accountable. Sometimes this resulted in reprimands, a loss of fun activities, or other natural consequences. To a nervous system on hyper-alert, however, these consequences can be misinterpreted as new sources of potential threat. Behavioral incidents might now escalate rather than deescalate in intensity and feed into power struggles. Javier eventually learned ways to soothe himself when starting to escalate, which helped prevent loss-of-control episodes. In Chapter 7 we review five self-regulation strategies he also mastered that helped him in this regard.

With the benefit of hindsight, we can see the effects of interpersonal trauma on Javier's functioning at school. Without hindsight, it's not always easy to spot, especially when we're unaware of a child's life circumstances. One reason is that its symptoms can vary widely. Not all children, for example, exhibit the range of learning, behavioral, emotional, and physiological symptoms that

Javier did. Some might withdraw and grow increasingly depressed. Others might become distrustful of human relationships and have difficulty forming close bonds. Some, on the other hand, might attach to others too quickly. Complicating matters even further, traumatized children often fail to meet diagnostic criteria for PTSD. One study, for example, showed only 25 percent of them meeting diagnostic criteria (van der Kolk and Pynoos, 2009). Not seeing the diagnosis mentioned anywhere in previous assessment reports, those involved in creating intervention plans may dismiss the impact of prolonged traumatic stress exposure on day-to-day functioning. Javier serves as a good illustration. Although his daily functioning was significantly affected by interpersonal trauma, his behavioral and emotional difficulties at school were not found to be consistent with PTSD diagnostic criteria, and nowhere in any reports was his trauma history considered to be a factor in his ongoing difficulties. Rather, his difficulties were felt to be more willful, intentional, manipulative, and attention-seeking.

This is not uncommon even today, since schools are often unaware of children's trauma histories. As a result, those impacted by interpersonal trauma may be treated instead for emotional disorders, behavioral disorders, or other conditions, all of which infer that the underlying source of difficulty lies within the child. This was evident in a study comparing the frequency of behavior problems among inner-city African American and white children. Initially, results showed behavior problems to be higher among African American children. When researchers controlled for traumatic stress exposure, however, rates were equal (Bryant-Davis, 2003).

Everyone who knows Javier today views him as a very resilient person. No one who knew him at age nine, however, viewed him as a particularly resilient child. At that time, he appeared to be inattentive, easily irritated, and unable to effectively control his behavior. We had little difficulty describing Javier's problem areas; we had great difficulty capturing his resilience.

This brings us to an important question. For an otherwise normal child, what does resilience look like—behaviorally, emotionally, and physiologically—after living in six different foster homes, following removal from a neglectful mother who suffered from severe mental illness and drug addiction, compounded further by ongoing difficulties at school? It's a very important question, because if we can't capture expressions of resilience under these conditions, rest assured, neither will the child.

To truly appreciate how resilient Javier was during his younger years, we have to also appreciate contextual influences, more specifically, how exposure to prolonged traumatically stressful experiences can affect otherwise normal children. At age nine, Javier's difficulties felt permanent, pervasive, and personal, and not because he lacked resilience. Rather, it was because life experiences provided no compelling evidence to the contrary. (In Chapter 6, we explore how we might begin to convey these and other important points in the assessment reports we write for school-age children growing up under similar conditions).

Our discussion thus far has explored how traumatic stress exposure can affect a variety of learning and behavioral functions in otherwise resilient children. When Javier first began school he was exposed to another environmental risk: poverty. This is an environmental risk often overlooked on assessments such as the one he completed in fourth grade. Yet it may help explain his low reading comprehension score. To better understand the connection, let's start with a simple exercise.

Read the following paragraph.

A newspaper is better than a magazine. A seashore is a better place than a street. At first it is better to run than to walk. You may have to try several times. It takes some skill but it is easy to learn. Even young children can enjoy it. Once successful, complications are minimal. Birds seldom get too close. Rain, however, soaks in very fast. Too many people doing the same thing can also cause problems. If there are no complications, it can be very peaceful. A rock will serve as an anchor. If things break loose from it, however, you will not get a second chance. (Burton, 2008, p. 5; Jones, 2002)

Now read the paragraph again, keeping in mind one word: kite.

The sentences now have an entirely different, much more obvious meaning. What this simple exercise illustrates is that it's possible to read fluently, yet not be able to fully grasp the significance of what we're reading.

To extract different levels of meaning from the material we read, we rely on background knowledge, including the knowledge of words and concepts. By the time children first begin attending school, they may already vary enormously in this regard. By the fourth grade, Javier had fallen behind most other children in his ability to comprehend what he read. Unlike Carl, he didn't struggle as a result of dyslexia. What he appeared to lack was a fund of knowledge comparable to most other fourth-graders, including knowledge of words and concepts. This affected his ability to comprehend what he read.

THE IMPACT OF BASIC ECONOMICS

What might cause a child to enter school knowing fewer words than other children? According to the results of a remarkable study by Betty Hart and Todd Risley (1995), one reason could relate to basic economics.

For two and a half years, Hart and Risley had researchers spend an hour a month in the homes of 42 families, each raising a one- to two-year-old child. Researchers documented every word that parents spoke to the child, even nonword utterances. Families shared many characteristics. All were loving parents from diverse cultural backgrounds. All were free of serious emotional or psychological problems. All of their children were developing normally, free of any known problems or disabilities. By design, the only real difference between the families was income. Some were poor, some were affluent, and some were in the middle. Initial findings came as no real surprise. Developmentally, all children learned to speak on time. As soon as those first words were uttered, families celebrated in an enthusiastic way. Reaching this significant developmental milestone was as much a celebration for a poor family as for a rich one. As the children grew, they all developed normally. By the time they reached age three, they all were effective speakers. By age nine, when the children were in third grade, all were performing fine. Researchers observed that with the loving help of their parents, all 42 children mastered language.

But what researchers also observed was that the higher a family was on the economic ladder, the more language their young child was exposed to, language in the quantity sense. What's more, the differences were striking. Researchers estimated that by age four, an average child growing up in the home of a family on welfare would have cumulative experience with 13 million words, an average child growing up in the home of a working-class family would have cumulative experience with 26 million words, and an average child growing up in the home of an affluent family would have cumulative experience with 45 million words.

Researchers then discovered a correlation between the amount of young children's language experience and their rate of vocabulary growth, vocabulary use, general accomplishments at age three, and their level of school performance at age nine. Although all children were doing fine in school, some were doing much better than others, which seemed correlated to how many words they knew and their degree of earlier language exposure.

At age four, Javier was removed from his mother's custody, having lived much of that time in impoverished surroundings. From what he can recall, the years following his removal were rather tumultuous as well. When he began school he appeared at least qualitatively on par with most other children. With respect to his fund of general knowledge, however, he was behind, and remained so for many years. This included his knowledge of words and concepts. This may help explain why his reading comprehension skills lagged behind many of his other skills.

CONTEXTUAL INFLUENCES: SOCIAL CONTEXT

1. The Transforming Power of Meaningful Work

After his graduation from high school, Javier felt in control of his life for the first time. In college, he was able to choose his classes, arrange his own schedule, and plan out his day.

He lived in a dorm for the first two years of college, then in an apartment with two roommates, also students. His tuition and living expenses were covered by a scholarship and a student loan. His personal initiative to pursue both allowed him to attend college and then graduate school.

Javier is viewed by his colleagues as an excellent clinician. His employer at the community clinic has publicly recognized him for his many contributions. Students he mentors at a local junior college look up to him. Some have also had difficult lives and, as a result of knowing Javier, have grown more confident and hopeful about their future. He is loved deeply by his wife and adored by his daughter. Whatever he may have felt in years past, today he feels that he matters to many people on many levels and has much to contribute to the lives of others.

Anyone who knew Javier when he was growing up in foster care would be quite surprised that he became a mental health professional who spends much of his workday reaching out to help children and youth, including those in foster care. "Other kids I knew in foster care couldn't wait to free themselves from the system. I decided to help try to change it," he says.

2. Raising the Bar and Leveling the Playing Field

Javier earned his master's in social work and has been encouraged by one of his former professors to consider pursuing a doctorate at some point in the future. He prefers to spend the next several years gaining more experience in his field, but is not ruling out the possibility of going back to school someday. He has no difficulty setting the bar high.

In contrast to his earlier school years, Javier seemed to have had less difficulty with academic subjects in college and graduate school. As the academic material grew more intellectually challenging, it appeared as though he had an easier time mastering it. He did, however, seek out some of his professors now and then for help in better understanding a particular topic or concept discussed in class. Comprehending lengthy and complex reading material also remained somewhat of a challenge. Javier learned that by obtaining certain textbooks over the summer and reading through them or even perusing them before classes began in the fall helped his comprehension. He also occasionally sought help from tutors, again in subjects requiring that he read and comprehend lengthy, abstract material. Tutors were typically older students who excelled in these subjects.

Like Carl, Javier eventually developed effective strategies for completing tasks he finds tedious and boring. When writing case notes at work, he listens to music. When listening to lectures at professional conferences, he doodles on a notepad. When having to read lengthy chapters in textbooks, he listens to an audio recording of the book and reads along at the same time. Through trial and error, he figured out that people who have difficulty completing important but uninteresting tasks are often better able to complete these tasks when providing themselves added stimulation through a different sense modality (Rotz and Wright, 2005).

Javier struggled when it came to listening to his professors and taking notes at the same time. (For more information on his note taking and other writing challenges, log on to the web page.) To navigate around these challenges, he began using a digital pen, which records the speaker and links notes written on a page to the speaker's actual words. When Javier returns home or back to the office, he simply taps a word he wrote down and the pen replays the audio portion of the lecture at the time he wrote it.

In college and graduate school, Javier knew where to look for help. He knew whom to turn to for advice on which tools, technologies, strategies, or resources would help him navigate areas of difficulty. His transactive memory was strong, and it continues to serve him well. As a struggling young student, however, seeking help was unthinkable. Instead, he spent much more time denying that any problems even existed. In situations where differences represent threat and danger, we know that it can make far more sense to appear inconspicuous rather than different.

3. A Change of Scenery: The Value of a Fresh Start

College life represented more than a fresh start for Javier. It represented "a chance to feel normal." Says Javier, "A lot of times I was embarrassed to tell kids at school I was a foster child. My good friends knew and that was okay. But I really didn't want anyone else to know. If felt embarrassing. It didn't feel normal. I began feeling differently my freshman year in college. For the first time in my life I actually felt normal. It's hard to explain what that feels like if you've never felt that way."

LIFE EXPERIENCES—IN CONTEXT

4. Personal Pathways to a Sense of Mastery

Javier enjoys a strong sense of mastery in many areas, including in his profession. He is recognized as a compassionate and skilled therapist capable of developing trusting bonds with hard-to-reach children, teens, and families. Clients who are slow or unable to warm up to others are often quick to warm up to Javier. When he encounters a particularly challenging clinical situation, he meets the challenge head on. "I actually prefer challenging situations. My colleagues know this. They're always referring clients to me who they feel I would be much more effective working with." When it comes to clinical matters, Javier believes there's a light at the end of the tunnel, no matter what the challenge. He feels uniquely skilled in helping those he treats to see this as well.

5. Seeing Human Intelligence in a New Light: Not How Smart We Are But How We Are Smart

As with many others who succeed in the field of health care, Javier's intrapersonal and interpersonal strengths serve him well. He is skilled at using introspective thinking abilities to better understand why he reacts the way he does when faced with different clinical situations. His skills in this regard afford him the opportunity to grow professionally. He is also very aware of and sensitive to people's perspectives, moods, and feelings, and he excels in the ability to connect emotionally with others, including those in distress. When it comes to performing tasks requiring intrapersonal and interpersonal skills, proponents of multiple intelligence theory would describe Javier as gifted.

6. When Difference No Longer Signals Danger

More Labels, Not Fewer
Husband, father, social worker, therapist, colleague, mentor, insightful, compassionate, hard-working, resilient. There are a number of different labels that people use to describe Javier, and today, these are the same labels he uses to describe himself. He is

confident in his abilities and hopeful about his future. In earlier years, he felt embarrassed by being a foster child in foster care. Now he does presentations at his agency, local schools, and other organizations on the needs of children in foster care, often referring to his own experiences when making an important point.

Seeing Abilities as Malleable

As noted, there a number of benefits derived from adopting a growth mind-set. Growing up, Javier had a fixed view of his intelligence. He believed others in school were smart, but he was not. Today, we can infer from his work ethic that he views intelligence as malleable. His growth mind-set has allowed him to benefit from new learning experiences without feeling devalued by mistakes and setbacks.

Seeing Interpersonal Trauma in Historical Context

If we could go back and ask those who knew Javier at age nine what he would be doing 20 years later, few, if any, would have predicted his career choice. He certainly would not have predicted it. Moreover, few would have predicted the understanding and compassion he feels for his mother. Javier eventually learned more about her life and difficult childhood. Neglected by her own mother, she also grew up in foster care, but it was at a time and in a community where caring homes were far less available. She eventually ran away at age 15 and lived with a variety of men, who repeatedly abused her. Although she also suffered from the effects of interpersonal trauma, it occurred before professionals knew much about the link between traumatic stress exposure and mental health challenges. Javier understands the link well, professionally and personally, in historical context. Rather than harboring anger toward his mother, he now feels compassion.

Traumatic events in Javier's life represented central themes. He eventually learned to view them instead as life episodes (Terr, 2003, 2009, 2013). In his work with traumatized children and youth in foster care, he's helping them learn to do the same. However, he feels that we still have a ways to go. He reads assessment reports written about children suffering the effects of trauma that read much like reports written about him between ages 8 and 17. These reports failed to accurately capture how trauma was affecting his life. If captured more accurately, others might have come away with different impressions of his inherently resilient qualities in the face of very difficult emotional experiences. More important perhaps, he may have come away with these same impressions. As we now know, the meaning others attach to our adversities can influence the meaning we attach to these same adversities. (In Chapter 6, we explore how assessment reports might better capture the resilient qualities of children growing up under extremely stressful conditions. A separate section on the web page has also been created to further explore this topic.)

7. Translating the Pain of Our Past into Meaningful Action on Behalf of Others

Javier chose a career that provides him the opportunity to give back to others what he feels others gave to him. He also spends some of his free time mentoring children and youth currently residing in foster care. They see him as a role model. Some have told him that just knowing him personally has helped them feel more hopeful about their future. (To read more, log on to the web page.)

RELATIONSHIPS—IN CONTEXT

8. Beating the Odds Thanks to Those Who Changed the Odds

Safety Nets

During his earlier years, Javier set the bar low. He had little idea of what was in store for him down the road and seemed concerned with simply making it through each day. His foster parents, however, had a far more hopeful view of his future and what he was capable of attaining. They had dreams for him, which in time became his dreams as well.

Javier benefited from a strong safety net. It included his foster parents and foster siblings. It also included teachers, social workers, therapists, a tutor who worked with him throughout high school, and a close friend. The more time he spent talking about his safety net, the more he realized how strong it was and still is.

Connecting with Those Who Legitimize Rather Than Stigmatize

By the time Javier reached high school, he had become quite skilled at distancing himself from students who were quick to ridicule and shame others, and equally skilled at connecting to friends who were quick to support and encourage others. To this day, he remains very skilled at doing this, and often tries to help the children, youth, and families that he works with learn to do the same.

9. Growing Closer and Stronger as a Result of Difficult or Traumatic Life Events

In his work with traumatized children and youth, Javier often draws on new research in the field of post-traumatic growth. This has helped him better understand his own journey. The term "post-traumatic growth" was coined in the mid-1990s by clinical researchers Richard Tedeschi and Lawrence Calhoun (2012). Their studies reveal potential growth in the following five general areas following major life crises, several of which appear consistent with Javier's areas of growth:

1. increased awareness of new opportunities and new possibilities one was unaware of before.
2. personal relationships that grow stronger and emotional connections to others who suffer that grow deeper.
3. greater awareness of personal strength, despite also being more aware of a greater sense of vulnerability to traumatic events beyond one's control.
4. valuing life more than before and growing more appreciative of things that previously might have been taken for granted.
5. experiencing a deeper spiritual life, sometimes resulting in a change in one's belief system.

While Tedeschi and Calhoun (2004a, b) remind us that post-traumatic growth should not be construed as the opposite of post-traumatic stress, research shows that it's conceivable that from intense pain and distress can also come growth. Javier is a good illustration of this. Today he feels emotionally stronger than at any other time in his life. He has a number of people to thank for this. He named his wife, his foster parents, some of his teachers, and a social worker who guided him through foster care, among others.

Relationships as Malleable

Entirely understandable yet erroneous perceptions (see Chapter 1) can lead caring people to think in fixed and inflexible ways. During his earlier school years, such was the case with several of Javier's teachers. Over time, understanding and compassion replaced misunderstanding and blame. Today, Javier looks back on his relationships with many of his teachers fondly. He remains in touch with one in particular, who teaches a high school life skills class. Javier has been invited to speak to her students on several occasions.

10. Our Greatest Source of Strength: Each Other

Javier had a long list of turning points, among them enrolling in college, completing graduate school, and finding his current job. When relating turning points to people he has known, the list grew longer and the conversation more emotional. He spoke at length about his foster parents and their unwavering love and support. He spoke at length about a social worker he came to know and care about deeply. She was the one who found him his permanent foster home. The two remained in close contact up through his high school graduation. He spoke at length about a college professor who took a special interest in him and mentored him in several courses, eventually encouraging him to pursue a graduate degree. When applying for his current job, he had an advantage in the form of glowing letters of recommendation from that social worker and professor, both of whom knew the agency director and whose opinions carried considerable weight. He spoke about a previous therapist who helped him understand not only his own traumatic past, but also his mother's traumatic past. In college, Javier met his future wife, who inspired him to work hard and not give up when courses became difficult. He mentioned their marriage and the birth of their child as turning points.

LINDA

*"Every child is an artist. The problem is how to remain an
artist once he grows up."* —*Pablo Picasso*

Linda started kindergarten at age five as an artist and managed to
remain one. "My parents were really hoping for a scholar, though.
My mom's a teacher, my dad's an engineer. School meant a lot to
them. They were both A students. And they expected their children
to be A students too. Which my older brother and sister were. But
not me. I struggled to get Cs and Ds. And in some classes couldn't
even manage that. To my parents, this was unacceptable. For years I
agonized over not being able to live up to my parents' expectations. I
felt I disappointed them. I let them down. They truly believed I could
get straight A's if I would simply try my best. But I really felt I was
trying my best. It didn't matter. I'd still fail, or at best, barely pass."

At age 25, Linda began studying art in college and eventually
earned a B.A. in fine arts. Currently an aspiring artist in her spare
time, she is a happily married 35-year-old mother of two and an
art instructor at the college where she earned her degree. It's said
that every child in a family grows up in a different family. Linda
knows her parents loved her just as much as they loved their other
children. But being an artist didn't count for much; being gifted
in school did. It took decades for Linda to create a life where her
strengths and talents could take center stage.

Like with Carl and Javier, Linda experienced challenges in areas
associated with executive function, specifically those we rely on to
organize work, plan assignments, manage time, and hold information in mind long enough to reach a goal or solve a problem (working memory). These challenges probably explain much of why she
performed so inconsistently on tests. "I would study for days and
days for my exams and know the material. Then, on the day of the
exam, I would forget everything. People would constantly tell me
that I didn't study hard enough. But I did. And I knew the material.
I just couldn't remember it when I was tested on it."

Looking back at some of her earlier test scores, there were
occasions when Linda remembered what she had studied quite
well. How she performed depended more on how the test was

constructed. On multiple choice tests, for example, she did fine. On essay exams she often failed. One reason may be that multiple choice tests helped her find the information in memory. The correct answer was printed right there on the page, and all she had to do was recognize it. Essay exams required that she locate the information in memory on her own, then organize it in a way that would allow her to effectively and coherently communicate it in writing. That was hard for her to do in light of her learning profile.

Imagine comparing Linda's memory for what she studies to a file cabinet in the corner of your office. Picture filing papers away in the cabinet but doing so randomly. When you need to retrieve a single piece of paper, you have to look in every single file. Linda would study and study but not know how to file the material away in a manner that would allow her to retrieve it later. People with strong study and organizational skills tend to be very good at prioritizing, categorizing, and sorting material when studying. Essentially, they know how to file information away so that it's easy to retrieve. Not Linda. When she studied for exams, all information was treated equally. Nothing was stored in a way that would make it easy to retrieve, but the information was actually in there. Multiple choice tests showed her where to find it. Linda really was trying hard to pass her exams. Sometimes she did. Unfortunately, her uneven ways led to two misperceptions: if she would only try harder she would surely do better, and anyone who could do as well as she did at times, should be able to do that well all the time, if they really cared.

In middle school and high school, Linda was under the care of a psychiatrist who treated her for clinical depression. Her doctor believed her depression caused her problems in school. In retrospect, Linda believes it was actually her problems in school that caused her depression. Comparing her life back then to her life today, she finds that the adult world has been kinder to her than the world she lived in as a child. The adult world values a range of different strengths, artistic and otherwise. But this is not always the case when we're young.

What was less apparent back then was how Linda's struggles at school affected her at home. With two siblings who were straight-A students and parents who deeply valued school success, Linda felt she could never be the child her parents wanted her to be. She says,

"I would have given anything to be the straight-A child they wished for. They thought I didn't care, but they were wrong. I really did care." To Linda, there was a disconnect between her actions and her desired outcomes, in her mind at least. In some respects, she experienced a similar disconnect at home. In her mind, no matter how hard she tried, she could never achieve at school what her brother and sister could achieve and, as a result, could never live up to her parents' expectations—a perception that decades later she realized was totally incorrect.

CONTEXTUAL INFLUENCES: SOCIAL CONTEXT

1. The Transforming Power of Meaningful Work

Linda has always been passionate about expressing herself through art, and years after graduating from high school she decided to pursue her passion. It was a decision she feels has helped transform her life. She currently balances her work as an aspiring artist with her many other important roles, among them, wife, mother, teacher, and mentor.

2. Raising the Bar and Leveling the Playing Field

Linda feels that she still experiences learning challenges, although they no longer interfere with her ability to successfully handle daily demands and responsibilities. She uses different tools, technologies, and strategies to navigate the difficult areas. She programs her cell phone with reminder messages throughout the day, uses organizing tools on her computer to help her manage time and complete the tasks she begins, and attends a weekly support group, where she and others brainstorm strategies to help one another organize their day and achieve their goals.

3. A Change of Scenery: The Value of a Fresh Start

Linda did poorly at the first university she attended. "I felt lost. Classes were too large for me." She then switched to a much smaller private college, which she described as "a wonderful learning environment." There were far fewer students per class, and she had the opportunity to get to know her instructors, some of whom she continues to communicate with. She describes one previous instructor in particular as a close and trusted friend.

LIFE EXPERIENCES—IN CONTEXT

4. Personal Pathways to a Sense of Mastery

Projects that Linda takes on as an artist and as a college instructor are sometimes difficult, sometimes frustrating, and sometimes fraught with unanticipated challenges. She's undeterred. She is confident in her ability to successfully complete projects she undertakes.

If Linda could magically transport herself back to middle school or high school, she would probably still struggle as she did decades ago. "I'm not all that different today than I was back then. I still do the same things well and still struggle in some of the same ways, too." Today, though, things going right in her life far outweigh things that continue to challenge her.

5. Seeing Human Intelligence in a New Light

Linda enjoys significant strengths in areas that call into play visual spatial abilities. It's no surprise that she loves art. It's also no surprise that she feels so fulfilled now that she has the opportunity to teach art and express her artistic gifts around others who share a similar passion. As a struggling child, she believed that her poor grades meant that she was not very smart. Today, she believes there are many different ways of being smart.

6. When Difference No Longer Signals Danger

More Labels, Not Fewer

Linda is a wife, mother, artist, teacher, and mentor, among other roles. She is described by family and friends as creative, energetic, kind, compassionate, and as a self-starter. She has learned to see herself in relation to others and the world through these and other positive labels. Unlike in years past, she views her few persisting challenges in the context of her many impressive strengths.

Seeing Abilities as Malleable

Linda's approach to art projects, or really any project that draws on her creative talents, reflects a malleable view of abilities. Interestingly, this same mind-set eventually extended to the academic arena. In college, there were classes she prepared for in advance, months before the class actually began. This allowed her the extra time she needed to master difficult reading material and course content that she felt she would be unable to master during the regular semester. On several occasions, she sought tutoring for courses she found challenging. On some occasions, she was also able to retake tests that she initially scored poorly on. When she sets her sight on a goal today, Linda usually tries very hard, is reluctant to give up, and knows how to treat mistakes and setbacks as learning experiences. She seems to have made the transition from a fixed mind-set during earlier school years to a more malleable or growth mind-set today. Her artistic and creative strengths have helped pave the way.

Seeing Challenges in Historical Context

In college, Linda became increasingly interested in the topic of clinical depression when it was discussed in one of her psychology courses. The class discussion resonated with her, and as a matter of personal interest, she began researching its causes and the latest and most effective treatments. She remains well informed about the condition, particularly the link between clinical depression and learning problems. She knows better than most that depression can affect learning, but also that learning problems can sometimes lead to depression. She is aware that when she was in middle school and high school, less was known about the link between learning challenges on one hand and clinical depression on the other. Her awareness in this regard is derived in part by her ability to understand mental health challenges in their historical context.

7. Translating the Pain of Our Past into Meaningful Action on Behalf of Others

As Linda became more understanding of her earlier challenges, she began advocating on behalf of others who struggled as she did during her earlier school years. She volunteers for a local nonprofit organization that helps children and families overcome various challenges, serving as a member of their board of directors and on their fundraising committee. (Carl volunteers for the same organization and serves on the same board.) She also mentors several students at the college where she teaches, most of whom struggled as she once did. As was the case with Carl and Javier, once she gained a new understanding of her specific challenges, she became increasingly interested in reaching out to help others with similar challenges.

RELATIONSHIPS—IN CONTEXT

8. Beating the Odds Thanks to Those Who Changed the Odds

Safety Nets

Linda was treated for clinical depression in middle school and high school. At the time, she had been growing increasingly sad and irritable. Despite the pressure she felt to perform better at school and the disappointment she felt her problems were causing her parents, she always felt a strong emotional connection to her family, particularly her mother and sister. She often drew on their love and support during difficult emotional periods. She also enjoyed a strong emotional connection with her best friend, with whom she remains in close contact.

Connecting with Those Who Legitimize Rather than Stigmatize

Linda has always felt supported by her family and her closest friend. Today, she also enjoys the support of her husband, her children, and her colleagues. She feels no shame or embarrassment about her learning differences or any events of the past. She remains thankful that the important people in her life legitimize rather than stigmatize differences. Looking back to her years in middle school and high school, however, she remembers how difficult it was to talk openly about her depression, fearing others would judge her or reject her. She also recalls how little she and others knew back then about mental health challenges, and she can remember how students who experienced these challenges were often ridiculed. Back then, it made sense to simply suffer in silence, which she chose to do. Except for her immediate family and closest friend, no one knew she was being treated for depression.

9. Growing Closer and Stronger

Today, Linda sees her earlier struggles in a different context. She feels they helped make her a stronger, wiser, and more insightful person. She is also grateful to her parents, her sister, and her close friend for their support. Though misperceptions can lead caring people to think in fixed and inflexible ways, this was not the case with her support network. They remained compassionate, nonjudgmental, and hopeful of better days for Linda down the road.

10. Our Greatest Source of Strength: Each Other

Linda says that her decision to go back to college was one of several different turning points in her life. Her first attempt ended unsuccessfully. "It was a difficult decision to try college again." She re-enrolled, this time at a college that proved to be a much better fit. Choosing a career in art was also a turning point. Linda says that no one she knew at the time believed that it was possible to earn an income as an artist. "I needed to at least try."

When asked to think about turning points in the context of personal relationships, the conversation grew more emotional. Among those she felt most grateful to were her parents. Linda now believes her parents inspired her to always try her best and never give up. She remembers how much they cared, unconditionally, and how much they sacrificed for their children. "They just had no idea that I learned differently than my brother and sister did." In college, Linda had the chance to meet art instructors who shared her passion. She valued these relationships, to the extent that today she includes them as turning points. In their presence she felt appreciated, accepted, and understood. These relationships also helped validate her career choice.

Carl, Javier, and Linda are different people who grew up at different times under different conditions. Yet, they share several things. They all experienced difficulties in school, albeit for different reasons. Their difficulties manifested themselves in ways that seemed confusing and paradoxical to others, including their parents (and foster parents), teachers, and even the health care professionals who treated them. Their confusing ways in turn resulted in misinterpretations on the part of those who cared deeply about them. These perceptions then led to ineffective interventions, ultimately resulting in disappointing outcomes. But in time, Carl, Javier, and Linda rebounded from their difficult past and eventually carved out meaningful and productive lives for themselves. Although their journeys from challenged children to successful adults involved different pathways, on closer examination, we find them benefiting from similar contextual influences.

PAM

Pam is well known in her community as a skilled nurse practitioner and tireless advocate for those whose lives have been affected by interpersonal violence, including bullying. Those who know her personally know her as a warm and loving mother, grandmother, and wife. As a child, Pam was an A student who enjoyed going to school. She worked hard, earned good grades, was well liked by her teachers, had a number of good friends, and always seemed very confident in her abilities. But in seventh grade her life at school changed dramatically. Attending a junior high school much larger and less personal than the small school she attended from kindergarten through grade six, she was tormented, ridiculed, and physically threatened almost daily by two of her classmates. Pam soon learned that the two girls were acting under the direction of a third, a ringleader, an attractive and popular classmate whose mission was to make the lives of girls she was envious of miserable. Weeks into the start of her first semester of junior high, Pam became her number one target.

Pam attended school at a time when far fewer people were aware of the harmful effects of bullying. Many at the time treated it as a rite of passage. Today, on the other hand, a number of experts treat bullying as a form of interpersonal abuse. Bullying represents one person with power tormenting another person who feels powerless to stop it. It's not a conflict that needs to be resolved, a fight that needs to be stopped, or harmless horseplay.

Thanks to authorities on bullying prevention, among them Rachel Simmons (2002), Pam knows now that her experiences were hardly unique. When Simmons was eight years old, her best friend rounded up her other friends and convinced them not to play with her. At the time, Simmons thought she was the only child this had ever happened to. Many years later as a graduate student, she would learn otherwise. While attending graduate school in England, Simmons sent out e-mails to women she knew in the United States, asking them to ask every woman they knew, three questions: "Were you ever tormented or teased by another girl?" "Explain what it was like." "How has it affected you?" Within 24 hours she was flooded with messages describing incidents some of the respondents were sharing for the first time. She followed up with in-depth interviews, both with school-age girls and adult women, exploring the impact these incidents had on their lives. In the youth violence research literature, these incidents are now seen as examples of "relational aggression," an often overlooked form of bullying that researchers say is more common in girls than boys. Simmons's findings culminated in her 2002 book *Odd Girl Out*.

Pam's academic struggles in seventh grade must have been confusing to her teachers. After all, she was capable of performing so much better and demonstrated this in years past. Furthermore, there were days when she appeared focused, attentive, and motivated to try her best—on the days her tormenters were not around. For very different reasons, Pam was uneven in how she handled day-to-day functions at school. In years past, she could do the difficult things easily. Now, even easy things appeared difficult, at least sometimes. On the execution end, Pam's functioning seemed inconsistent and unpredictable. She affectionately recalls the encouraging comments of teachers, counselors, and other adults she felt connected to at school, comments like, "We know you could do better, Pam." "We've seen you do it." "Just try harder."

Can feelings of social disconnection affect our ability to consistently and predictably do what we otherwise know how to do? Possibly, based on a study conducted by social psychologist Roy Baumeister and colleagues. The study showed that college students who perceived their futures to be void of meaningful relationships scored lower on cognitive tasks, not because of feeling distressed but as a result of less access to executive function skills necessary to perform up to one's cognitive capacity. A follow-up investigation also found them scoring lower on complex cognitive problem-solving tasks requiring memory retrieval skills (Baumeister, Tenge, and Nuss, 2002; Cacioppo and Patrick, 2008). (To learn more about these studies, log on to the web page.) It's important to remember that these studies were performed with college student volunteers, so we await the results of future research to see if these results generalize to more real-life social experiences. Yet results do suggest an interesting link between experiences of social isolation and social rejection on the one hand and our ability to perform cognitively on the other, including our ability to execute skills we may be able to execute better under more accepting conditions. For those enduring bullying and other toxic peer-on-peer behaviors at school or in the workplace, Baumeister and colleagues may be shedding light on another explanation for why resilient and capable people can sometimes know what to do yet be inconsistent and unpredictable in doing it.

In the summer before Pam began eighth grade, her mother moved the family to a community about 30 miles away. For Pam, this meant a new school and a fresh start. With the threat of daily violence removed, she began to thrive. She formed new friendships, again started earning straight A's in her classes, and once again felt hopeful about her future.

Rachel Simmons heard a number of stories from women who changed schools and began to thrive. Although changing schools can also be disruptive, she writes, for some it represents a fresh start.

A lengthier discussion of how bullying affected Pam at school, and how other contextual influences also contribute to her now successful life, can be found on the web page.

BILL

Bill, our last portrait of resilience, proves that in some cases it may only take one misperception to transform an otherwise resilient child into a demoralized young adult: that the true measure of human intelligence is school performance. Those that are able to achieve good grades in school must be smart, and those unable to achieve good grades are not.

Bill owns a small plumbing company in Southern California. He has been happily married for over 30 years and is the father of two grown children, both college graduates with successful careers. He is also known around the community for the many hours he volunteers for local causes, especially those serving military veterans.

Over 35 years have passed since Bill attended school, yet he remembers some of his experiences in great detail. "They were probably some of the hardest and most embarrassing times of my life. No matter how hard I tried, I could never keep up. Reading for me was especially difficult. It still is." Surprisingly, Bill's teachers and counselors were not that concerned about his academic challenges, at least not in earlier grades. He was considered to be a late bloomer, and teachers and counselors believed that late bloomers were simply immature and, given time, would eventually catch up. Unfortunately, research is showing that this may not always be the case. In a longitudinal study that tracked 403 students from 12 Connecticut communities from 1st through 12th grade, investigators found that struggling readers in early elementary school grades remained, on average, behind their same-age peers through the end of high school (Shaywitz et al., 1999). In the absence of research-validated intervention, said the investigators, poor readers in early grades tended to remain poor readers throughout their school lives. Bill actually never caught up. To help close the gap, in ninth grade his school had him repeat the school year. It didn't help. When he was retained again in 11th grade, he decided to drop out of school. He did so for one reason: attending school made him feel "stupid." "Every time I didn't understand something the teacher said, it reminded me of how stupid I felt. Every time I took a test I felt the same way. It got to a point that I just couldn't stand it anymore. So I just quit going to school."

After coming to the attention of the juvenile justice system as a result of chronic truancy, he enrolled in an alternative school. At age 18, he then joined the army. Bill's military experience proved to be among the major turning points in his life. He credits the army with providing him the opportunity to learn his trade—plumbing. After his discharge from the service, he started his own plumbing business. With the help of his wife, who handles the bookkeeping, inventory, and other business-related functions, the business has grown steadily over the years and continues to provide financial security.

Bill's story bears similarity to a select group of middle-aged men who researchers began following from the time they were adolescents. They were originally part of a larger group sample of 456 adolescent males serving as controls in Sheldon and Eleanor

Glueck's landmark outcome study of incarcerated youth with significant delinquent histories (Glueck and Glueck, 1968). (The study is discussed further on the web page). Study participants were all assessed at age 14 on a battery of tests that included the Wechsler Bellevue Test of Intelligence, an early version of the currently used Wechsler Intelligence Scales. Participants were then reinterviewed at ages 25, 30, and 47. Psychiatrist and researcher George Vaillant studied the mid-life outcomes of three groups drawn from the 456 control group participants. Two of the groups had IQ scores well below average (average IQ of 80), whereas those in the third group had IQ scores that were well above average (average IQ score of 115). Of the two lower scoring groups, one enjoyed significantly better mid-life outcomes than the other. Their outcomes, in fact, were comparable to the high IQ group.

Years ago, Bill was assessed on a battery of cognitive and educational tests and received scores similar to those in Vaillant's two lower scoring groups. Today, his quality of life exceeds that of Vaillant's high IQ group. Vaillant's major finding was that IQ score at age 14, as measured by the Wechsler Bellevue Test of Intelligence, does not predict mid-life success (Vaillant and Davis, 2000). Bill is living proof.

Among the factors that did predict mid-life success was a stable career identity. Bill has never aspired to a career or profession that required a college education. He has always been drawn to jobs where he could either fix or build things. With the help of friends and family, he built his own home from scratch. When something breaks and needs repair, he usually can fix it himself. It's no surprise that he loves his work. His job allows him to do the things he enjoys doing and does well.

Bill has other important qualities as well, among them a very warm and engaging manner. He has a long list of loyal customers who have used his services for years. Many consider him not only their plumber but also a friend. Bill is gifted in those social, emotional, and relationship skills that allow people to connect easily with those they meet and sustain these relationships over time. He always remembers being able to connect in this way, even as a child. His skills in this regard help explain his 30-year marriage.

Personal qualities contributing to Bill's success support Vaillant's findings. Among those in the low IQ group doing well at mid-life,

Vaillant found that relationship skills were actually more important than cognitive skills. Successful mid-life adults in the low IQ group were able to sustain intimate relationships over time. As a group, they also experienced rewarding marriages. In addition, they scored high on measures of "generativity," defined in part as a willingness to assume responsibility for the next generation and think beyond one's own self-interests. They actually scored higher on these measures than did those in the high IQ group. For those in the low IQ group doing poorly at mid-life, researchers were able to predict these poor outcomes based on social, emotional, and relationship skills, not on IQ score or level of education.

As a group, those with low IQ scores doing well exhibited strengths in areas involving manual dexterity. Bill excels in areas that weigh heavily on manual dexterity skills, in addition to visual spatial and tactile-kinesthetic skills. In all likelihood, these skills were also present in abundant supply decades ago, when he was struggling in school. Unfortunately, they mattered little back then.

Although he never realized it back then, Bill also possessed a number of other qualities necessary to do well in life. These included an impressive level of successful intelligence, an array of real-world problem-solving skills, and perhaps most important, the wise and courageous qualities we find in "social heroes."

A lengthier discussion of the qualities that helped Bill eventually carve out a meaningful and productive life appears on the web page. Also included is a discussion of the contextual influences that helped him achieve his current life success.

SUMMARY

- It turns out that a lot of people exhibit paradoxically uneven learning, behavioral, and/or emotional profiles. What's more, they can exhibit them for different reasons. Yet, as school-age children, their paradoxically uneven ways led parents, teachers, and others to the same five erroneous perceptions, which led to the same unfortunate results.
- On occasion, we see uneven profiles among those experiencing a variety of learning challenges, including those affecting processing skills, memory retrieval skills, as well as a host of other learning functions.

115

- We can also see these uneven profiles in those suffering the effects of prolonged traumatic stress exposure and in children affected by bullying.
- Those who struggled as children but currently enjoy successful lives appear to benefit from similar contextual influences.
- These contextual influences appear entirely transportable to a child's school day. As a result, there's reason to believe they may help children who struggle at school.
- Appreciating the important role that these contextual influences can play begins by recognizing and overcoming common contextual blind spots.

PART II

What Can Be

At varying times during their childhood years, the people introduced in part I all succumbed to risks and adversities (neurodevelopmental and/or environmental) that culminated in years of school failure. Decades later, they're all leading successful lives. Contextual influences changed the odds. In part II, we explore how these influences can prevent children who are exposed to similar risks and adversities from enduring similar years of school failure. We also explore how these influences can prevent an array of potential health, mental health, and life adjustment problems down the road.

New remedies require abandoning five erroneous perceptions so that we might be guided instead by five new, more empirically validated ones. But as we learn in Chapter 5, abandoning them can be far more difficult than we might think, largely because of common contextual blind spots. In the chapter, we discuss how to overcome these blind spots, thereby paving the way to new perceptions and ultimately new remedies.

In an effort to alert readers to special considerations when attempting to improve later life health outcomes, brief introductory remarks precede Chapters 6, 7, and 8. As we'll see, improving these outcomes appears to require additional practices.

In Chapter 6, we present a variety of practices that can support, highlight, and reinforce contextual influences observed in the lives of those who successfully rebounded from difficult childhoods.

Chapter 7 extends the discussion to specific strategies for improving emotional self-regulation and self-control skills, both of which are subsumed under the executive function umbrella and are associated with a wide range of later life outcomes.

In Chapter 8, we continue our discussion of improved later life outcomes from a different perspective. We highlight contributing influences to Carl's eventual success in changing his unhealthy ways and illustrate how children might benefit from similar experiences if we first change our perceptual lens.

Chapter 9 explores additional benefits to children currently at risk for later life criminal behavior and incarceration.

Chapter 10 explores how our new perceptions can strengthen the protective properties of an innovative approach to fostering family strengths and resilience and reducing the incidence of child maltreatment.

At first I thought I might be exaggerating the impact that a few erroneous perceptions can have on the lives of children, youth, parents, teachers, and families. But I came to realize that I may have actually been underestimating their effects. It turns out that these misperceptions can persist for a lifetime, in some instances doing serious harm to people's relationships and their careers. But, this doesn't have to happen. In many instances, we know how to prevent these outcomes, and in the process repair and strengthen our closest personal and professional relationships, as we'll learn in Chapter 11.

William Bruce Cameron once said, "Not everything that can be counted counts, and not everything that counts can be counted." These words serve as a fitting summation of lessons learned from those enjoying lives well-lived, despite enduring years of school failure, as we'll see in Chapter 12.

Chapter 5

※

PREVENTING THE RISE AND EXPEDITING THE DEMISE OF ERRONEOUS PERCEPTIONS

RECOGNIZING AND OVERCOMING OUR COMMON CONTEXTUAL BLIND SPOTS

For a number of children who exhibit paradoxically uneven learning and behavioral profiles, the following five new perceptions (to counter the misperceptions detailed in Chapter 1) can allow greater access to important contextual influences (contextually expressed protective processes), which in turn can guide us to a new array of practices that can improve the quality of many of their lives, now and into the future.

1. It's indeed possible that some people can be capable of doing difficult things easily yet find easy things difficult for reasons that have nothing to do with laziness or moral character. Although it's always important to try your best, the key to success in these simpler areas may not come down to trying harder, but trying differently.

2. It's entirely possible for someone to know what to do yet have difficulty consistently, predictably, and independently doing what they know, in part because they call into play different skills. Improving the ability to consistently, predictably, and independently do what one knows, therefore, sometimes requires learning an entire new set of strategies.

3. There are many different ways of being smart, some of which can't be measured by how well one does in school.

4. Resilient people sometimes think and act differently in places they find threatening and dangerous as opposed to places they find warm and friendly, particularly when those threatening and dangerous places also feel stigmatizing, inescapable, and beyond their ability to control or influence. To really appreciate human resilience, one needs to appreciate contextual influences, the visible and not-so-visible situational factors and personal circumstances affecting our lives.

5. These contextual influences can determine whether we endure in the face of adversity or are stretched to our limits of emotional endurance, which helps explain why some of the most resilient people may struggle significantly to get through a typical day.

The simple solution, then, is to replace the five misperceptions with these new ones. Unfortunately, though, it's not that easy. It turns out that misperceptions form quickly and die slowly. The good news is that we now know a lot more about how to prevent them from forming. Or if we're too late, we now also know a lot more about how to expedite their demise. In either case, the key lies in our ability to appreciate the often inconspicuous role that common contextual blind spots play in the perceptions we form and the conclusions we reach about the events, conditions, and experiences occurring in people's lives.

In this chapter, we discuss some of these contextual blind spots, how they can subvert greater human understanding, and how we can prevent this from happening. We begin with a discussion of a particularly common one, referred to here as a "context deficit disorder," and known in the social psychology literature as the fundamental attribution error. We follow with a discussion of cognitive dissonance, another common blind spot. Then we discuss a blind spot that affects how we see ourselves in relation to others and to the world and can make it difficult for us to see life's challenges in a new light. We follow with a fourth blind spot: the inability to see resilience in context. This can prevent us from understanding the resilient ways of those who struggle simply to make it through a normal day. We conclude with a discussion of a fifth blind spot, one that occasionally affects our ability to see evidence-based practices in context. (The discussion of contextual blind spots continues in a later section of the book, when we explore their impact on our closest personal and professional relationships).

CONTEXT DEFICIT DISORDER, A.K.A. THE FUNDAMENTAL ATTRIBUTION ERROR

There's a contextual blind spot that we all seem to experience from time to time, and it prevents us from accurately perceiving how events and experiences in a person's environment can negatively influence how they respond in a particular situation. Social psychologists have known for some time about this flaw in our judgmental machinery, this context deficit disorder. Their studies show that when it comes to explaining people's actions, we tend to favor explanations that overestimate character or moral fiber. We're inclined to believe that people do things because that's the way they are. It's their nature. It's not that we believe context doesn't matter or that we're oblivious to the impact that uncontrollable events play in determining how people might act in different situations. We are well aware of the forces they exert and often factor them into the perceptual equation when making meaning of behavior. But usually we reserve this kinder perceptual view for judging our own behavior, rather than the behavior of others. Social psychologists coined a term to explain this common contextual blind spot. They refer to it as the "fundamental attribution error" (Ross and Nisbett, 1991). It goes something like this. When it comes to understanding the mysterious and confusing actions of others—peculiarities or inconsistencies in their day-to-day behavior as well as the ultimate direction others' lives have taken—we can be quick to assume that people are basically getting what they deserve. If they handled things differently, if they made different choices, if they tried harder, things would have turned out differently. Situational factors or the context within which behaviors occur may well take a back seat when it comes to our meaning-making ways. When it's about others, character trumps context. When it's about us, we tend to be acutely sensitive to potential contributing forces propelling us to act in certain ways. Moreover, we're much quicker to use them as reasons to explain why we might be doing the things we're doing—context trumps character.

Why is this? According to some researchers, it's all a matter of our primary focus of attention. We are extremely aware of the surrounding events and experiences affecting ourselves. We can't see or feel the world as others do, so we have no way of really knowing how contextual influences might be affecting them (Aronson, 2000).

As human observers, we see the person and we see the behavior. Context is invisible. Even when we're made aware of it, it can be open to so many different interpretations. How can we know which one is accurate? It's much easier to just judge the person and attribute behavior to character or moral fiber.

If we're unaware of this common contextual blind spot, erroneous perceptions won't sound mistaken. To the contrary, they'll make great sense. Recall how frequently Carl's parents and teachers relied on facts, fear, and force to help him change his ways. But these tactics didn't result in Carl becoming a more fluent reader. He needed a particular type of intervention for that to happen. They also didn't help him navigate his struggles in at least some areas of executive function. Specific strategies and interventions were required here as well.

Before moving on, we should also mention that this contextual blind spot has a flip side. Not only is the meaning we attach to the behavior of others sometimes less than accurate, the meaning we attach to our own behavior can be less than accurate as well. Our context deficit disorder can sometimes cause us to underestimate the impact of context on other people's behavior and overestimate its impact on our own. Students with profiles similar to Carl's may fail to appreciate the control they actually have in changing their ways.

WHEN THINKING WE'RE RIGHT TRUMPS BEING RIGHT: COGNITIVE DISSONANCE AND ERRONEOUS PERCEPTIONS

It turns out that the common misperceptions, once formed, can become so entrenched that contradictory views may be summarily dismissed. This includes views that are far more accurate than those we've been clinging to. In fact, in some cases, despite being provable, these new views may serve to strengthen existing misperceptions. Social psychologists have known about this second flaw in our meaning-making machinery for some time. Even the most open minded among us are susceptible to psychological forces that can promote misunderstanding. The good news is that human understanding can eventually win out, but only if we can spot and counteract the effects of cognitive dissonance.

Hundreds of studies have been conducted over the years showing how the theory of cognitive dissonance helps explain some of our most irrational, hard-to-believe behaviors. According to the theory, when having to contend with new information that contradicts strongly held personal beliefs, we may find ourselves experiencing a state of mental tension—known as cognitive dissonance. One way to alleviate this uncomfortable state is to cling tightly to our originally held beliefs, regardless of how true and accurate the new information might be. Logically it would seem simpler to change our beliefs in favor of the new, more accurate information. But cognitive dissonance theory proves that sometimes the exact opposite occurs. Research has shown that when it comes to our strongly held beliefs, being right can sometimes take a back seat to *thinking* we're right. We have a tendency to self-justify or interpret information in ways that corroborate what we already believe (Aronson, 1995).

Self-justification actually helps us get through the day. If we didn't self-justify, we would endlessly question our beliefs and behavioral choices. But our self-justifying tendencies have a serious downside. They make it harder for us to change our beliefs when new and more accurate information runs counter to what we believe. Self-justification shouldn't be confused with lying or being untruthful. If anything, it's lying to ourselves to convince ourselves that what we believe is right. And the engine that drives self-justification, social psychologists say, is cognitive dissonance (Aronson, 2010; Festinger, 1957; Tavris and Aronson, 2007).

COGNITIVE DISSONANCE IN ACTION

Imagine that you're a heavy smoker and have tried to quit smoking many times. You hear over and over that smoking is very bad for you, that it can cause cancer and other health problems. You've tried to quit but can't seem to break the habit. One way to alleviate the resulting mental tension is to convince yourself that you're not a heavy a smoker, only a moderate one. Studies in cognitive dissonance have found that many heavy smokers do just that. Researchers asked 155 people who smoked one to two packs of cigarettes a day whether they considered themselves to be either moderate or heavy smokers and also whether they were aware of the harmful effects of their habit. Results showed that those most aware of the long-term health consequences were more likely to see themselves as only moderate smokers. Those less aware were more likely to rate themselves as heavy smokers. Based on cognitive dissonance theory, another way to eliminate the mental tension is by simply denying the credibility of studies that link smoking to cancer. Research shows that this is often what happens. When the surgeon general first announced the health hazards of smoking, researchers found that 90 percent of nonsmokers accepted the report as factual, compared with only 60 percent of smokers (Aronson, 1995, 2010; Kassarjian and Cohen, 1965).

Cognitive dissonance theory shows us that when we leap to an erroneous perception, one we strongly believe to be true, we can completely discard a more accurate, even provable counter-perception. Furthermore, when presented with this counter-perception, our existing misperception may grow stronger.

Another potential outcome is possible: we can form an entirely new misperception, one that includes elements of the old mistaken one and of the new one. To illustrate this, imagine having a conversation with a young child who believes the world to be flat. To the child's way of thinking, it's flat because that's what allows people to stand on it without falling off. You explain to the child that the world is actually round. Then you ask the child to draw a picture of the world, and the child makes it in the shape of a pancake. It's round, and you can still stand on it without falling off (Bransford, Brown, and Cocking, 2000). Young children aren't the only ones who distort incoming information to fit their original point of view—we're all guilty of this. From time to time, we start with a misperception or misunderstanding, place new information over it, and rather than having a more accurate picture create a more elaborate misperception.

The five understandable yet erroneous perceptions were covered in detail in Chapter 1. Review them and notice how each represents consonant (or consistent) beliefs, as opposed to dissonant (or contradictory) beliefs.

Now read through the following statements. Notice how they represent beliefs that are dissonant (contradictory), as opposed to consonant.

1. Some people can be capable of doing difficult things easily yet find easy things difficult for reasons that have nothing to do with laziness or moral character.
2. It's entirely possible for someone to know what to do yet have difficulty consistently, predictably, and independently doing what they know.
3. There are many different ways of being smart, some of which can't be measured by how well one does in school.
4. Resilient people sometimes think and act differently in places they find threatening and dangerous as opposed to places they find warm and friendly.
5. Some of the most resilient people may struggle significantly just to get through a typical day.

Once we're aware of how cognitive dissonance can support existing misperceptions and prevent us from accepting new and more accurate ones, our mind-sets are open to change. Insight into the nature of cognitive dissonance strengthens our capacity for greater human understanding by allowing us the opportunity to override a major psychological force contributing to human misunderstanding. This has significant implications for the important people in our lives who may have been affected by our misperceptions. We're now in a better position to see the challenges and adversities affecting their lives in a whole new light. The question is, are *they*?

PRESERVING OUR SELF-VIEWS

It turns out that the same forces that can prevent us from seeing the challenges of a loved one in a new light may prevent them from doing this as well. Research shows that once we've formed our personal self-views, we may be inclined to distort and discount incoming information about ourselves in ways that support these self-views. If we've come to see ourselves as incapable, for example, we may be more likely to accept new information that corroborates this view and discount new information showing that we're actually very capable. Furthermore, this can occur even when it's undeniable that the new information is true and accurate. According to social psychologist William Swann (1996), there are several common yet faulty assumptions about the nature of our self-views and one of them is that we're all motivated to think well of ourselves. To the contrary, research suggests we may be more motivated to preserve the views we already have, good or bad, healthy or damaged. Swann and his colleagues have conducted a number of studies to illustrate this. In one study, volunteers were asked to listen to positive and negative judgments others had formed about them. Those who viewed themselves positively were more likely to remember the positive comments, and those who viewed themselves negatively tended to remember the negative ones. Participants tended to remember comments that confirmed their self-views.

Other studies seem to support the same conclusion: our self-views, once formed, are not easy to change. Perhaps this shouldn't come as a big surprise. Over the course of many years, we've had a lot of practice learning to see ourselves the way we do. Swann suggested another explanation, one related to a sense of personal control. Researchers find that the more uncontrollable our outside world feels, the more important it can be to control our inside world. We have a need for psychological order, according to Swann. Knowing who we are in relationship to our world provides this, even when the place we believe we occupy in the world might not be very positive. By controlling our inside world, we're better able to predict what to expect from others and the world.

HUMAN RESILIENCE—IN CONTEXT

For Carl, school was a threatening and dangerous place. For his brother, Steven, on the other hand, school was warm and friendly. But as different as their school experiences were, Carl and Steven shared one thing, something we all share: a nervous system wired for survival. That nervous system functions very differently in situations that we perceive as threatening and dangerous than it does in situations perceived as warm and friendly.

To the parts of our brain that cue our emotions and propel us to action when we feel survival is at stake, danger is danger (Bremner, 2001; Dosier, 2002; Siegel, 1999). In an instant, different hormones and chemical messengers rush through us, mobilizing our bodies to divert energy from things that can wait—like reading this, for example—to things that can't.

What we think, how we feel, and how we act can vary a great deal depending on whether we perceive conditions as safe and harmless or as threatening and dangerous. As a result, fighting on and persevering under threatening and dangerous conditions can look a lot different behaviorally, psychologically, and physiologically than doing so under safe conditions. To appreciate human resilience, therefore, one needs to appreciate contextual influences. Herein lies another contextual blind spot: Sometimes we appear to have difficulty perceiving human resilience in context.

After the terrorist attacks of September 11, 2001, some thought the Twin Towers might have collapsed because they weren't strong enough. Many didn't realize how strong they actually were. We've learned since that even very strong buildings have their limits of endurance. The same is true for resilient individuals. We are aware of this as a result of our ability to perceive human resilience in context.

In preparation for the next chapter, which explores a range of practices for improving the lives of struggling children and their families, it's timely that we explore an additional contextual blind spot, one that best follows the one we just discussed. Let me introduce it with a true story, an illustration of how even experienced mental health professionals can ask the wrong question at times.

EVIDENCE-BASED PRACTICES—IN CONTEXT

At a conference several years ago, a workshop presenter described to an audience of 100 professionals a program designed to connect children living in group home facilities with distant family members, many of whom were unaware of the child's circumstances.

According to the presenter, children in these group homes were placed there by social service officials because their parents were unable to care for them, either because the parents were incarcerated or suffered from serious drug-related problems. Often, these children exhibited emotional and behavioral challenges, which were directly related to or seriously exacerbated by their separation from their parents. While the group homes provided mental health services to address these challenges, what these children really needed were loving homes. According to the presenter, this was essentially the program's mission: connect children living in group homes to extended family members. And it was working. Children were being placed in homes with caregivers who would welcome them into their family. They could stay there permanently, or if their parents' lives significantly improved, they could live with their parents. Social service officials were strong and vocal supporters of the program. Many said they would be doing the exact same thing if they had the resources. As the formal part of the presentation came to a conclusion, the presenter asked if there were any questions. The first question came from a person in the back of the auditorium. He introduced himself as a mental health professional at a Midwest treatment center. After praising the presenter for the excellent work that he was doing, he then asked the following question: "Is your program evidence-based?"

That question was a beautiful illustration of our occasional inability to view evidence-based practices in context.

Practices should be supported by research showing them to be effective. After all, research-validated practices have improved the quality of countless lives. But those of us immersed in the world of evidence-based practices have to also remain mindful that some people struggle with learning, behavioral, and emotional challenges not as a result of underlying disorders but because of unmet human needs. By failing to remain mindful of this, we run the risk of pathologizing their suffering. What are examples of universal human needs? In addition to the obvious ones required for us physically to survive, there is the need to feel loved, the need to feel we matter and contribute something important to the world, the need to feel that our actions control our destiny, and the need to feel connected to others. Some would consider this the short list.

Evidence-Based Practices in the Context of Universal Human Needs

It bears repeating that not all resilient people beat the odds. In fact, some of the most resilient people struggle significantly just to get through a typical day. Some struggle not because of a lack of resilience, but as a result of unmet needs. Some feel unsafe. Some feel they don't belong. Some feel they don't matter. Some feel they have little to contribute. No doubt, evidence-based practices can play a role in helping them enjoy better lives down the road. But so can a greater appreciation of the role of these universal needs and greater efforts on the part of all of us to address them.

WHAT CAN BE

By way of review, erroneous perceptions need not transform resilient children into demoralized young adults. In many instances, these damaging outcomes can be prevented and the prospects for a successful school career and successful adult life improved. These outcomes are achievable with greater awareness of the often inconspicuous role that contextual influences play in the quality of our lives. To access these influences, however, we may first have to recognize and overcome common contextual blind spots such as those discussed here.

Greater awareness of contextual influences can improve our lives at any age. As we'll see in the chapters that follow, these influences can help children transform school failure into school success. They can help prevent a host of later life health, mental health, and life adjustment problems. They can help strengthen areas of executive function, including emotional self-regulation and self-control. And they can repair and improve our closest personal and professional relationships. In exploring "what can be," we have barely scratched the surface.

SUMMARY

- The key to changing misperceptions lies in our ability to appreciate common contextual blind spots and the conclusions we reach about the events, conditions, and experiences occurring in people's lives.

- Context deficit disorder, also known as the fundamental attribution error, leads us to favor explanations for others' behavior that overestimate character and underestimate contextual influences. When it's about our own behavior, the reverse if often true.

- Cognitive dissonance theory shows us that when we leap to a misperception, one we strongly believe to be true, we may discard a more accurate, even provable counter-perception. When presented with this new perception, our existing erroneous perception may grow even stronger.

- The same forces that prevent us from seeing another's challenges in a new light may prevent them from doing so as well. Once we've formed our own self-views, we may be inclined to distort new incoming information about ourselves in ways that support these views and discount new information that runs counter to them.

- Fighting on and persevering under threatening and dangerous conditions can look a lot different behaviorally, psychologically, and physiologically, than fighting on and persevering under safe conditions. At times, we appear to have difficulty perceiving human resilience in context.

- Some children struggle not because of a lack of resilience but as a result of one or more unmet universal needs. Evidence-based practices (viewed in context) can play a role in helping them enjoy better lives down the road.

INTRODUCTORY REMARKS TO CHAPTERS 6, 7, AND 8

The Kauai Longitudinal Study found that a significant number of those who beat the odds as children (54.5 percent of the men and 41.2 percent of the women) reported health-related symptoms decades later. What was particularly surprising was that their health-related symptoms were twice that of high-risk peers who developed coping problems as teens (Werner and Smith, 2001). Children similar to Steven, in other words, were at greater risk for health-related problems decades later than were children similar to Carl! According to some experts in the field, one possible reason may have to do with the added stress they endured (Masten, 2014). Beating the odds may have been more psychologically demanding than we realized, resulting in added stress that eventually affected health outcomes. In preventing health problems, it's important to be thinking about how to change the odds for *all* children growing up exposed to multiple risks and adversities.

In addition, children who struggle in areas of emotional self-regulation and self-control are also at significantly greater risk for health-related problems (as well as many other negative outcomes) down the road. What's more, this risk may even exist in the absence of high ACE scores.

In preventing negative later life health outcomes, therefore, we may need to tackle the problem on several fronts. First, we'll want to create a school day that significantly alleviates elevated stress levels of children exposed to multiple risks. Second, we'll want to create the opportunity for these children to have resources available to help them learn to see these events in a new light, if they choose to discuss them. In Chapter 6, specific ideas for addressing these considerations appear under the contextual influence they most closely align with. Third, we'll want to help children with weak emotional self-regulation and self-control skills learn how to improve these skills. We devote an entire chapter to this (Chapter 7). We focus on five self-regulation strategies in particular. Collectively, they make up what Stanford University researcher James Gross refers to as the process model of emotion regulation (Gross, 1998; Gross and Thompson, 2009). Evidence suggests that the more we employ them effectively, the better we will be at regulating and controlling our emotions (Southam-Gerow, 2013). Over the course of their adult years, Carl and Javier each mastered these self-regulation strategies. Today, each seems far more skilled in regulating emotions and controlling behavior. In Chapter 7, we provide specific ideas on how teachers, parents, and health care professionals can help children become increasingly skilled in these areas as well.

We devote another chapter (Chapter 8) to three agents of change that eventually helped Carl master a new behavioral lifestyle that reduced the likelihood of serious health problems. These agents of change correspond to three contextual influences we previously showed to be transportable to a typical school day. There's reason to believe that agents of change (contextual influences) can prevent some children from experiencing health-related problems later. As before, however, accessing these agents of change (contextual influences) requires that we abandon five familiar erroneous perceptions and replace them with new, more empirically validated ones.

Finally, improved emotional self-regulation and self-control skills can potentially buffer a great many children from behavioral risks we know to be hazardous to our health—smoking, poor nutrition, a sedentary lifestyle among them. Chapters 6, 7, and 8 provide ideas that help all children improve emotional self-regulation and self-control skills.

Chapter 6

~~~~~

PREVENTING SCHOOL FAILURE, ONE SCHOOL DAY AT A TIME

CONTEXTUAL INFLUENCES THAT CAN CHANGE THE ODDS

Recall from Chapter 2 that protective processes are not the equivalent of programs or practices, nor do they equal treatment strategies or techniques. However, any number of different programs, practices, strategies, or techniques can foster protective processes (Prochaska, Norcross, and DiClemente, 2002). Recall also that contextual influences are made up of the same properties and serve the same functions as do protective processes. Protective processes neutralize or outweigh the potentially harmful effects of multiple risk exposure, and so do contextual influences. The term "contextual influences" however, draws attention to our context-sensitive ways, particularly our gift for contextual thinking. There are many different contexts within which protective processes can express themselves, and the term "contextual influences" provides the opportunity to begin exploring them. These influences can best be understood as contextually expressed protective processes.

PERCEPTIONS, PROCESSES, PRACTICES

Our five new perceptions allow easier access to contextual influences. Contextual influences, in turn, guide us to a new array of compatible practices. Our five new perceptions (presented in Chapter 5) thus represent an important starting point for preventing school failure and a host of negative later life outcomes, one school day at a time. (An illustration of the five erroneous perceptions and these five new perceptions appears on the web page).

Contextual influences that can change the odds operate on at least three levels: (1) socially (externally); (2) emotionally, psychologically, and spiritually (internally) by helping us see life experiences in a new light; and 3) relationally.

Socially, these influences create contexts where children feel they belong and have something important to contribute, regardless of their differences. These are social settings where they are encouraged to raise personal and educational expectations (raise the bar) and also learn to use tools, strategies, and accommodations to strengthen or navigate challenges (level their playing fields).

Emotionally, psychologically, and spiritually, contextual influences assist children in developing a sense of mastery by valuing, celebrating, and reinforcing effort, struggle, and the ability to treat mistakes as learning experiences. They redefine intelligence in ways that recognize diverse areas of intellectual strength and talent. They help children perceive challenges in a new light, one that no longer associates these challenges with feelings of threat and danger. In later grades, they provide opportunities to transform the pain of one's past into meaningful action on behalf of others.

Relationally, these influences draw on the power of bystanders to help legitimize rather than stigmatize learning, behavioral, and other challenges. In addition, they provide struggling children experiences that years later will be seen as positive turning points in their lives.

All programs and practices selected for discussion here support and strengthen one or more contextual influences in the lives of adults who overcame a difficult past, including years of school failure. A number of programs and practices are supported by research. Others represent innovative efforts drawn from the personal and professional experiences of teachers, health care providers, and others. All are intended to serve as illustrations, not prescriptive recommendations.

Although programs and practices will be discussed in relation to particular contextual influences, they can often support and strengthen a number of other influences as well.

Several of the programs and practices are also described in greater detail on the book's web page. New programs and practices will be added to the web page on an ongoing basis.

The discussion of contextual influences occurs in the same order as in other chapters. The practices reviewed here are described separately. This is not to imply they should be replicated in isolation, separate from other practices targeting co-occurring sources of risk. To the contrary, bundling practices in ways that address co-occurring risks is recommended, given what we now know about the effects of multiple risk exposure. Research shows, for example, that it's rarely one childhood risk or one adverse life experience that leads to school failure, aggressive and violent behavior, or other serious mental health, physical health, and/or life adjustment difficulties. Rather, it's usually the presence of several risks and adversities in combination. Furthermore, when these risks and experiences exist in combination, beating the odds will be very difficult in the absence of protective processes. The good news is that there are practices that not only foster protective processes but also target specific childhood risks. Some target specific neurodevelopmental risks, others risks that are more environmental in nature. To neutralize the impact of multiple risk exposure, then, the key may lie in combining these practices in ways that address their cumulative impact. Researchers who study resilience through the life span make a similar argument with respect to protective processes. For example, when Werner and colleagues cite protective processes that can outweigh the effects of multiple risk exposure, they don't cite one process but several in combination. The same argument could be made with regard to programs and practices. In combination, they exert a more powerful effect than when provided individually.

SOCIAL CONTEXT

1. The Opportunity to Do What We Love to Do and Do Well: The Transforming Power of Meaningful Work

Important Jobs Performed Well
Students who find school to be a threatening and dangerous place may feel they have little to contribute. In an effort to address

this, some schools are creating important jobs for students to perform, giving them the opportunity to contribute in meaningful ways. Some examples:

- School ambassador: Among students who enjoy talking (but not at the most appropriate times), some turn out to be excellent school ambassadors. Their job is to give persons visiting the school a tour of the campus. Talking is part of the job description. As tour guides, the more they converse, the better the tour.
- Tutor: Students are paired with younger students in lower grades. Student tutors help these younger children with academic subjects, class projects, and/or homework assignments.
- Assistant resource specialist: Responsibilities include reminding students to turn in homework assignments each morning and being available during designated hours after school for students to contact (via text messaging, e-mail, or by phone) in case they forgot to write down that day's homework assignment.
- School or class artist: The student's drawings or other works of art are displayed in class and around the campus. At one school, a teacher had her class artist draw a large picture of a tree, which she prominently displayed in the front office. Pictures were then taken of other students in class and placed on the drawing to represent the tree's leaves. The photos placed on the tree gave the student's artistic creation added importance. At another school, one student had the job of cartoonist, and she drew monthly cartoon strips for her class.
- Computer specialist: For students with an interest and expertise in digital technologies, responsibilities include helping other students understand how to use these technologies. Tasks may also include helping prepare teacher or other professional presentations that require the use of a computer and/or other technologies.
- Communications specialist: The job requires delivering messages from class to class or class to office. This is an excellent role for students who have difficulty sitting still for long periods or who perform better when given more opportunity to move about physically.

- Intern: In some communities, local businesses and organizations are teaming up with schools to provide students with community-based internships. One high school in Southern California has a collaborative relationship with a large community health care facility. As part of their collaboration, high school students do internships in one of the facility's hospitals, working several months of the year alongside nurses and other medical staff. Students have real-world experiences working at the hospital, and many excel, with some doing far better handling these experiences than they do handling academic or other school-related tasks.
- Hall monitor: The following true story is a reminder to not underestimate the impact of valued roles on people's lives, children included.

At the 2008 Olympics in Beijing, nine-year-old Lin Hao had the honor of walking alongside NBA basketball star Yao Ming as they led the Chinese Olympic Team into the stadium for the opening ceremonies. The boy was given the honor as a result of his heroic actions following a devastating earthquake in Sichuan Province that same year, one that killed tens of thousands people and left millions homeless. While walking down a corridor at his school, the earthquake struck, and the school building collapsed, trapping the child under the rubble. He managed to free himself from the debris, but rather than focus on his own personal safety, he chose to free a fellow student from the collapsed building. He then went back into the building to free another student. When later asked about his heroic efforts on behalf of his classmates, Lin Hao replied, "I was the hall monitor. It was my job to look after my classmates" (CBBC Newsround, 2011; Zimbardo, 2011).

Creating Opportunities to Contribute: Other Examples

On Saturday mornings at a comedy club in Los Angeles, professional comedians coach students on comedy techniques in preparation for a stand-up routine each will perform in front of a live audience. The participating students are currently in foster care. Each enjoys a wonderful sense of humor, only their comedic ways sometimes get them in trouble at school. Their stand-up routines, on the other hand, are greeted with thunderous applause.

At least once a week, an eighth-grade teacher at a Northern California middle school meets before school with a student having difficulty following class discussions. During these meetings, the teacher coaches the student on the material to be covered later that morning in class. They discuss background information related to a specific question the teacher intends to ask the class about the material. They brainstorm answers. When they arrive at a correct one, the teacher gives the student the option of raising his hand when the question is asked in class. The student is told that if he chooses to raise his hand, the teacher will call on him. Feeling prepared to give the correct answer in front of his classmates, the student typically raises his hand when the teacher asks the question. The teacher later learned that prior to their early morning meetings, the student had never raised his hand in any class before, much less answered a teacher's question correctly in front of other students.

Psychologist Robert Brooks (2013) tells a story about five students with significant behavioral challenges who dramatically improved their behavior when given a special job by a social worker at their school. The job required that they interview other students to determine why they either like or do not like coming to school. Before starting the job, the five students often missed school. Soon after starting their job, they began attending school regularly. Even more surprising, according to Brooks, is that they actually remained at school after the school day ended so they could participate in committee meetings exploring why students like or do not like coming to school.

Students remember school experiences where they felt they made a contribution. When a group of inner-city sixth graders were asked to think back to the previous school year and describe things that made them feel successful, creative, or proud, they mentioned activities like tutoring a younger child or designing playhouses that were donated to preschools (Barron et al., 1998; Bransford, Brown, and Cocking, 2000).

The Jigsaw Classroom

The brainchild of retired University of California, Santa Cruz social psychology professor Elliott Aronson, the jigsaw process provides all students with responsibilities that show they belong and have something important to contribute. The process begins by assigning students to jigsaw groups. Each student in the jigsaw group is assigned a critical piece of a lesson plan and required to become an expert on it. Next, students meet in expert groups with others assigned with the same part of the lesson. Teachers work closely with students in expert groups to ensure they effectively master their part of the lesson. They return to their original jigsaw group as experts and help fellow group members master their area of expertise. Other group members do the same. Since the model was first introduced in the 1970s, a number of studies have corroborated its benefits. Research shows that students engaging in the jigsaw process grow more understanding of and empathic toward their classmates and master academic material as well as or better than when similar material is taught in more traditional ways. Aronson's jigsaw formula has also helped create emotional bonds between ethnically and racially diverse students who previously viewed one another with suspicion and mistrust (Aronson and Patnoe, 1997; Katz, 2002b, 2010c). Those interested in learning more about the jigsaw process are encouraged to visit the jigsaw website at http://www.jigsaw.org. A more in-depth understanding of its history and empirical support can also be found in Aronson (2000). (Reminder: Lengthier descriptions of many of the programs and practices discussed here, including jigsaw, appear on the book's web page.)

Specialisterne

Qualities that render us at a disadvantage at school can sometimes be highly valued at work. Consider, for example, the Specialisterne story. Specialisterne is a high-tech company based in Copenhagen, Denmark that provides a range of consultation services to other high-tech firms throughout the country. What's unique about the company is that its workforce is comprised of high-functioning adults on the autism spectrum. Many of the employees also have ADHD as an additional diagnosis. Their unique characteristics, considered liabilities in other situations, provide them with an advantage at Specialisterne (Katz, 2013c). The company was started in 2003 by Thorkil Sonne, a former technical director in the telecommunications industry, and the father of a teenage son with high-functioning autism.

2. Raising the Bar and Leveling the Playing Field

A number of successful adults who did poorly in school remember the countless hours that dedicated teachers, health care professionals, mental health specialists, and others spent trying to help remediate their deficits and level their playing fields. Many also remember how embarrassed they felt accepting such help. As a result, many eventually stopped accepting it. Many also stopped trying their best. By lowering the bar, they avoided the public humiliation of trying, failing, and bringing yet more attention to differences and challenges they associated with threat and danger.

No doubt, it's important to level the playing field. But we also have to remember to raise the bar. This has not always been easy. Fortunately, help has arrived from an unexpected source: people who did poorly in school but are doing well in life. A number of those who were eventually able to rise above their earlier school difficulties have created programs designed to help others who struggle as much as they did in years past. Some programs are in the form of mentoring models, others in the form of specific practices, some a combination of the two. Several examples are provided here.

WhyTry: Christian Moore is a licensed clinical social worker from Orem, Utah, who struggled with a number of learning challenges. He knows firsthand how demoralizing these challenges can be to school-age youth who are unable to see them in a hopeful new light. So he created WhyTry, a program that helps children do this. The program is composed of 10 visual analogies that correspond to 10 problems or challenges often encountered by students who learn differently. Reinforced by a series of experiential learning activities and music, visual analogies show students how to reframe and rise above these problems or challenges. All lessons and activities relate back to the central question, "Why try in life?," more specifically, "Why try in life when challenges and pressures feel overwhelming and insurmountable?"

When effectively replicated, WhyTry can help struggling students raise the bar and level their playing field. Students learn to see that creative solutions to difficult problems really exist and that by choosing these solutions, new freedoms emerge, self-respect grows, more opportunities appear, and motivation to succeed increases (Katz, 2006). The program is currently in use in thousands of schools, mental health centers, and correctional facilities in the United States, Canada, and abroad. To learn more about the model, visit the WhyTry website at http://www.whytry.org.

Eye to Eye: A national after-school mentoring model, Eye to Eye helps students learn to see labels in a hopeful and empowering light. The model pairs trained college or high school mentors succeeding in spite of learning or attentional challenges with younger students struggling with the same challenges. Mentor and mentee spend time together, share personal experiences, and collaborate on projects. Struggling children have the opportunity to see firsthand that people with the same challenges can have successful academic careers and lead very satisfying lives. They also discover that success doesn't just happen—students need to determine how they learn best, find the tools they need to navigate their challenges, and learn how to ask for what they need. Who better to help them learn these things than their Eye to Eye mentors? It's a simple idea that appears to be yielding significant results. Research conducted by Harvard University Graduate School of Education and Columbia University Teachers College, as cited by Eye to Eye, shows that 82 percent of children participating in the program view their mentor as the kind of student they want to be; 73 percent feel their mentor helped them learn how to ask for the things they need to succeed in school; and 87 percent reported that being a part of Eye to Eye got them thinking about what they're good at. Mentors reportedly benefit from the experience as well: 89 percent felt that being part of Eye to Eye made them better advocates for addressing their own learning differences, and 81 percent agree or strongly agree that Eye to Eye helped them to think about their own learning styles (Katz, 2009c, 2013d). Eye to Eye has chapters on a number of college campuses throughout the United States. Chapters have also been started on some high school campuses as well. To learn more about Eye to Eye, readers are encouraged to visit their website at www.eyetoeyenational.org.

Those familiar with Eye to Eye may also be familiar with the work of its cofounder, Jonathan Mooney, coauthor of the book *Learning Outside the Lines* (Mooney and Cole, 2000). In the book he discusses his personal journey from struggling student to successful adult. Jonathan has also written a second book, *The Short Bus: A Journey Beyond Normal* (2008).

Raising the Bar and Leveling the Playing Field: Student Examples

An increasing number of students affected by learning, behavioral, or other differences no longer associate their differences with threat and danger. Having learned to see their challenges in a new light, many are more motivated to raise the bar and level the playing field.

At an innovative high school in Southern California, a ninth-grade student with significant writing difficulties approached the school resource specialist for ideas on how to navigate these challenges. The student was introduced to a voice-activated software program that translates speech to text. With coaching from a fellow student skilled in this technology, the previously struggling writer is now able to communicate his thoughts clearly and coherently. One of his teachers actually told him that he was a "gifted writer," a compliment he said would have been unthinkable before.

An eighth-grade middle school student prone to severe anxiety attacks, including test anxiety, approached the school's psychologist for resources to assist her in preventing these attacks. She was introduced to a local therapist in her community who specializes in treating anxiety disorders in children through cognitive-behavioral and mindfulness-based approaches. The student has responded very well to treatment and no longer suffers from anxiety attacks. Her test anxiety has significantly decreased as well, and her grades have improved. The psychologist also introduced the student and her parents to the website http://www.worrywisekids.org. Information and resources there have helped the entire family better understand the nature of anxiety symptoms, including when these symptoms are considered clinically significant, evidence-based approaches for reducing and preventing them, and helpful resources for schools.

With the help of his parents, school counselors, and a volunteer from the local Learning Disability Association chapter (http://www.ldanatl.org), a tenth-grade student diagnosed in earlier grades with dyslexia spent a month researching programs designed to remediate reading disabilities. The student selected a reading specialist trained in a research-validated intervention shown to be effective in helping remediate dyslexia. He enrolled in a summer program under the direction of the reading specialist and by the end of August had gained three years in his reading comprehension and reading fluency skills.

The three students described here live in different communities, attend different schools, and struggle with different challenges. Yet, they share some things in common. They each now realize that they are far more capable than they once thought. They all now expect more of themselves than in times past and as a result have chosen to elevate their future goals. All are now eager to learn about tools, technologies, strategies, and accommodations that can help them reach their goals. All no longer see their differences as shameful or embarrassing. To the contrary, their struggle to succeed in the face of their challenges is seen as a testament to their resilience. Once they learned to see their challenges in a new light, it had a dramatic effect on their desire to raise their personal and educational expectations and level their playing fields.

3. A Change of Scenery: The Benefits of a Fresh Start

Students who struggle in one school may be capable of succeeding in another, depending on the social climate. Recall Pam's experience (see Chapter 4) in seventh grade compared to her experience at her new school a year later. In seventh grade, she was demoralized, the result of ongoing incidents of bullying. In eighth grade, she was a straight A student who felt safe, secure, and confident about her future. Pam's success at school was not the result of trying harder, but a change of scenery.

The Impact of Social Climate on School Performance
Social climate can have a significant impact on school performance. British psychiatrist Michael Rutter showed this in a study he conducted that compared two schools made up of students drawn from the same economically disadvantaged neighborhood. He observed that one school reported more truancy problems, more behavioral and academic difficulties, and a delinquency rate three times higher than the other. Student outcomes varied less as a result of differences in students and more as a result of differences in schools. The more protective school employed better classroom management strategies, provided more structure in the classrooms,

and also seemed to foster important social and cognitive skills (Rutter, 1979a).

Rutter's findings illustrate the potential benefits derived from a change of scenery. Other studies suggest the same. Psychologist Russell Barkley (2002) cites three different federal studies showing improved outcomes for families who relocate to new neighborhoods where neighbors watch over children and where new peer influences replace previously disruptive ones.

Changing the Social Climate of a Classroom

Practices that successfully change the social climate of a classroom, particularly the social dynamics, can potentially represent a fresh start for struggling students. This was illustrated in a landmark study that followed the developmental trajectories of highly aggressive first-graders in several Baltimore public schools. Results revealed that aggressive first-grade boys in classrooms with few other aggressive boys were about 2.7 times more likely to have serious problems with aggression in middle school years later when compared to a control group of middle school peers. This was in stark contrast to aggressive first-grade boys in classrooms with similarly aggressive students, who were 59 times more likely to have serious aggression problems six years later when compared to the control group (Kellam, 1999). Researcher and prevention specialist Hill Walker refers to this finding as the "oh no level of significance."

In the study, contextual influences played a significant role in how aggressive first-graders fared down the road. In a follow-up study, researchers demonstrated that by neutralizing these contextual influences, they could reduce negative outcomes among aggressive first-graders years later. Within randomly selected first-grade classrooms, they had teachers implement the Good Behavior Game, which provides children with immediate payoffs in a social context for good behavior. Fellow classmates actually root for one another to control themselves. Since the game lasts for only a few minutes, even children with poor self-control skills can win (Katz, 2004a). Aggressive first-graders who played the game were rated by middle school teachers five years later as less aggressive than aggressive first-graders who didn't play the game (Kellam, 1999). Even more surprising perhaps, by ages 19 to 21, they were also significantly less likely to meet criteria for antisocial personality disorder and less likely to be involved in illegal drug use (Kellam and Chinnia, 2003).

Contextually speaking, there are different ways to enjoy a change of scenery and the benefits of a fresh start. It's not always a matter of moving to a new place, as was the case with Pam. Researchers who introduced the Good Behavior Game into randomly selected first-grade classrooms also provided a change of scenery. They changed the social context for at least some aggressive first-graders and in the process managed to improve the odds of a better adjustment years later.

Johns Hopkins University researcher and developmental epidemiologist Shep Kellam served as principal investigator for these landmark studies. In addition to the Good Behavior Game, Kellam cites other preventive measures that further reduce negative outcomes down the road. These include practices designed to improve reading ability, as well as those that involve parents more directly in classroom activities targeting reading and behavioral skills (Kellam and Chinnia, 2003). Kellam has been involved in designing and evaluating prevention models that include these components, with promising results.

Despite the number of studies showing the effectiveness of the Good Behavior Game, it's not as widely used as one might expect. One possible reason is that the administration instructions accompanying the free downloadable public domain version are not as simple to follow as some had hoped. Dennis Embry came up with a remedy. Working in conjunction with researchers involved in the above-mentioned studies, he developed a more user-friendly version known as the PAX Good Behavior Game (described next). What's more, he incorporated a number of other practices as well, expanding its potential benefits to children at risk for serious later life health, mental health, and life adjustment problems.

PAX Good Behavior Game: Given the results of the Dunedin Study, it's perhaps no surprise that the PAX Good Behavior Game (PAX GBG) is gaining more attention now than ever before, since studies show it to be a very effective tool for helping young children learn to control their behavior. The game is simple to play. Children develop a vision of a wonderful classroom. What would they wish to see, hear, feel, and do more of and less of? The things they want more of are called PAX, which stands for peace, productivity, health, and happiness. The things they want less of are called Spleems, which are unwanted behaviors. Children are then divided into small teams, usually two to five teams per class. Teams try to commit as few behavioral errors (Spleems) as possible within a designated period of time, initially measured in minutes. To win the game, teams must commit three or fewer errors. Winning teams earn rewards, usually in the form of brief, fun activities. To make the game fair, children with weaker self-control skills are equally distributed among groups. As children become more familiar with the game, it's played for longer periods of time. Groups change throughout the school year so that each child has a chance to repeatedly win the game with all of the other children. Children eventually learn to predict what PAX and Spleems are for each activity in real time, greatly enhancing self-regulation. The use of the special words allows the spread of the strategy to any instructional or classroom activity as well as assemblies, buses, cafeteria, after-school programs, and many other situations where children must use self-regulation. Within weeks teachers generally notice a significant decrease in impulsive and disruptive behaviors. They observe children actually rooting for each other to control themselves.

Behavioral Vaccines: Just as a vaccine inoculates people from contracting disease, Embry believes that "behavioral vaccines" can inoculate children from serious behavioral problems down the road. "Our society is crying out for behavioral vaccines," he says. "We're crying out for simple, inexpensive behavioral practices that can be incorporated into children's lives in order to prevent major life problems down the road" (Katz, 2014c). Longitudinal studies were showing that the original Good Behavior Game functioned much like a behavioral vaccine. To strengthen its inoculation powers and prevent other serious problems down the road, Embry's next step was to bundle it with other potential behavioral vaccines. It's hard to accurately convey in a few short sentences how many simple, yet powerful practices are incorporated into this game. There are practices to help children feel they belong, connect with other children, improve emotional self-regulation skills, and learn to generalize new behavioral skills to other settings and times of the day. There are also strategies for helping parents reinforce new behavioral skills at home and procedures for helping teachers measure behavioral gains on an ongoing basis. Some schools now even incorporate components of the game into 504 Accommodation Plans and individual education plans.

To children, PAX GBG is simple and fun to play. To those with an eye toward prevention, it's a direct link between research and practice, with potential population level benefits. It's these potential population level benefits that Embry has always been the most interested in. His vision is to see PAX GBG incorporated into every elementary school classroom in the country. He and colleagues have actually been calculating the possible long-term benefits, not only in terms of children's long-term health and well-being but also in terms of cost savings.

Reviewed next are other examples of practices that have been shown to effectively change the social climate of a classroom. Examples of school-wide social climate changing practices follow.

The Concentration Game: In a game developed by Annimieke Golly, from the University of Oregon's Institute on Violence and Destructive Behavior (http://www.uoregon.edu/~ivdb/), young children practice working quietly at their desks for a specified period of time while their teacher tries to draw them off task with very distracting behaviors (the funnier, the better). The teacher might be so bold as to knock a book off a child's desk, for example, fake having a temper tantrum, or start cracking jokes or making wisecracks. If children can stay focused on their work and not get distracted for the specified period of time, the class earns a point. The activity is repeated on an ongoing basis throughout the year for systematically longer periods of time. Children try to beat their previous score (measured by minutes in which no one became distracted). As children get increasingly better at ignoring distractions, they earn more points, which get cashed in for surprise class rewards. But more important, children also learn an automatic behavioral response when a classmate is acting out or causing a distraction. Golly finds that acting out incidents often decrease significantly as a result (Golly, 2002). According to IVDB co-director Hill Walker (2001), weaving interventions like these into classroom is particularly important for what he refers to as "early starters," kindergartners and first-graders whose aggressive and out-of control-behaviors in the classroom, on the playground, and at home are precursors to more serious behavior problems down the road.

Variations in Temperament and Goodness of Fit: Barbara Keogh (2003) and colleagues evaluated kindergartners randomly assigned to four different elementary school classrooms. Results showed that children's temperaments were similar from classroom to classroom. This came as no surprise, since they were randomly assigned. What was a surprise was that in one of the four classrooms, a significantly higher number of children were reported to be at risk. To Keogh, a pioneer in the study of temperament and its impact on school performance, the reason was obvious. In that one classroom, there was a poor fit between a child's temperament and the context of the classroom.

We are all born with a unique temperament. Differences in temperament translate into corresponding differences in how we express our emotions, relate to people, and see the world. In 1956, Stella Chess and Alexander Thomas initiated the New York Longitudinal Study, one of the best-known prospective longitudinal studies of human temperament to date (Chess and Thomas, 1987, 1999). The study identified nine different categories of temperament, each of which can be rated from high to low: activity level, rhythmicity (regularity), approach or withdrawal, adaptability, sensory threshold, intensity of reactions, quality of mood, distractibility, and persistence and attention span. Beginning in early childhood these categories tend to cluster into three broader patterns of temperament, referred to as "easy," "difficult," and "slow to warm up." Children with easy temperaments—about 40 percent of Chess and Thomas's sample—adapt well to new situations, warm up quickly, make friends easily, and get along well with others. In contrast, children with difficult temperaments—about 10 percent of their sample—have more difficulty adapting to new situations, aren't always easy to get along with, and are much more prone to temper outbursts. Children with slow-to-warm-up temperaments, about 15 percent of the sample, also tend to have a hard time adapting to new situations, are more likely to withdraw or shy away from situations they find difficult or uncomfortable, and as the phrase implies, often need more time to warm up to others.

Thanks to the work of Keogh, Chess and Thomas, and other pioneers in the field, teachers, parents, and health care professionals have a better understanding of why normal variations in children's temperaments—including normal variations in skills related to self-control—can render a child at risk in one classroom and not in another. It's all about the fit.

Changing Social Climate School-Wide

Positive Behavior Intervention and Supports (PBIS): A previous surgeon general's report estimated that roughly 20 percent of youth under age 18 are in need of mental health services (U.S. Department of Health and Human Services, 1999). For a number of these children and youth, their emotional and behavioral challenges are more than likely affecting their ability to succeed at school. How can schools ever hope to address the mental health needs of so many students? In an effort to address the problem, prevention experts developed a comprehensive prevention model known as school-wide positive behavior intervention and supports (SWPBIS, or PBIS). The model weaves together three levels of preventive intervention (see figure 6.1), starting with a series of strategies designed to create a safe school climate, improve all students' social and behavioral abilities, and prevent problems before they emerge (primary or universal intervention). School staff are called on to reinforce each student's successes and accomplishments and to teach all students the same three to five behavioral expectations (e.g., "be safe," "be respectful," "be responsible"). Woven seamlessly into the three-tier prevention model is a second tier of preventive

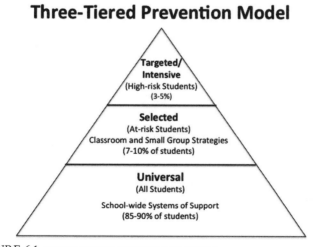

Three-Tiered Prevention Model

Targeted/Intensive
(High-risk Students)
(3-5%)

Selected
(At-risk Students)
Classroom and Small Group Strategies
(7-10% of students)

Universal
(All Students)
School-wide Systems of Support
(85-90% of students)

FIGURE 6.1 THREE-TIERED PREVENTION MODEL

practices intended to help students identified as at-risk. These are children and youth whose problems will likely escalate without special help of some kind (secondary or selected prevention). The model's third tier incorporates intensive interventions (tertiary or targeted prevention) to address the emotional and behavioral needs of a school's most vulnerable students (Katz, 2002a, 2004b).

Developed by Jeffrey Sprague and Annemieke Golly at the University of Oregon's Institute on Violence and Destructive Behavior (IVDB), BEST Behavior represents one of the most widely replicated SWPBIS models in the United States. Since rolling out their original version of the model, Sprague and colleagues have expanded it to include additional practices consistent with findings from the youth violence prevention literature, risk and resilience literature, and family-friendly system of care values and principles (Katz, 2004b; Sprague and Golly, 2004).

RtI for Behavior and Academics: Sprague and colleagues have been refining ways to weave BEST Behavior's three-tiered prevention practices within a response to intervention (RtI) paradigm (see figure 6.2).

Schools successfully applying RtI are better able to identify the first signs of learning, behavioral, emotional, and/or social difficulties in children. This then allows them to provide empirically validated interventions that can potentially steer developmental trajectories in a more positive direction, thus preventing more serious problems from emerging later (Katz, 2009b). Unique to the paradigm is its ongoing (formative) assessment process known as progress monitoring, which provides a continuous picture of a child's response to intervention. If interventions are successful, they can either be continued or faded out. If unsuccessful, more intensive interventions can be implemented, and again monitored closely to determine their effectiveness. This represents a significant departure from how children have traditionally qualified for additional help for learning, behavior, social, or emotional difficulties. Referred to as the "wait to fail" model (Sprague et al., 2008), students traditionally have had to struggle and fail, sometimes for years, before their difficulties were determined to be serious enough to meet special education eligibility criteria. Those interested in learning more about this innovative prevention paradigm are encouraged to visit the IVDB website at http://uoregon.edu/~ivdb/.

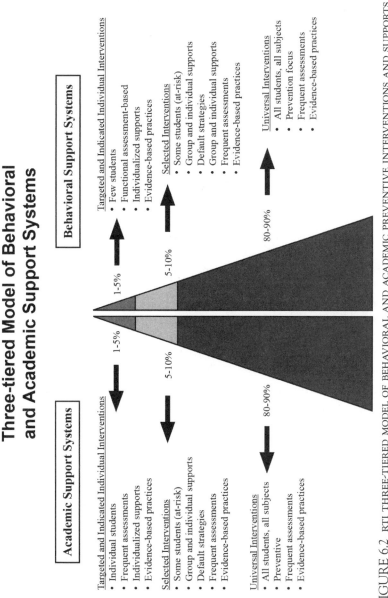

Three-tiered Model of Behavioral and Academic Support Systems

Academic Support Systems

Behavioral Support Systems

Academic Support Systems

Targeted and Indicated Individual Interventions
• Individual students
• Frequent assessments
• Individualized supports
• Evidence-based practices

1-5%

Selected Interventions
• Some students (at-risk)
• Group and individual supports
• Default strategies
• Frequent assessments
• Evidence-based practices

5-10%

Universal Interventions
• All students, all subjects
• Preventive
• Frequent assessments
• Evidence-based practices

80-90%

Behavioral Support Systems

Targeted and Indicated Individual Interventions
• Few students
• Functional assessment-based
• Individualized supports
• Evidence-based practices

1-5%

Selected Interventions
• Some students (at-risk)
• Group and individual supports
• Default strategies
• Group and individual supports
• Frequent assessments
• Evidence-based practices

5-10%

Universal Interventions
• All students, all subjects
• Prevention focus
• Frequent assessments
• Evidence-based practices

80-90%

FIGURE 6.2 RTI THREE-TIERED MODEL OF BEHAVIORAL AND ACADEMIC PREVENTIVE INTERVENTIONS AND SUPPORTS

The Wraparound Planning Process and SWPBIS: For children, youth, and families affected by multiple risks and adversities, an innovative strengths-based model of care offers new hope for better days. The model weaves together system of care principles, including the wraparound planning process, with school-wide positive behavior supports (SWPBS). System of care principles are familiar to mental health and child welfare professionals, but less so to educators and other professionals who work in schools. SWPBS, on the other hand, are familiar to those working in school settings but less so to those working in the fields of mental health and child welfare. These paradigms share common properties, which may be why they go together so nicely. For example, both are strengths-based and focus attention on what's going well. Both study conditions contributing to things going well and explore ways to change or redesign living and learning environments to reflect these conditions so that things can go well more often and in other settings. Both are family- and teacher-friendly. Each views parents and teachers as full partners in designing interventions. Both rely on a team effort, where members tailor services to meet individualized needs. When interventions fail, they try to learn from the experience to modify interventions so they'll work better. Both represent alternatives to deficit-based models that often feel stigmatizing to the very people the services are designed to help (Katz, 2007).

Lucile Eber is an Illinois educator known nationally for her groundbreaking work in linking the SWPBS world with system of care principles and the wraparound planning process. Those interested in learning more about her work in Illinois and elsewhere are encouraged to visit the Illinois PBIS website at http://www.illinoispbis.org (also see Eber, 2003, 2006).

Restorative Practices: An increasing number of schools across the United States are embracing restorative practices as a guiding philosophy for creating a safe, respectful, and inclusive school culture. Many were initially attracted to these practices by studies showing their effectiveness in preventing and reducing suspensions and expulsions, which are known to occur more frequently among students of color and those with learning and behavior challenges. Many have since learned that other benefits accrue once these practices are effectively implemented. These include greater levels of trust among and between students, teachers, and others in the school community (Katz, 2015a).

Effectively implementing restorative practices requires a school-wide commitment to a very different way of relating to one another. Those engaged in wrongdoing, for example, will be asked to respond to several restorative questions: What happened? What were you thinking about at the time? What have you thought about since? Who has been affected by what you have done? In what way? What do you think you need to do to make things right? Those who are harmed respond to restorative questions as well: What did you think when you realized what happened? What impact has this had on you and others? What has been the hardest thing for you? What do you think needs to happen to make things right? Questions are typically posed during teacher-led group meetings referred to as circles, which include other classmates and/or others in the school community. Circles occur continuously, not just in response to wrongdoing but also as a way for students and staff to get to know each other better and function more effectively as a group. Circles build a sense of community. All voices are heard, all share in making important decisions, and all share in experiences providing opportunities for developing greater trust, respect, empathy, and mutual understanding (Mirsky, 2014). To learn more about these and other informal and formal restorative practices, visit the International Institute for Restorative Practices (IIRP) website at http://www.iirp.edu.

PeaceBuilders: "Praise people," "give up put-downs," "seek out wise people," "notice and speak up about hurts," "right wrongs," and "help others." These are six principles for everyone at school to model, practice, celebrate, and reinforce. When enough people do—students, teachers, administrators, bus drivers, secretaries—the school climate improves; fewer injuries, acts of violence, and discipline problems are reported; absenteeism decreases; and students enjoy new opportunities to contribute and feel they belong. Closer examination of these six principles reveals that they speak to the quality of our relationships. It's no surprise that a number of school administrators committed to sustaining this model report that relationships at school seem to grow stronger: relationships between students, relationships between adults, and relationships between students and adults (Katz, 2008a). PeaceBuilders also provides a language for recognizing strengths ("praise people") and for speaking out in response to those who stigmatize and devalue others ("give up put-downs," "notice and speak out about hurts," "right wrongs," "help others"). Students struggling with different challenges often feel accepted and valued at schools that are successfully implementing the model. PeaceBuilders is designed to reach beyond school and into homes, businesses, recreational centers, and other public places in the community. To learn more visit their website at http://www.peacebuilders.com.

Heroic Imagination Project (HIP): PeaceBuilder practices increase compassion, help validate and legitimize differences, and provide students with the feeling that they belong and have something important to contribute. But for some students, school can remain a threatening and dangerous place. One reason for this is that dangerous incidents frequently occur "in the shadows," outside of adult sight. Students being targeted and who are powerless to defend themselves will need others to speak up on their behalf. Unfortunately, others may choose not to, sometimes out of fear, sometimes because they're unsure of what they can do to help, or sometimes simply because they prefer not to get involved.

The Heroic Imagination Project (HIP) provides a remedy. The program teaches students to be "social heroes." A social hero is a person who steps forward to help a fellow student in danger, for no personal gain, and at some personal risk. According to HIP's developers, we are all social heroes in waiting. Each of us will encounter a situation at some point where we will have to make a difficult choice: step forward on behalf of someone we know to be in personal danger, or choose what might feel like the safer option: doing nothing. When that time comes, those of us equipped with the right tools will step forward. HIP provides us with the tools (Katz, 2011b).

The project is the brainchild of Phil Zimbardo, whose Stanford Prison Experiment in the 1970s dramatically illustrated how a toxic social environment can lead otherwise normal people to do very abnormal things. To learn more about HIP, visit their website at www.heroicimagination.org.

The Olweus Bullying Prevention Program (OBPP): While a few effective school bullying prevention practices have already been cited

154

(PeaceBuilders, Heroic Imagination Project, PBIS, restorative practices), the Olweus Bullying Prevention Program (OBPP) remains the most empirically validated model. At OBPP schools, students and adults are guided by four universal behavioral principles: (1) we will not bully others; (2) we will try to help students who are bullied; (3) we will include students who are left out; and (4) if we know that somebody is being bullied, we will tell an adult at school and an adult at home (Katz, 2009d). The model is made up of four interlocking components—school-wide, classroom, individual, and community. OBPP practices target all four levels. To learn more about the program, visit. http://www.clemson.edu/olweus/index.html.

Project-Based Learning: At a small cluster of project-based schools in Southern California, teachers create lesson plans that translate academic tasks into real-life project-based experiences. The model appears to be matching well with students who evidence a range of uneven learning and behavioral profiles. Based on anecdotal accounts, the prevailing culture of these schools may override the potential harmful effects associated with the five erroneous perceptions. Should future research prove this to be the case, there may be several reasons. The model deemphasizes repetitive tasks performed for lengthy periods of time at a desk, and places far more emphasis on hands-on problem-solving tasks. Students work in collaboration with other students, while being coached by their teachers and academic aides. The testing process is different as well. Students are required to present their completed projects to their teachers, parents, and fellow students. Over time, children often become very skilled at presenting in front of groups.

For at least some struggling students, these project-based schools may be providing quality of life benefits that were not realized in previous schools. This was the conclusion reached by many of those in attendance at a meeting that was held at one of these schools. The meeting included 20 sets of parents and their children, all of whom had various learning or behavioral challenges. They were joined by a group of psychiatrists who were there to learn more about their current school experiences, particularly the potential mental health benefits that may have accrued. While the vast majority of students and parents felt their lives had improved significantly since arriving at their current school, it wasn't only the innovative model they

155

spoke about. They also mentioned the close relationships they had formed with teachers and other school personnel. Many had good relationships with teachers and others in previous schools, but in their new learning environment relationships generally seemed closer and stronger. This was by design. Prior to a student's first day at the school, each family received a call and then a visit from a teacher or other staff member who would serve as the student's advisor and mentor until the student graduated. At the conclusion of the meeting, psychiatrists in attendance were more aware of the potential impact of positive school climate on child and family well-being. Given the right social context, simply going to school had the potential to improve lives and buffer children and families from risks and adverse experiences associated with a range of negative life outcomes.

LIFE EXPERIENCES—IN CONTEXT

Students whose differences trigger feelings of threat and danger, not surprisingly, can also find school to be a threatening and dangerous place. Fortunately, a number of these students are learning to see their differences in a new light and, in the process, learning to see school in a new light as well.

4. "There's Never Anything So Wrong with Us That What's Right with Us Can't Fix": Personal Pathways to a Sense of Mastery

"Who Had a Great Struggle Today?"

Stanford psychologist Carol Dweck recommends that teachers ask students at the end of the school day, "Who had a great struggle today?" Rewarding and celebrating struggle helps foster a malleable or growth mind-set. Drawing on Dweck's research, some teachers keep a jar on their desk with a label that reads, "Who had a great struggle today?" Next to the jar is another jar with marbles. At the end of the day, students (or teachers) who can identify a great struggle are asked to place a marble in the jar. If you had two great struggles, then two marbles go in the jar, three great struggles, three marbles, and so on. If the class can fill the jar with all the marbles by the end of the week, the whole class gets a surprise reward, compliments of their teacher. The message is clear: in this class, we value struggle.

One teacher now keeps a second jar on her desk with the label "Who learned from a mistake today?" Each day, students are asked to remember a mistake they made, one they learned from. For each mistake a marble is placed in the jar. Fill the jar up with marbles by the end of the week and the whole class gets another surprise. The message here is also clear: in this class we don't fear making mistakes. In this class, that's how we learn, from our mistakes.

"We Recognize the Hurts That We Cause Others," and "We Right Our Wrongs"

The six PeaceBuilders principles were discussed earlier. The fourth and fifth principles, "we recognize hurts that we cause others" and "we right our wrongs," can work in combination to help foster a sense of mastery. Recognizing hurts requires taking responsibility for our actions. Recognizing the impact that our actions have on others provides the opportunity to right our wrongs and learn from our mistakes. By modeling and practicing these principles students are also modeling and practicing how to translate mistakes into learning experiences.

In some PeaceBuilder schools, teachers send parents short congratulatory text messages, e-mails, or postcards once or twice a week recognizing a student's achievement, such as working hard on an activity and not giving up, treating a mistake as a learning experience, recognizing a hurt, righting a wrong, reaching out to help another student, or achieving a learning or behavioral accomplishment. Celebrations are wide-ranging. This small act of recognition has meant a great deal to some families who say that in the past, whenever they received something from the school in writing or via phone call, it was always bad news.

Some schools who currently model PeaceBuilders principles have taken this idea a step further. Parents are asked to send text messages, e-mails, postcards, or letters back to the school, thanking the teachers and others for the help they give to their child. By engaging in these reciprocal acts of recognition, adults in the child's life are modeling important relationship skills. Children witness firsthand how the adults in their lives find the good in others and pay attention to it. These acts of recognition also serve as a reminder to parents, teachers, and other school staff of the power of modeling. Modeling can serve to strengthen relationships or drive people apart. Adults whose interactions with one another have been tense, conflictual, and negative may, without realizing it, be modeling the same behaviors they're trying to teach a child to avoid.

5. Seeing Human Intelligence in a New Light: It's Not How Smart We Are, But How We Are Smart

Research shows that we have it within our power to change our mind-set. People with fixed mind-sets can learn to see their abilities as malleable, regardless of age or background. How can we help those of us with fixed mind-sets develop more flexible or "growth" mind-sets? For students in middle school at least, Brainology, a web-based interactive program, may be the answer.

Brainology: Drawing on advances in our understanding of brain plasticity, Brainology's fun, animated, interactive lessons teach students how the human brain physically changes itself when exercised. Learners develop a new understanding of brain functions, including how thinking occurs, how learning and memory work, how we can develop and change our own brains, and most important, how we can use knowledge of the brain and its functions to improve our study habits and grow our skills in and out of school (Katz, 2015b). Pilot data compiled on over 300 New York City middle school students is impressive. Children taught to view intelligence as malleable demonstrated improved motivation and higher math scores in relation to a control group comprised of similar age peers. To assess change, researchers used a set of scales designed to measure key motivational variables, including beliefs about intelligence, beliefs about effort, and helpless versus mastery-oriented responses to failure. Researchers also relied on teacher observations (Blackwell, Trzesniewski, and Dweck, 2007). Lessons in the pilot study were instructor-supported rather than purely software-based (Katz, 2008b).

Brainology's lessons extend well beyond middle school. Studies show that a fixed mind-set favors personal and professional goals that allow us to look smart and avoid challenges that might result in mistakes. In contrast, a growth mind-set favors goals that challenge us, stretch us beyond our abilities, and provide us the opportunity to learn from mistakes. A growth mind-set pushes us to raise the bar. A fixed mind-set makes us to think twice about doing so. According to Dweck (2006), when people move from a fixed to a growth mind-set, they also move from a judge-and-be-judged to a learn-and-help learn approach. Dweck has observed this among couples, coaches, athletes, managers, workers, parents, teachers, and students. For teachers and students, it can mean a classroom climate where raising the bar while leveling the playing field is the cultural norm rather than the exception.

Researchers in Germany observed a relationship between teacher mind-set and student achievement. Teachers with fixed mind-sets believed incoming students who achieve differently were permanently different. Students in their classrooms who began the school year in the high-ability group ended the school year in the high-ability group, and students who began in the low-ability group ended in the low-ability group. Teachers with more malleable mind-sets believed all students were capable of developing their skills. Students in their classrooms, in both high- and low-ability groups, improved significantly (Dweck, 2006). Those interested in learning more about Dweck's research are encouraged to read her 2006 book, *Mindset: The New Psychology of Success*. Those interested in learning more about Brainology, including how the program is also being successfully adapted to both lower and higher grades, can do so by visiting its website at http://www.mindsetworks.com.

Multiple Intelligences (MI): Some schools are weaving MI theory's eight intelligences throughout the school day, providing students with opportunities to engage in activities that draw attention to strengths that may lie beyond academic areas. Students at these schools often feel "gifted." MI proponents say they're probably right. They're gifted in one or more of the eight areas highlighted in Gardner's model, and school provides the opportunity to showcase their gifts every day (ABC News, 1993).

WhyTry activities (discussed earlier) draw on Gardner's principles in teaching the 10 WhyTry lessons. Principles are represented through visual analogies, each accompanied by activities that call into play different intelligences (auditory, visual spatial, tactile-kinesthetic), thereby accommodating those with diverse learning styles.

6. When Difference No Longer Signals Danger: Seeing Strengths and Challenges in a New Light

Challenges no longer signal threat and danger if they can be seen in a new light. Seeing challenges in a new light is far easier when teachers, fellow students, and others at school see them in a new light as well. The following practices and resources can help.

Assessments that Highlight Strengths and Explain Challenges in the Context of Strengths

Assessments in the past focused primarily on deficits and weaknesses. More recently, a number of mental health professionals, educators, and other service providers have shifted their focus and conduct assessments that capture personal strengths and talents. They still assess for specific challenges, but they communicate these findings in ways that can allow students, their families, and their teachers to understand challenges in the context of strengths. To illustrate, the following introduction appears in the assessments conducted at our center in San Diego, both with children and with adults. It's intended to provide readers with a better understanding of the context within which we wish our findings to be interpreted.

Interpreting Assessment Results: Learning trajectories are unique. They vary from person to person. Some of us demonstrate a consistent learning curve with steady gains over time. Some of us demonstrate a relatively flat learning curve and then suddenly spike when a skill is mastered. And some of us demonstrate a jagged learning curve with information mastered, then forgotten, then mastered again. When taking into account how unique our learning trajectories are, it can be very risky trying to predict a person's future learning accomplishments. It gets riskier still when we factor in one other often overlooked variable. We seem to have this uncanny ability to learn and grow in new and surprising ways in areas that we find to be personally meaningful and stimulating. These may be areas that, up to this point in our lives, we have had little exposure to, but may have exposure to some time down the road. In addition, how people view their abilities often determines the expectations they set for themselves. If people see their abilities as fixed, for example, "I am smart" or "I am not smart" they may miss valuable opportunities to achieve the goals they have set for themselves. In reality, many of our cognitive skills are malleable. People have the potential to improve their abilities in a variety of cognitive domains through new advances in technology, persistence and effort. All things considered, our wish is that assessment results such as these never be used to close our minds as to our potential future accomplishments, but rather to open them.

When explaining assessment results to children, my colleague Gretchen Gillingham (personal communication, May 1, 2015) ends the meeting by providing the child with a gift bag. Each gift is removed and explained. The child's parents are told about the gift bag beforehand and are asked to listen carefully to the explanations so they can continually reinforce the message at home. The first gift is a small, squishy, rubber-like brain, which symbolizes the many important strengths the child possesses. For some, strengths may lie in visual spatial areas, for others, tactile-kinesthetic areas, for others, it's a love of mechanical things. The intended message behind the squishy rubber-like brain is "It's not how smart we are, but how we are smart." The next gift is a small plastic flashlight. "There are brighter days ahead. The world needs your gifts, even though it may not feel that way now. Keep your spirits up." The next gift is a compass. "This is to remind you of all the tools, technologies, and supports that are available to help you level your playing field. Remember, keep the bar high, and level that playing field." The next gift is a page filled with photographs of well-known people who share similar learning and/or behavioral profiles. Photographs are accompanied by brief descriptions of the struggles each endured many years earlier. The last gift is a business card with a wrapped piece of chewing gum taped on the back. "This to let you know we're going to stick by you. We're here to help, not only now but in years to come."

Gillingham reminds children and families that it's not unusual for us to get a call from college students, graduate students, and people who have long since achieved their career goals, who participated in an assessment such as this many years earlier. At the time of their assessment, many struggled mightily in school. Today, many are successful in life.

Often included in the gift bag as well is a small rubber ball. "The ball is to symbolize your ability to bounce back." The ball is an introduction to a discussion about resilience, or the ability to remain strong or even grow stronger in the face of challenging situations. A number of children have never heard the term "resilience." Knowing the meaning of the term is key to the reframing process, because to see life experiences in a new light, we need a vocabulary that allows us to tag them in a new light.

Trauma-Informed Assessment Reports

Recall the following question from our earlier discussion of Javier's childhood experiences. For an otherwise normal nine-year-old, what does resilience look like—behaviorally, emotionally, and physiologically—after living in six different foster homes following removal from a neglectful mother with severe mental illness and addiction to drugs, compounded by ongoing difficulties at school? As was noted, it's a very important question, because if we can't capture expressions of resilience under these conditions, rest assured, neither will the child.

One way to capture these expressions of resilience is through assessment reports. The following section now appears at the beginning of reports we write for school-age children who we believe to be affected by very stressful conditions:

Extreme Stress and Its Impact on the Learning Process

Researchers now know that extreme stress can potentially affect a number of functions we rely on to succeed in school. It can affect our ability to concentrate, to retrieve information, to remain focused on our goals, and to control and regulate our emotions. This is the short list. Other functions can be affected as well. Researchers also now know that we all vary in how extreme stress can affect these functions. Different students will be impacted in different ways. Furthermore, our inherent resilient nature may not protect us from these effects. Resilient school-age children exposed to prolonged and extreme stress may be susceptible to learning problems associated with these conditions. Complicating matters even further, these learning problems may persist, even when extremely stressful conditions no longer prevail. It's been said that we can at times bring our past to our present, and such may be the case for students who at one time in their lives suffered the effects of exposure to extreme stress.

We know that students suffering the effects of extreme stress exposure can suffer more if their struggles are attributed solely to controllable conditions from within (willful disobedience, laziness, a lack of resilience), rather than uncontrollable conditions from without. We are working hard to write our reports in an effort to prevent this from happening.

The study of extreme stress exposure and its impact on the learning process is an evolving field, and we continue to learn from the field's experts. We will be updating our reports to include new advances in the field as we become aware of them.

(For educators, psychologists, and other health care professionals interested in further discussing how we can hone our skills at writing both strengths-based and trauma-informed reports, please visit the web page, where a separate section has been created specifically with this goal in mind.)

Resources That Celebrate Differences and Help Us See Challenges in a New Light

A number of available resources celebrate human differences and help those struggling with differences see them in a new light. Some were highlighted in previous sections, including Eye-to-Eye and WhyTry. Five additional resources are highlighted here: the Movement of Imperfection, Change the View, Active Minds, LETS Erase the Stigma, and Collaborative and Proactive Solutions.

"Shut Up About Your Perfect Kid" and the Movement of Imperfection: Gina (Terrasi) Gallagher and Patty (Terrasi) Konjoian (also known as the "Shut Up" sisters) extend an open invitation to join their Movement of Imperfection. It's a movement dedicated to helping "imperfect parents" of "imperfect children" learn to see their children's differences in a new light. Actually, it's a movement that helps all of us see differences in a new light. Gina and Patty's journey began soon after their daughters' difficulties were given diagnoses (Asperger's syndrome and bipolar disorder, respectively). The names were frightening and confusing. Professionals seemed to be speaking in a foreign language, using terms Gina and Patty didn't understand. School meetings felt like it was "us versus them," rather than a team working together. To learn more, they read books, which left them feeling only more depressed. The world seemed more interested in what their children couldn't do rather than what they could do.

The straw that broke the camel's back was having to listen to friends talk endlessly about their high-achieving "perfect" children. Gina didn't know whether to laugh or cry. Blessed with each other and "the ability to find humor in almost anything," the sisters chose laughter. They decided to create a movement, one that encouraged parents who might be feeling as they do, "to come out of their messy closets" and embrace the imperfections that lie within all of us. They wrote a book, *Shut Up About Your Perfect Kid*. Soon after, they started a business, Shut Up Industries, and then the Movement of Imperfection.

Gina and Patty are providing countless individuals—children, families, and adults—a new and different roadmap. In their funny and irreverent way, they help all of us see beyond our imperfections so that we can value our true qualities (Katz, 2010a, 2012c). Those interested in joining the Movement of Imperfection can do so by visiting the website http://www.shutupabout.com.

"Change the View": In a culture that stigmatizes those who struggle with learning, behavioral, or emotional challenges, some people still manage to rise above them. They find the courage to accept these challenges head on, and they work hard to succeed in spite of them. There are others who take it a step further. They choose to publicly share their unique journey with us so that we might learn from their experiences. Then there are others who take it even further than this. They create videos, helping the whole world understand challenges such as theirs in a hopeful new light. Sponsored by Children's Mental Health Ontario (CMHO), Change the View is the home of YouTube videos about mental health and other challenges, each trying to legitimize and destigmatize the challenges portrayed.

Videos address three specific questions: (1) "How can we help our friends instead of turning our backs on them?" (2) "How do we talk about it?" (3) "How do we show everyone that any problem can be worked out with a little kindness and understanding?" These videos often represent actual voices of those experiencing the challenge described and/or their friends and family members. Change the View also chooses yearly prize winners for the best videos, as determined by a panel of CMHO judges. Winners are chosen based on a range of criteria, including originality, creativity, clarity, and persuasiveness. Viewers soon see that all videos try to communicate a simple, yet important message: "One in five youth struggle with mental health challenges. It's time to end the stigma, and change the view" (Katz, 2012a). Those interested in viewing videos can do so by visiting the YouTube channel at http://www.youtube.com/user/changetheview2012. Those interested in learning more about the project are encouraged to visit the CMHO website at http://www.kidsmentalhealth.ca.

Active Minds: Through its rapidly growing network of campus-based, student-led chapters, Active Minds is helping remove the negative perceptions around mental health at colleges and universities throughout the United States. It does so by drawing on student voices. College students with mental health challenges reach out to help other students with similar challenges to let them know they no longer have to suffer in silence. They also provide presentations to others on campus and in the community to help alleviate the stigma associated with mental illness. In some communities, Active Minds volunteers reach out to younger students with mental health challenges, again in an effort to alleviate their shame and embarrassment and to let them know there is hope.

The Washington, D.C.–based nonprofit organization is the brainchild of Alison Malmon, who started the organization in 2001 following the tragic loss of her older brother to suicide. She created Active Minds to help prevent feelings of hopelessness among those with mental health challenges and to let them know that people experiencing such challenges can lead successful lives (Katz, 2011d). A sampling of Active Minds' national and campus-based programs can be found at http://www.Activeminds.org.

LETS: According to psychologist and researcher Stephen Hinshaw, stigma represents the single most important issue facing the entire mental health field today. Whether it's a function of their age or particular stage of development, school-age youth seem to feel its effects the most. But not all youth succumb to its effects. To the contrary, some are choosing to fight back. They are part of a program known as *LETS*, an acronym for Let's Erase the Stigma (Katz, 2013a). Hinshaw, an expert in the field of stigma prevention, serves as the co-director of research.

LETS youth are young people from all walks of life choosing to speak up about mental health challenges and doing so in a way that presents these challenges in a new and more hopeful light. Many experience mental health challenges themselves and thus speak from personal experience. They feel empowered and unafraid. In speaking openly, they also provide a sense of acceptance, belonging, and solidarity with those who experience similar challenges. To quote a LETS club member: "Everyone has a story. If you knew my story . . . you might change your mind about me." To learn more about LETS, visit http://www.lets.org. Those wishing to learn more about the impact of stigma on the lives of those with mental health challenges, including recommendations for preventing and reducing stigma, are encouraged to read Hinshaw's 2007 book on the subject, titled, *The Mark of Shame.*

Collaborative and Proactive Solutions (CPS): As an alternative to interventions that view all behavioral, social, and emotional difficulties as willful, manipulative, or the result of inconsistent parenting, psychologist Ross Greene created a treatment model based on an entirely different philosophy: "Children do well if they can. If they're not doing well, something must be getting in their way, and adults need to figure out why so we can help." Greene calls the model Collaborative and Proactive Solutions (CPS).

To help these children, Greene believes we need to start by seeing challenging behaviors through "a new set of lenses." He says, "Your explanation guides your interventions. And faulty explanations lead to faulty interventions." When challenging behaviors are viewed through the lens of lagging skills, it's easier to think of how best to incorporate experiences into the struggling child's life that can help strengthen these skills (Katz, 2011a). CPS does just that. The approach has helped countless numbers of parents, teachers, school administrators, and health care professionals see a host of challenging behaviors through a new set of lenses, a necessary first step, says Greene, in successfully implementing CPS's many other unique and innovative components.

Three Common Approaches to Handling Challenging Behaviors: According to Greene, adults have three options for resolving problems they encounter with children prone to challenging behaviors. They can solve the problem unilaterally (plan A), which involves the imposition of adult will, often with adult-imposed consequences attached ("You'll do it my way and that's it"; "I'll count to three—1, 2, 3"). For children lacking the necessary skills to behave better, Greene finds that plan A can actually precipitate rather than prevent challenging behavioral episodes. A second option involves solving problems collaboratively (plan B, discussed below), which is the replacement for plan A. The third option (plan C) requires setting aside an unsolved problem for a time in favor of higher priority problems.

Plan B involves three steps (or ingredients): (1) empathy; (2) define the problem; and (3) invitation. The empathy step involves gathering information from the child to achieve a clear understanding of his or her concerns about an unsolved problem. The premise is that it's impossible to come up with a viable solution to a problem without understanding (from the child's perspective) what's causing the problem in the first place. In the define the problem step, the adult's concern is articulated. The invitation is often a brainstorming process aimed at working toward a solution that is mutually satisfactory. It addresses the concerns of both parties and it's also realistic.

What should be clear, according to Greene, is that CPS places the emphasis on repairing relationships and improving communication. This is largely accomplished through the process of solving problems collaboratively. Greene's model, first articulated in his book *The Explosive Child*, is known to many parents and professionals as Collaborative Problem Solving. As a result of legal action, Greene now calls his model Collaborative & Proactive Solutions (CPS). To learn more about CPS, visit http://www.livesinthebalance.org.

More Labels, Not Fewer

"School artist" is a label. The same is true for "school ambassador" and "computer specialist." One or two previously embarrassing labels often no longer feel embarrassing in the context of more positive ones. Students who have the opportunity to wear many important hats at school or in the community also have the opportunity to be identified by many positive labels.

Seeing Abilities as Malleable, Not Fixed

Brainology (discussed earlier) helps middle school students develop a growth mind-set. The program's lessons teach students to view abilities as malleable rather than fixed. Visitors to the Mindset Works website (http://www.mindworks.com) can also learn how schools are drawing on Dweck's research to teach students at all grade levels to see their abilities as malleable.

Seeing Challenges in Historical Context

Carl, Javier, Linda, and many others have benefited a great deal from their ability to perceive challenges in historical context. They include parents, teachers, and others seeking to improve the lives of children who learn differently. Today, they recognize that recent advances are providing new hope for better lives down the road. Learning specialists, for example, are identifying important areas of previously unrecognized strength in children's lives and using these strengths to help them overcome or navigate these differences. In addition, we now know about techniques for teaching children to read and write, when in years past those children would have been thought incapable of learning to do so. These same advances are improving the lives of adults with similar challenges. Contrast these advances with the prevailing views of the past. When IQ tests were first introduced less than 100 years ago, those scoring in the lowest ranges were classified either as "moron," "imbecile," or "idiot," depending on how low they scored. Although some may find it hard to believe now, in years past these were accepted terms in the professional literature!

Viewed in historical perspective, there are a great many areas of challenge we can cite to show how far we've come in understanding and improving the lives of those affected by them. Few are more dramatic than challenges on the autism spectrum. Today, early childhood intervention programs for children on the spectrum are producing outcomes once thought of as unattainable. Contrast these positive outcomes with commonly held views of only a few decades ago, when autism was believed to be caused by cold and rejecting parenting practices. A term used in the professional literature at the time to capture these practices was "refrigerator mothers," a phrase that had devastating effects on many families caring for an autistic child. (Those wishing to learn more about the term and its impact on families are encouraged to view the documentary *Refrigerator Mothers*, produced by Kartemquin Films; visit http://www.kartemquin.com/store/product/KTQ0040).

Through a historical lens, we can see how far we've come in our ability to see these and other challenges in a new light. In time, this can also allow those affected by these challenges to see them in a new light as well.

7. Translating the Pain of Our Past into Meaningful Action on Behalf of Others

After overcoming the stigma associated with their differences, a growing number of students are stepping forward to help fellow students do the same.

- A high school student at a school in Northern California gave a presentation to her class on the nature of her mental health challenges, which included an explanation of how her symptoms can manifest themselves at school and what strategies, tools, and accommodations can help. Her best friend is planning to give the same presentation to her class in the near future.
- A high school student with learning and executive function challenges spends several days a week mentoring middle school students with similar challenges and coaching them on how to better advocate for their needs.
- Several students at a high school in the Midwest started a club that focuses on reducing stigma associated with learning, behavioral, mental health, and other challenges. Club members have struggled with these challenges for years and want to help fellow students see them in a new light. (For other examples, log on to the web page.)

Helping Others Overcome the Stigma Associated with the IEP Process and Special Education Services

A college student who mentors an eighth-grader with reading and writing challenges similar to his own has the younger child join him from time to time on his visits to his college's Office of Students with Disabilities. The eighth-grader sees his college mentor speaking with resource staff on ways to level his academic playing field. Prior to witnessing this, the eighth-grader had been extremely embarrassed about having an IEP at school and even more embarrassed about receiving special education services. He no longer feels this way, having seen how similar services are helping his mentor reach his future career goals.

Remaining Mindful of Stress Levels in Children Who Beat the Odds

The Kauai Longitudinal Study revealed that resilient children who continued to function well despite exposure to multiple risks still had high rates of health-related symptoms decades later (Werner and Smith, 2001). This presents an interesting dilemma. Since these children may be doing very well in school, what can be done to alleviate conditions that may be placing them at risk for later health issues? Complicating matters even further, at least some may want to keep attention away from stresses in other life areas, preferring not to share personal experiences with teachers, counselors, or others at school. Three potentially helpful recommendations include (1) providing experiences that increase an awareness of their resilience in the face of challenging life events; (2) insuring that they learn to view their difficult life experiences in a new light; and (3) alleviating potentially elevated stress levels in their lives.

1. Learning to see oneself as resilient: A class project at a middle school asked students to write about a person who they know or have read about who has shown resilience in the face of difficult life experiences. Students were asked to talk to the class about why they chose this person and how he or she displayed strength and courage. The project helped students appreciate the many different ways children, families, and adults display resilience in the face of challenging conditions.

Change the View videos (mentioned earlier) provide examples of resilient youth sharing stories of difficult life experiences so that others are more understanding. Their stories have inspired other students confronting challenging situations to do the same.

A simple gift, such as the rubber ball we include in our gift bags, symbolizes the child's ability to bounce back. We sometimes include a clothespin in our gift bag, given to parents in recognition of their ability to "hold things together" for their family under very difficult conditions.

Important jobs performed well: editor of "Profiles in Courage": Working under the supervision of a teacher, resource specialist, school psychologist, or other school staff member, the student prepares stories (written, oral, or through photos) that document courageous behaviors of students at school (and/or their family members).

2. Viewing difficult life experiences in a new light: developing a meaningful connection with someone older who lived through similar experiences can potentially help a child legitimize their feelings, even when conversations steer clear of these experiences. Often, this can occur through a mentoring relationship, where an older student serves in a coaching or tutoring role.

3. Alleviating potentially elevated stress levels: opportunities to engage in ongoing aerobic exercise, mindfulness practices, and other activities help us regulate our emotions and can also potentially alleviate elevated stress levels. (See web page for additional recommendations and resources.)

RELATIONSHIPS—IN CONTEXT

8. Beating the Odds Thanks to Those Who Changed the Odds

Safety nets provide critical support in times of need. Safety nets composed of others who legitimize rather than stigmatize differences can do even more. They can rekindle a resilient child's spirit and restore a demoralized child's sense of hope. If we look closely, we'll also see that every school has an enormous pool of untapped resources for accomplishing this—called "bystanders." If what they believe in grows stronger than what they're afraid of, they have the power to transform our lives—all lives, not just the lives of children in school. To gain a better sense of their capacity for doing good, three illustrations are provided next, the first involving the actions of residents of Billings, Montana, the second involving actions of residents living in a Chicago neighborhood, and the third involving actions of residents living in New York City immediately following the events of September 11, 2001.

The Transforming Power of Bystander Behavior

"The opposite of love is not hate, it's indifference."
—*Elie Wiesel, Nobel Peace Prize laureate*

In 1993, hate crimes in the city of Billings, Montana, were on the rise. In a relatively short period of time, a Native American family's home was spray painted with swastikas, African American church members were harassed, tombstones in a Jewish cemetery were overturned, and bricks were thrown through windows displaying menorahs. Rather than remain passive bystanders, the citizens decided to fight back. A painters' union task force painted over racist graffiti. Religious and community leaders sponsored human rights activities in support of African American churchgoers. And the *Billings Gazette* published a full-page printout of a menorah in their newspaper, which 10,000 people in Billings publicly displayed in their homes and businesses (California Work Group, 1995).

People in Billings were willing to stand up on behalf of others in need of their help. They did so for no personal gain and at significant personal risk. Hate crimes eventually declined, and Billings became an example to the nation of the transforming power of bystander behavior.

On Chicago's West Side, local residents were confronted with a serious problem. Drug dealers were starting to do deals in daylight on street corners their children would pass by on their way to and from school. It was only a matter of time before drugs would be running rampant throughout the neighborhood. How did they solve the problem? Barbecues. Whenever neighbors saw drug dealers starting to take over a local street corner, they would rush in, lawn chairs in hand, and host a giant barbecue. They continued hosting barbecues on the corner until the dealers left. It worked. Dealers eventually moved on (Marshall, 1997).

From the perspective of human history, 9/11 represented an

uncommon catastrophic event of mass destruction, occurring in a moment's time at the hands of a few. Following these rare catastrophic moments, author Steven Jay Gould (2001) reminded us that human history also reveals an interesting counteractive force, one that propels an infinitely greater number of us to rebuild, in a way that leaves us feeling stronger than before. Gould refers to this counteracting force as "the great asymmetry." He observed it in the hours, days, and weeks following 9/11, when New Yorkers came to the aid of other city dwellers.

For the residents of Billings, Chicago, and New York, their convictions outweighed their fears. What they believed in was stronger than what they were afraid of. Together, they helped transform threatening and dangerous places into warm and friendly ones. It's a testament to the power of bystander behavior and the role it can play in validating differences, alleviating fear, restoring hope, and reconnecting lives.

Some organizations are now drawing on these transforming powers to improve the lives of children, including those with learning, behavioral, and other differences. Among them is Not in Our School (http://www.nios.org). It's a campaign that inspires students to create an atmosphere of acceptance and inclusion for all students at school, regardless of their differences. Students learn how to be active "upstanders," rather than passive or indifferent bystanders. The campaign was inspired by another campaign, Not in Our Town, a nationwide movement that encourages people to work together in their communities to stop hate and foster safe and inclusive environments (http://niot.org). The movement was inspired by a documentary by the same name (California Working Group, 1995), which captured the courageous actions of the citizens of Billings to fight back against hate crimes. It turns out that the same formula that helped Billings change the odds can also help change the odds for a significant number of struggling students at school.

Other programs that we've highlighted, among them, the PAX Good Behavior Game, PeaceBuilders, the Heroic Imagination Program, and the Olweus Bullying Prevention Program, also draw on the good that can come from bystanders when they choose to step forward to help others.

9. Growing Closer and Stronger as a Result of Difficult or Traumatic Life Events

Relationships as Malleable

Students with growth mind-sets who learn to view relationships as malleable may be buffered somewhat from the effects of bullying. Students with fixed mind-sets, on the other hand, may be susceptible to greater harm. Carol Dweck (2006) cites the following study by Sheri Levy to illustrate. In the study, eighth-graders were presented with a vignette in which a student at school was being bullied by a group of more popular students. The bullying occurred daily and in front of others. Each student was asked to imagine that they were the person being bullied, then write about what they would think and do. Results showed that those with fixed mind-sets were more likely to take the experiences personally and believe that what others were saying about them was true. They also wanted revenge. Eighth-graders with growth mind-sets, on the other hand, were less likely to perceive the cruel comments as true and more likely to attribute them to personal problems experienced by the bullies. Rather than seeking revenge, they were more interested in getting help for the bullies.

Unfortunately, given time, growth mind-sets can succumb to the effects of bullying and fall prey to fixed and inflexible views of abilities and relationships. This seemed to have been the case with Pam who, if you recall, was bullied repeatedly in seventh grade. She came to believe that what the other girls were saying about her was true. In this respect, it resembled perceptions of students with fixed mind-sets. What was different in Pam's case was that she seemed more intent on hurting herself rather than others.

The good news is that growth mind-sets can be restored when students once again attend a school where they feel they belong. This was the case with Pam. Eighth grade represented a fresh start in a safe school environment and the quick return of a growth mindset.

New school experiences seemed to also positively transform the mindset of Bill's grandson. (Recall that we met Bill in Chapter 4.) Prior to high school, his grandson always performed poorly in school. The five misperceptions were among the reasons for this. He excelled at difficult tasks but struggled with simple academic ones, particularly reading. He also lacked organizational skills. By eighth grade (his last year of middle school), he had all but given up. In ninth grade, he enrolled in a small project-based high school similar in structure and philosophy to the ones discussed here. Teachers at the school were trained on how to translate lesson plans into meaningful hands-on projects. Interestingly, even in his new school Bill's grandson still struggled to read. He was also as disorganized as ever. His struggles persisted, but his spirit returned.

In eighth grade, Bill's grandson viewed his abilities and his relationships as fixed and inflexible. He gave up at the first sign of difficulty, never asked for help, and believed that teachers and students viewed him as unintelligent. In ninth grade, he tried hard, rarely gave up, learned from his mistakes, asked his teachers for help when needed, and dreamed of attending college someday. His views of his abilities and his relationships went from fixed to malleable in one year. Teachers were now seen as caring, and success at school was seen as possible, with effort.

Learning to Think Socially: According to Michelle Garcia Winner, social thinking represents the key ingredient to mastering the skills necessary to make better social and emotional connections. Social thinking involves several components, among them the ability to take into account how others see things, the ability to empathize with how others feel, the ability to appreciate how the things we say and do affect others, and the ability to do all of these things in a matter of milliseconds. For some of us, this comes easy. For others, it does not. According to Garcia Winner, some people, including children, experience the equivalent of a learning disability in social thinking. Her innovative model, the ILAUGH Model of Social Thinking, is designed to improve these skills (Katz, 2011c). ILAUGH is an acronym representing six empirically supported social cognitive skills, each representing an important part of the model's assessment and intervention process: initiation of communication, listening with our eyes and brain, abstract and inferential language/communication, understanding perspective, Gestalt processing/getting the big picture, humor and human relatedness. Additional information about Garcia Winner's work can be found on the website http://www.socialthinking.com.

The ILAUGH model is being used throughout the country to help individuals of all ages develop the skills necessary to make and maintain a friendship. For children fortunate enough to benefit from the model, their gains may help improve the quality of their lives decades later. Consider, for example, a study that looked at two aspects of social relationships, one related to peer acceptance/rejection, the other related to friendships—whether a child had a friend. Results revealed that by their 20s, the effects seemed additive. If you were rejected and also had no friends, adjustment problems were more likely. Separately, though, these effects were less evident. Researchers speculated that if you were rejected in grade school but had a friend, you may have been buffered (Erdley et al., 2001). Perhaps this was the case with Carl prior to losing contact with his two closest friends.

10. Our Greatest Source of Strength—Each Other: A Closer Look at Turning Points

Question 1: Were there specific turning point experiences or second-chance opportunities that help explain how or why your life changed for the better?

Question 2: Still on the matter of turning point experiences or second chance opportunities, are they related to specific people in your life? People who make you feel grateful that they were or continue to be part of your life.

People who rebound from adverse childhood experiences, including years of school failure, can usually identify turning point experiences that created possibilities for a more meaningful and productive life. Answers to question 1 speak to these possibilities. Answers to question 2 speak to those who open the door to these possibilities.

Those who open these doors are often unaware of the role they play in helping struggling children eventually rebound from a difficult past. This was the case for a colleague of mine who works as a program director at a foster care agency. This is no longer the case, thanks to a chance meeting with Jim, a former foster child he counseled many years ago. Today, Jim is married, fathers a young child, and holds down a good job. This is quite a departure from his days in foster care. At age 17, he was failing in school, threatening to drop out, and refusing help. He had also been picked up by the police, along with three friends, when one of them broke into a convenience store and stole some items. My colleague spent a great deal of time speaking on Jim's behalf to juvenile probation workers, school officials, even a juvenile court judge who was considering placing Jim in a center for juvenile offenders. There's little doubt that had he not spoken up for Jim in this way, the boy would have eventually been incarcerated. Fast forward 15 years. Jim is 32 now, and the two are reunited for the first time since his days in foster care. After catching up with one another, Jim spontaneously began sharing how grateful he was for the help my colleague provided to him during what he described as the most difficult time of his life. He felt that without this help he would have likely found himself in even more trouble with the law, as, in fact, turned out to be the case with some of his friends from that time. Jim said he had always wanted to share these thoughts with my colleague and knew he would do so if they ever met again.

Jim knew some things about turning points that my colleague had not known prior to this chance encounter but, thanks to Jim, is well aware of now. Turning points play an important role in overcoming a difficult past, and human relationships play an important role in opening the door to these turning points. Our greatest source of strength may truly be each other.

FINAL THOUGHTS

Without ever realizing it, each day, teachers and other caring individuals at school provide struggling students with potential turning point experiences. Some are creating important jobs for students who never enjoyed the feeling of accomplishment that comes from assuming a meaningful and valued role. Some are coaching students before school on a question to be asked during class later, providing the opportunity to correctly answer the question in front of other classmates. Some use mistake jars and other strategies to help students learn to perceive setbacks as learning experiences. Some take the time to send letters, postcards, e-mails, or text messages to parents celebrating students' accomplishments. Some spend time after school tutoring students in subjects they find difficult. Some allow students rendered at a serious disadvantage by virtue of their challenges to demonstrate mastery of a subject in ways they learn and communicate best.

Individuals who engage in these small acts of kindness often go unnoticed. This is unfortunate, since we know that the trusting bonds they form with struggling students will, in some instances, have far greater long-term significance than anyone probably realizes. Perceptions, processes, and practices notwithstanding, it's people like these that change the odds, one school day at a time.

SUMMARY

- Five new, empirically validated perceptions regarding commonly observed uneven learning and behavioral profiles allow easier access to contextual influences that can change the odds for struggling school-age children.
- The Kauai Longitudinal Study suggested that children exposed to multiple risks who "beat the odds" may actually be at greater risk for health-related problems decades later than children who succumb. Ensuring that their school day provides healthy outlets for stress reduction may help, as may opportunities to see themselves as resilient individuals working hard to rise above very challenging life circumstances.
- Contextual influences that can change the odds operate on at least three levels: (1) socially (externally); (2) emotionally, psychologically, and spiritually (internally) by helping us see life experiences in a new light; and (3) relationally.

Chapter 7

~~~~~

IMPROVING EMOTIONAL SELF-REGULATION AND SELF-CONTROL SKILLS, ONE SCHOOL DAY AT A TIME

Carl's brother, Steven, loved school. School also loved Steven. It wasn't only because he was strong academically and earned good grades. He was also very good at regulating his emotions and controlling his behavior. What's more, he learned quickly from his behavioral mistakes. When Steven broke a rule at school, he was punished and then never broke the rule again. He was the kind of student who responded well to facts and fear—so well that force never entered into the equation. This was not the case for Carl, and no one knew why. Few if any ever heard of the term "executive function," and even fewer recognized executive function challenges, particularly those affecting emotional self-regulation and self-control.

As a nation, we've committed significant amounts of time, energy, and resources to end illiteracy. We've made this investment because research has shown that strong reading skills translate to better lives down the road and a more productive nation. Should we be making a similar investment in improving children's emotional self-regulation and self-control skills?

A growing number of experts believe we should. Among them is Terrie Moffitt, Associate Director of the Dunedin Study, described by Michael Rutter as the most comprehensive longitudinal investigation of life outcomes to date (Moffitt, 2012). The Dunedin Study has been following the life trajectories of all babies born during 1972–73 in the city of Dunedin, New Zealand (1,037 in total). Moffitt's views are based on Dunedin Study results, which show a strong relationship between children's self-control skills and a range of later life outcomes, among them physical health and illness (a finding we highlighted earlier), criminal offending, addiction, heavy smoking, personal finances, saving for retirement, dropping out of high school, and unplanned single parenting. These outcomes hold regardless of IQ or social class. They also hold whether or not a child meets diagnostic criteria for ADHD. Though the Dunedin Study isn't designed to explore the impact of self-control interventions on later life outcomes, some study participants did manage to move up in their self-control ranking over the years, and improved self-control was associated with better outcomes (Moffitt, 2012; Moffitt et al., 2011).

The ability to control behavior represents one of many different emotional self-regulation skills. Emotional self-regulation skills allow us to adjust our emotions to the situation at hand. In some situations it's important to control our emotions, while in other situations it's important to express them. We also draw on emotional self-regulation skills when expressing positive emotions. Positive emotions seem to receive less attention than do emotions that upset us and cause us stress. We now know, though, that our ability to express positive emotions can go a long way in helping us cope with and regulate more negative ones (Fredrickson, 2000, 2001; Fredrickson and Losada, 2005).

Improving emotional self-regulation skills can have far-reaching effects on life outcomes. The majority of diagnostic categories of psychopathology, for example, are characterized by problems with emotion or emotional regulation (Werner and Gross, 2009). Research has also linked child neglect, physical abuse, sexual abuse, and early onset of maltreatment to increased emotional self-regulation problems and then to higher rates of externalizing problems, such as aggressive or delinquent behaviors. In contrast, better emotional self-regulation skills among similarly maltreated children predicted greater peer acceptance over time, which related to lower internalizing symptoms such as withdrawal, somatic complaints, anxiety, and depression (Kim and Cicchetti, 2010). In addition, a number of leading experts now view emotional self-regulation problems as among the executive function challenges commonly affecting people diagnosed with ADHD (Barkley, 2010b, 2011b).

Clearly, for those who struggle in regulating their emotions and controlling their behavior, improving in these areas can significantly improve the quality of their lives. What's more, Dunedin Study results suggest this to be especially true for children whose struggles in this regard place them at greater risk for a number of negative life outcomes, among them being poorer health. And the key to improving in these areas, whether affected by environmental factors, neurodevelopmental factors, or combinations of both, may lie in our ability to master five specific self-regulation strategies:

- Situation selection: selecting situations that are less likely to lead to emotional regulation problems.
- Situation modification: modifying a situation that is known to trigger emotional regulation problems.
- Attention deployment: using attention strategically in ways that distract us from the source of hard-to-regulate emotions.
- Cognitive change or appraisal: changing the way we view the situation or the way we think about our ability to manage the demands that the situation poses. Cognitive change can also involve changing the way we view our emotional reaction to a situation.
- Response modulation: attempting to alter our actual emotional response.

These five strategies make up what Stanford University researcher James Gross refers to as the process model of emotion regulation (Gross, 1998; Gross and Thompson, 2009). An emotional response can be broken down into four steps, according to Gross: situation, attention, appraisal, response (Barkley, 2010b; Gross, 1998; Gross and Thompson, 2009). A situation draws our attention to an event, which we then appraise to determine what it means, which leads to our emotional response. From these four steps emerge the five emotional self-regulation strategies. An increasing number of experts use Gross's model to help people improve how they regulate their emotions and control their behavior. The growing interest in these strategies is understandable. Evidence suggests that the more we employ them effectively, the better we become at regulating and controlling our emotions. This appears to be true for children and adults (Southam-Gerow, 2013).

Recall that during their childhood years, Carl and Javier had difficulty regulating their emotions and controlling their behavior. They've since grown far more skilled at managing these functions, possibly as a result of becoming more skilled in employing these strategies. Both have learned to find or create contexts in which they excel (situation selection). Each has become quite skilled at using different tools, technologies, and strategies to succeed at tasks that in years past were frustrating and upsetting (situation modification). Today, they no longer ruminate about daily problems, worry endlessly about their future, or overly focus on perceived criticisms about their capabilities (attention deployment). Each can see their challenges in a new light, and no longer attribute these challenges to flaws in their character or as the result of a lack of intelligence (cognitive change or appraisal). Both are very skilled at replenishing their emotional self-regulation fuel tanks. Doing so helps them remain calm and in control when faced with emotionally provocative situations that previously would have led to strong emotional reactions (response modulation).

Carl and Javier never had the opportunity to master self-regulation strategies during their childhood years. Fortunately, children who currently struggle in similar ways do. In the section that follows, we explore how we might help them do so.

The following discussion explores Gross's self-regulation strategies in greater depth. We provide examples of their effective execution (adaptive execution) and examples of ineffective execution (maladaptive execution). Barriers to effective execution are also reviewed so we might be more aware of how to navigate them (Leahy, Tirch, and Napolitano, 2011; Werner and Gross, 2009). The discussion explores how these strategies relate to the contextual influences highlighted earlier. Learning to successfully regulate our emotions and control our behavior may provide greater access to these contextual influences. The reverse appears to be true as well. Greater access to these contextual influences may also improve our ability to regulate emotions and behavior. While the process model of emotion regulation is relevant to adults wishing to improve their emotional self-regulation skills, in the following discussion we focus greater attention on ways to improve these skills in children.

FIVE SELF-REGULATION STRATEGIES

Situation Selection

Situation selection involves looking ahead and predicting which situations are likely to provoke us and which are not. Persons who successfully select out of situations that trigger hard-to-regulate emotions and into situations where emotions are more easily managed are executing situation selection adaptively.

Students who avoid situations that no longer pose threat or danger are expressing situation selection less adaptively. Learning that a situation no longer poses the danger of losing control requires exposure to the situation. Avoidance prevents exposure, which prevents the opportunity to learn from emotional experiences.

Situation selection may not always be as easy as it seems. Consider, for example, persons who associate certain new situations with traumatic life events in similar past situations. The human brain is remarkably proficient at storing detailed memories of experiences causing us serious harm, including emotional memories of the situations within which these experiences occurred. These memories can involve sights, sounds, smells, or other sensory sensations, all potential reminders of both the experience and its context. Social contexts that trigger these emotional memories may well be avoided until we learn to associate them with a greater sense of emotional safety. As mentioned earlier, "The cost of treating a stick as a snake is less, in the long run, than the cost of treating a snake as a stick" (LeDoux, 1998, p. 186).

Situation selection speaks directly to the role of social context and its potential impact on emotional self-regulation skills. In relation to adults, children have less opportunity to select out of certain social contexts and into others. This poses a particular problem in social situations where differences are sources of shame or ridicule. Social contexts like these increase exposure to emotional triggers, potentially leading to hard-to-regulate emotions. Students unable to select out of these situations are at greater risk emotionally, behaviorally, and psychologically. Providing students access to social climates that validate differences and reduce perceptions of threat and danger can reduce this risk and possibly result in improved emotional self-regulation and self-control. In the previous chapter, a number of helpful programs and practices were discussed (the Jigsaw Classroom, PeaceBuilders, the Heroic Imagination Project, the PAX Good Behavior Game, and PBIS, to name a few). When successfully replicated, they show students that social climates can be changed in ways that create a sense of acceptance, safety, belonging, and purpose for all students, including those with challenges. In addition, students also see the role of social context in determining the quality of a school day and the potential benefits derived from well-executed situation selection.

Situation Modification

Situation modification also speaks to the importance of social context in regulating emotions and controlling behavior. Students who can successfully "raise the bar" and "level the playing field" are better able to navigate learning, behavioral, and other challenges that may have triggered hard-to-regulate emotions.

Students who can successfully distance themselves from a specific student who triggers hard-to-regulate emotions are employing situation modification successfully. Situation modification can be maladaptive when it interferes with our ability to perform successfully. In the example above, distancing ourselves from a student we don't get along with to the point that we skip going to class would be maladaptive.

In the previous chapter, a number of programs and practices were discussed that can potentially strengthen skills that lend themselves to the effective expression of situation modification, among them, PAX GBG, Collaborative and Proactive Solutions, and the ILAUGH model of social thinking.

Attention Deployment

Research shows that some children as young as four years already know how to use attention strategically to control behavior. Children who do not know this can be taught to do so. Furthermore, learning to do so can potentially result in improved life outcomes many years later. These are among the findings from a study by Walter Mischel et al. (2011). The study, which has come to be known as "the marshmallow experiment," explored the ability of four-year-olds to control their behavior and delay gratification. In the study, a researcher had a child sit at a table in a room with no other children around. On the table, placed directly in front of the child, was a marshmallow. The child was told that he or she would be left alone in the room for a few minutes, and during this time would have a choice: either eat the one marshmallow now, or wait a few minutes and earn a second marshmallow. The actual waiting time was 15 minutes. About two-thirds of the children were able to wait the full amount of time and earn their extra marshmallow. It wasn't easy. Some would sing songs to themselves. Others covered their eyes. Others walked around the room. In each instance, children were trying to distract themselves from the temptation of gobbling up the marshmallow. A third couldn't resist.

Mischel conducted a follow-up study with the original four-year-olds at age 16. Surprisingly, four-year-olds who couldn't resist eating the marshmallow scored an average of 200 points lower on their SATs than those who waited. They also had more difficulty paying attention, more difficulty handling stressful situations, more difficulty maintaining friendships, and more behavior problems at home and school. Mischel and colleagues conducted a second follow-up study years later, when the original four-year-olds were in their late 30s. Results were significant. Four year-olds who ate the marshmallow had, on average, more problems with drugs, and also a higher body mass index.

Why were some children able to wait and others not? According to Mischel, the crucial skill was "strategic allocation of attention" (Lehrer, 2009; Mischel et al., 2011). The key to avoid devouring the marshmallow was to figure out how not to think about it. As noted, children who effectively delayed gratification would do things like walk around the room, cover their eyes, and sing songs to distract themselves. In fact, children who attended only to the marshmallow were also the children most likely to eat it. Four-year-olds who employed effective strategies showed early signs of an ability to think about their thinking, a process referred to as metacognition. Mischel and colleagues eventually showed that by teaching impulsive responders how to do other things besides thinking about the marshmallow, children who previously couldn't wait could wait the full 15 minutes.

"Please Don't Eat the Marshmallow": KIPP schools are college-preparatory charter schools that have been in the news recently for how effective they've been in helping low-income inner-city children reach college (Katz, 2010b; Lehrer, 2009; Mathews, 2009). KIPP stands for the Knowledge Is Power Program. KIPP schools set the bar high. Students typically start school at 7:30 AM and finish at 5:00 PM, attend occasional Saturday classes, and go to school several weeks during the summer. This provides students more time to focus on core classes (math and reading). KIPP schools place particular importance on self-control. Mischel and colleagues began working closely with KIPP Academy, a school in Philadelphia, on ways to teach young children strategies to improve self-control and delay gratification. To symbolize the school's efforts, students wore shirts prominently displaying the slogan "Pease Don't Eat the Marshmallow."

Working Memory and the Strategic Allocation of Attention: Working memory may play a bigger role than previously thought in determining who among us will eat the marshmallow. Under the direction of University of Michigan psychologist and neuroscientist John Jonides, researchers administered computer-based neuro-psychological tests on 55 of the original marshmallow experiment participants, who were now 40. Neuropsychological tests measured how well these subjects could control the contents of working memory. Recall that Mischel observed that children who were able to delay eating the marshmallow were also able to not think about it. This required the ability to keep competing thoughts in working memory instead of focusing entirely on the marshmallow. Results showed that those who successfully refrained from eating the marshmallow on average scored higher on neuropsychological measures of working memory and self-control at age 40 (Lehrer, 2009).

Deploying Attention Mindfully: Research suggests that mindfulness exercises help guide attention in ways that support emotional self-regulation (Zylowska, 2012). Those skilled in mindfulness practices learn to accept emotions nonjudgmentally, as normal human reactions. Clinicians who teach mindfulness practices often say that our emotional reaction to our emotional reaction leads to distress.

In other words, our emotions generate more emotions. Those who blame or shame themselves for emotions they feel or who believe those emotions are wrong and unacceptable may be suffering not as a result of their initial emotion, but as a result of their emotional reaction to an emotion. An increasing number of educators and health care professionals are introducing students to mindfulness training, with some schools incorporating mindfulness exercises into their curriculum.

Dialectical behavior therapy (DBT), acceptance and commitment therapy (ACT), and mindfulness-based cognitive therapy approaches are among the interventions that mental health professionals use to assist individuals strategically deploy their attentional resources in ways that increase emotional self-regulation and self-control (Werner and Gross, 2009). These and other related interventions help individuals distinguish normal emotions from emotions to emotions. Although these approaches have been used primarily with adult populations in years past, in more recent years clinicians have adapted them for use with children (Lee et al., 2008; Murrell and Scherbath, 2011; Perepletchikova et al., 2011).

Attention deployment speaks to the role of mastery in regulating emotions and controlling behavior. Those who practice ways to guide and deploy their attention to avoid self-regulation problems can eventually master these skills.

The PAX Good Behavior Game appears to be an effective tool for helping children learn to deploy attention strategically. Attention deployment can also be implemented maladaptively. Two examples are excessive rumination and excessive worry (Werner and Gross, 2009). To ruminate is to overthink a difficult situation or upsetting emotional experience. It's deploying too much attention to something that's causing distress. We do the same when we worry. The difference is that worrying is typically associated with the anticipation of something distressing happening in the future, whereas rumination is typically associated with distressing experiences of the past.

Distraction can also be used adaptively or maladaptively, depending on how much we rely on it. In appropriate doses it can be adaptive. If used excessively, it can prevent us from learning to manage challenging situations or cope with strong emotions (Werner and Gross, 2009).

Cognitive Change or Appraisal

Cognitive change involves changing the way we view a situation or how we think about our ability to manage the demands the situation poses. Cognitive change can also involve changing the way we perceive our emotional reaction to a situation.

Cognitive change or appraisal speaks to our ability to view challenges in a new light. Programs and practices that help students attach new meaning to challenges and differences serve to strengthen this self-regulation strategy. Examples cited in the previous chapter include PAX GBG, WhyTry, Eye-to-Eye, Active Minds, LETS, restorative practices, Change the View, Shut Up About Your Perfect Kid, CPS, and ILAUGH.

We see ourselves through the eyes of others, and this is particularly true during our childhood years. Those who view a student's challenges in erroneous ways can make it difficult for the student to cognitively change or reappraise challenges in a new light. Cognitive change can thus have a relational component.

People vary in the meaning they ascribe to their emotional reactions. These different meanings in turn influence how they react to their emotional experiences. Practices that help people accept emotions nonjudgmentally can help them execute this fourth self-regulation strategy successfully. On the other hand, believing that emotions are unacceptable or wrong and that it's never okay to feel angry or experience negative emotions increases the likelihood of expressing this strategy maladaptively.

In the psychotherapy research literature, the term "schema" is used to capture the meaning people ascribe to their emotional reactions. Robert Leahy, an expert in the field of cognitive therapy, outlined 14 different dimensions for understanding emotions, or emotional schemas. He also developed a self-report questionnaire, the Leahy Emotional Schema Scale or LESS, to assess where people fall on these dimensions (Leahy, 2002).

For some, learning to put new words to old pain may have to wait until their level of emotional distress decreases. Consider, for example, a phenomenon known as "speechless terror," or our inability to use language in the face of overwhelming emotional experiences. The phenomenon was observed in a brain imaging study involving persons suffering the effects of traumatic stress exposure. Researchers compared regional brain activity under two different conditions, one where participants listened to narrative accounts of traumatic experiences they had endured, and a second condition where they listened to a neutral story. When exposed to the first condition, Broca's area was relatively inactive. (Broca's area is the part of our brain that puts words to experience.) In contrast, a great deal of activity was observed in areas of the right hemisphere, particularly in the right visual cortex, an area associated with visual flashbacks. Heightened right hemisphere activity was also observed in regions used to evaluate the importance of incoming information and for regulating autonomic and hormonal responses to information. Studies like these suggest that under certain conditions, our brain may be capable of assessing danger on one hand but not capable of providing us the means to talk about it on the other, at least when the perception of danger generates extremely intense or frightening emotions (Rauch et al., 1996; van der Kolk, 2001). Some researchers believe those with serious psychiatric conditions, including those prone to sensory symptoms they feel unable to control, are susceptible to speechless terror as well.

Response Modulation

This strategy is called on when strong emotions have already been triggered. If executed successfully, our emotions remain regulated and our behavior under control. Mindfulness practices can be helpful here, as elsewhere. Accepting emotions nonjudgmentally, and avoiding a reaction to the emotion, increases the likelihood that a distressing emotion will pass. The PAX Good Behavior Game can help children gain skills here. A number of sensory strategies, including breathing and movement exercises, also help "lower the heat" when emotions begin to escalate.

Zones of Regulation: Leah Kuypers, an occupational therapist and social learning specialist, developed Zones of Regulation (The Zones for short) to help children with lagging self-regulation skills learn ways to effectively regulate themselves at school, at home, and in the company of their friends (Katz, 2012b). The curriculum categorizes states of arousal and emotional control into four color-coded zones: the red zone, where emotions are so intense that we feel out of control; the yellow zone, where emotions are not as intense, and we still have some control; the green zone, a calmer place, where we feel focused, alert, in control of our emotions, and ready to learn; and the blue zone, a low state of alertness, too low to get much work done. We know we're in the blue zone when we're not feeling well, when we're tired, or when we're too bored to focus. The Zones can be explained much as we would explain traffic signs. Red means stop. Yellow is a warning to slow down and be cautious. Green means we're good to go. Blue is like a rest area off the freeway, a place where we can stop, take a break, and get reenergized. Within the course of 18 lessons, children learn how to identify their different states of arousal and emotional control. Children who previously struggled when asked to explain how they feel now have a vocabulary for doing so. Children also learn about different tools for moving from one zone to another, including tools for staying in the green zone, the zone that children need to be in to function well in class (a lengthier description of The Zones appears on the web page).

Replenishing Our Emotional Self-Regulation Fuel Tank: In a study sometimes referred to as the "radish experiment," Roy Baumeister and colleagues demonstrated that self-regulation is indeed a depletable resource. In the study, college students were asked to solve geometric puzzles that were actually unsolvable, although subjects were not made aware of this. Before beginning the task, students were first seated at a table in a waiting room. On the table were three types of food: (1) freshly baked cookies, (2) pieces of chocolate, and (3) radishes. Students in one group were permitted to eat the cookies and chocolate, and students in another group were only permitted to eat the radishes. Radish eaters sitting at a table with freshly baked cookies and pieces of chocolate thus had to exercise a good deal of self-control. Results showed that students permitted to eat cookies and chocolate worked on the geometric puzzle task for roughly 20 minutes, as did a control group of equally hungry students not exposed to any food choices. The radish eaters, on the other hand, worked for roughly eight minutes. Resisting the cookies and chocolate required that they exert self-control. As a result, less of it was available to work on the demanding geometric puzzle task (Baumeister and Tierney, 2011; Baumeister, Vohs, and Tice, 2007).

For a number of people who struggle to regulate emotions and

190

control behavior, simply getting through a normal day can empty their emotional self-regulation fuel tanks. When they get home, they're exhausted and not feeling particularly well regulated. Children who struggle with these issues can find themselves in much the same boat after a normal school day. As was the case with Carl decades ago, when they get home they're in no mood for homework or for any activity requiring sustained periods of concentration, emotional self-regulation, or self-control. They're running on empty and need to refuel first.

According to Russell Barkley (2010b), a number of activities can replenish our emotional self-regulation fuel tanks. Regular aerobic exercise is among the best. A few minutes of relaxation or meditation can help as well. So can access to rewarding experiences that generate positive emotions. Having more opportunity to stretch and move can help. Different activities seem to work for different people. Experts often recommend that people try a number of different techniques to see which work best. Parents and teachers are asked to do the same with students. The key is to distribute activities throughout the day so that fuel tanks won't run low. Waiting until after school may be too late.

As with attention deployment, response modulation speaks to the role of mastery in regulating emotions and controlling behavior. Skills in modulating emotions when emotions are triggered can increase with practice. So can skills at replenishing an emotional self-regulation fuel tank.

Response Modulation under Extreme Conditions: Some situations are so life threatening, they're truly terrorizing. In these instances, it's not the reaction to the emotion that overwhelms us, but the initial emotion. Despite this, we still may need to function effectively. Apparently, some of us can learn to do so. Consider, for example, the job of a military fighter pilot. Mid-air combat can be terrifying. So can an aircraft malfunction or trying to land on a moving aircraft carrier thousands of miles from land. Fighter pilots have to think clearly and function effectively, despite these conditions. In his book, *Flourishing*, psychologist Martin Seligman (2011) describes how they are trained to do so. Rather than teaching trainees anxiety-reduction techniques, instructors instead expose them to feelings of terror in the cockpit. Then they train them to think clearly under these conditions. Trainers might send the jet into an actual nosedive and require the trainee to learn how to pull up to prevent the plane from crashing into the ground. Experienced fighter pilots who've spent time in combat come to expect moments of intense fear but still have to think clearly. The job demands effective response modulation under extreme conditions.

An illustration showing how several programs and practices mentioned in Chapter 6 can potentially support one or more of the self-regulation strategies appears on the web page.

SELF-REGULATION STRATEGIES: ADDITIONAL THOUGHTS

Evidence suggests that those who engage in effective strategies encompassing all five areas fare better at regulating their emotions and controlling their behavior than do others. As noted, this also appears to hold true for both children and adults (Southam-Gerow, 2013). Generally speaking, the earlier in the five-strategy sequence the intervention occurs, the greater the control exerted over the emotion. In other words, the earlier in the chain we interrupt the emotional event, the greater the emotional control we have over the situation (Barkley, 2010b).

The Role of Positive Emotions: When negative emotions get out of hand, the solution, logically speaking, is to focus on ways to reduce them. Some researchers now say that simply reducing negative emotions won't necessarily increase positive ones. The reason is that they serve different functions (Fredrickson, 2000, 2001; Fredrickson and Losada, 2005). Negative emotions serve as warning signals, alerting us to threat and danger. We couldn't survive without them. Positive emotions, on the other hand, motivate us to venture out, explore, and learn new things. They broaden our focus, not only about challenges but also about possibilities. We see the light at the end of the tunnel as a result of positive emotions. An unlimited number of thoughts, events, and experiences can trigger positive emotions. They're triggered by simple reminders of positive experiences, working intently on a personally meaningful goal, finally accomplishing the goal, and many other internal and external experiences as well.

Positive emotions can also play a role in successfully executing emotional self-regulation strategies. They motivate us to explore new situations and learn from new experiences (situation selection). They provide moments of relief in situations that previously may have only upset us or caused us stress (situation modification). They distract us from people, thoughts, or events that might otherwise cause problems in regulating emotions or controlling behavior (attention deployment). They serve as an enjoyable and rewarding by-product from seeing challenges in a new light (cognitive change or reappraisal). And they can potentially override what might otherwise be hard-to-regulate emotions once these emotions are triggered (response modulation). While positive emotions serve us throughout our lives, Seligman (2002) maintains that they're especially important during the childhood years. According to Seligman, they help build strengths and relationships and provide children with the emotional reserve they need to handle difficult life experiences. Positive emotions also drive exploration, which then drives new learning. New learning leads to new mastery, which leads to more positive emotions. It's a cycle that serves us our entire lives, but perhaps most during our childhood years.

"ME WANT COOKIE," "ME CAN WAIT": HOW SESAME STREET VISIONARIES ARE TRANSLATING DUNEDIN STUDY FINDINGS INTO PRACTICE

Dunedin Study results showed that children's self-control skills predicted a range of later life outcomes, including physical health and illness, criminal offending, addiction, heavy smoking, personal finances, saving for retirement, dropping out of high school, and unplanned single parenting. So compelling were these findings that Associate Director Terrie Moffitt recommended that entire societies seriously consider universal interventions to improve children's self-control skills, much as whole societies did years ago to end illiteracy.

The visionaries at Sesame Street are bringing Moffitt's recommendation one step closer to reality. They're helping preschool children learn strategies for improving self-regulation, self-control, and other executive function skills. And the help is coming from an unlikely source: Cookie Monster. Known for his *lack* of self-restraint ("Me want cookie!"), Cookie Monster is changing his behavioral ways ("Me can wait"). Since September 2013, Sesame

Street has featured him in a series of parodies (Cookie's Crumby Pictures), each requiring that he master strategies to help him regulate his emotions, control his behavior, and think ahead about the consequences of his actions. By watching Cookie Monster master these strategies, preschoolers can learn to do the same, especially before they start kindergarten, when these skills will prove extremely important to school and later life success. For decades, Sesame Street has been creating programs to enrich school readiness skills. Millions of preschoolers have benefited as a result. Few programs, however, have focused this directly on improving emotional self-regulation, behavioral self-control, and related executive function skills (Katz, 2014a).

Research shows that preschoolers who lack self-control skills will start kindergarten at a serious disadvantage (Blaire and Razza, 2007; Sesame Street Workshop, 2013). Visionaries at Sesame Street are hoping to remedy this. If successful, the benefits derived by preschoolers may extend well beyond kindergarten. For some, they will last a lifetime. Those interested in learning more about this important work are encouraged to log on to the Sesame Street Workshop website at http://www.sesameworkshop.org/season44/about-the-show/cookies-crumby-pictures/.

PAX Good Behavior Game: PAX GBG can potentially serve as one of the universal preventive interventions that Moffitt recommends for improving children's self-control skills. It's simple to learn, fun to play, and has been shown through a series of studies to reduce a range of later life negative outcomes. (To review several of these studies, visit http://www.nrepp.samhsa.gov/ViewIntervention.aspx?id=351.)

Tools of the Mind and the Irvine Paraprofessional Program (IPP) are two more programs that can help improve children's emotional self-regulation and self-control skills.

Tools of the Mind: Developed by Deborah Leong and Elena Boedrova of Denver, Colorado, Tools of the Mind teaches preschool and kindergarten-age children how to use different "mental tools" to exert greater control of their social, emotional, and cognitive behaviors. The program, which is composed of 40 individualized, imaginative play and learning activities, requires children to use private speech, planning, working memory, and other executive function skills in increasing amounts (Katz, 2009a). Results of a study conducted by Adele Diamond and colleagues showed that children enrolled in preschool classrooms using Tools of the Mind improved in their ability to resist distractions and temptations (inhibitory control), mentally hold information in mind (working memory), and flexibly adjust to change (cognitive flexibility). Simply by engaging in the fun-filled activities, children improved these skills and other areas of executive function (Diamond et al., 2007). Those interested in learning more about the program are encouraged to visit http://www.toolsofthemind.org. A comprehensive overview of the program's theoretical underpinnings can be found in Boedrova and Leong (2007). Tools of the Mind is based on the work of the Russian psychologist Lev Vygotsky. Boedrova worked with Vygotsky's students in Russia before coming to the United States.

The Irvine Paraprofessional Program (IPP): Students who struggle in areas involving emotional self-regulation, self-control, and mental processes under the executive function umbrella often know what to do, but may not be able to consistently do what they know (Barkley, 2010a, b; Goldstein, 2001). For many of these students, the problem is in doing or execution. With frequent reminders, prompts, and cues provided to them at the "point of performance," or within actual situations or settings that are typically problematic, the classroom for example, these students are often much better able to focus their efforts and control their actions (Barkley, 2013). The attractiveness of the IPP is that it provides a model for accomplishing this in a cost-effective manner (Katz, 2013b; Kirk, 1992, Kotkin, 1999; Ron Kotkin, personal communication, December 15, 2012). A major component of the model is the use of a paraprofessional classroom aide working alongside the teacher. The classroom aides are recruited from a group of undergraduate students who completed a series of classes that teach empirically validated strategies for helping children with ADHD. Teachers within the local school district who find themselves struggling to manage students in their regular education classrooms can call on these trained aides to assist them. The aide will design and implement a specific 10–12-week behavioral program that addresses the needs of the struggling student. The aide also assists the teacher in providing extra help and enrichment to the other students in the class (Katz, 2013b).

IMPROVING EMOTIONAL SELF-REGULATION AND SELF-CONTROL, ONE SCHOOL DAY AT A TIME

Carl, Javier, and many others who eventually learn how to better manage their emotions and control their behavior seem to have grown far more skilled at using Ross and Thompson's five self-regulation strategies. They have done so having never heard of them or having ever been coached by anyone familiar with them. In their adult years, Carl, Javier, and many others have also been able to access contextual influences discussed throughout the book. As noted on several occasions, these contextual influences (contextually expressed protective processes) appear to outweigh multiple childhood risks linked to a range of negative outcomes. Interestingly, Dunedin Study results show that childhood self-control problems may predict many of these same negative outcomes, including problems in parenting one's own children later (Moffitt, 2012).

Improving self-regulation skills and accessing contextual influences thus appear to be different pathways to a better quality of life. And for those struggling to overcome a difficult past, pursuing them in combination may yield benefits beyond those that can be achieved by pursuing each one alone. Pursuing both in combination may also be less complicated and time consuming than it might seem, as they overlap considerably.

SUMMARY

- Emotional self-regulation skills allow us to adjust our emotions to the situation at hand. In some situations it's important to control our emotions, and in others it's important to express them.
- We also draw upon our emotional self-regulation skills when expressing positive emotions. The ability to express positive emotions can go a long way in helping us cope with and regulate more negative ones.
- Self-control skills in childhood can predict physical health and illness, criminal offending, addiction, heavy smoking, personal finances, saving for retirement, dropping out of high school, and unplanned single-parenting.

- To help children and adults improve emotional self-regulation and self-control skills, an increasing number of professionals are focusing on five self-regulation strategies: situation selection, situation modification, attention deployment, cognitive changes or appraisals, and response modulation, or the process model of emotion regulation.

Chapter 8

~~~~~

IMPROVING LATER LIFE
HEALTH OUTCOMES,
ONE SCHOOL DAY AT A TIME

Recall that several years ago, Carl suffered a heart attack and required bypass surgery. Carl had to lose weight, exercise regularly, and change his eating habits. If he didn't make these behavioral changes, a future heart attack was likely.

Carl was presented with a life-or-death choice. He could change his behavioral lifestyle and live longer, or he could engage in his unhealthy ways and possibly die young. He heeded his doctor's advice. Soon after his discharge from the hospital, he began exercising and changed his eating habits. Unfortunately, though, these changes were short-lived, and within several weeks he reverted to his old behavioral ways.

The fear of death seems as though it would be sufficient motivation for people to change their behavioral lifestyle. This seems particularly so when you consider that behavioral changes are simple to understand and, at least in appearance, simple to do. But for many of us, behavioral change can be far more difficult than it appears on the surface. In our search for reasons for this, we find a few erroneous perceptions, similar to those we've seen before:

Misperception 1: Anyone capable of performing exceptionally well on intellectual, creative, artistic, or complex behavioral tasks that others find difficult is capable of performing equally well or better on tasks that others find easy. It's simply a matter of trying harder. The doctor's recommendations were simple. Anyone who can accomplish difficult things as effortlessly as Carl can, can certainly carry out a series of simple behavioral recommendations that most of us should be able to accomplish without much effort, especially when we consider that our very lives are depending on it.

Misperception 2: Anyone who knows what they're supposed to do in a given situation can be expected to consistently, predictably, and independently do what they know all the time. It's a matter of willpower. To avoid a heart attack in the future, Carl simply had to engage in new behavioral routines consistently and predictably. He knew these new behavioral routines and he appeared capable of following them, which he did for several weeks. But then inconsistency set in.

Misperception 3: The only explanation for why anyone would be unable to do one or both of the above is because they don't care, are lazy, or are lacking a real desire to change. Several weeks into his new behavioral lifestyle, Carl wasn't feeling much better physically than he had before his heart attack. Discouraged by what he perceived to be a lack of progress, he eventually reverted to his old ways. It wasn't that he didn't care, was lazy, or had no desire to change. Rather, he seemed unable to viscerally connect new behavioral routines with feeling better or living longer. In the absence of a sense of mastery over his new behavioral lifestyle, what emerged instead was a sense of futility.

Misperception 4: Resilient people of strong character can be expected to willfully refrain from unhealthy behavioral choices, regardless of the social situation. Contextual influences, in other words, count very little when it comes to refraining from these unhealthy behaviors. Carl's closest friend, with whom he often spent time on the weekends, rarely exercised, was overweight, and paid little attention to his eating habits. As was the case with Carl, he was at risk for serious medical problems as well. When he and Carl were together, Carl went back to his unhealthy behaviors.

Misperception 5: Believing as we do in misperception 4, it follows that resilient people of strong character are able to refrain from unhealthy behavioral choices. People who lack resilience and strong character, on the other hand, are not. Carl believed this to be true. After several failed attempts at behavioral change, he grew increasingly discouraged.

Carl eventually changed his ways and sustained these changes, to the delight of those who cared about him. But it wasn't the fear of dying that led to these changes, nor was it knowledge of the facts linking specific unhealthy behaviors to serious medical problems. As was the case decades ago, neither facts, nor fear, nor force helped Carl change. In retrospect, what did seem to help were some of the same contextual influences that allowed him to rise above other challenges in years past, challenges fueled by similar erroneous perceptions. And as the following discussion attests, these contextual influences correspond directly to the agents of change that author Alan Deutschman observed among heart bypass patients who successfully changed their ways as well.

FACTS, FEAR, AND FORCE VERSUS RELATE, REPEAT, REFRAME

In November, 2004, top experts in the field of health care were invited to speak at a private conference at Rockefeller University on the state of health care in the United States. We presently spend more money on health care than we can afford, and the costs are growing more expensive every year. Those in attendance were about to learn that these costs were consumed by a relatively small percentage of the U.S. population suffering from well-known diseases. These diseases related directly to specific behaviors: too much smoking, too much drinking, too much eating, too much stress, and an increasingly sedentary lifestyle. If we could manage to reduce smoking, drinking, and overeating; consume healthier foods; and exercise regularly, the nation could save a significant amount of money and the quality of our lives would improve. Attendees then learned that among heart patients who undergo coronary-artery bypass grafting, 90 percent will have not changed their behavioral lifestyle, despite knowing that healthier changes could potentially arrest the course of their disease (Deutschman, 2005, 2007). It turns out that Carl's story is a familiar one to a number of experts in the field of health care. According to journalist and writer Alan Deutschman, people who have already undergone major heart surgery, who know their disease can grow worse if they don't change, who know it's within their power and control to change, and who know they may die if they don't change, seem to find dying easier than changing.

To convince people to change so they won't die, Deutschman says we typically rely on three approaches, each of which fails more than we realize: facts, fear, and force. Instead of the three F's, he says, we need to focus on the three R's—relate, repeat, reframe.

Relate, Repeat, Reframe

Although a majority of coronary bypass patients reverted to a behavioral lifestyle putting them at serious medical risk, some did make permanent changes. Deutschman found three key change agents contributing to their successful turnabout. First, they formed a relationship with a person or community of people that inspired hope (relate). They believed those they were now connected to— mentors, partners, role models, or others—had the knowledge, methods, or strategies to help them change. New attachments led to new beliefs. New beliefs led to new hope.

Second, these new relationships helped them learn new behavioral skills. With practice, these behavioral skills began to feel natural and automatic (repeat), so much so that they were eventually able to execute them without giving them much thought. If relationships sold them on the belief that they had it within their power to change, repetition provided the practice to master skills they would ultimately need to achieve and sustain change.

Third, they eventually viewed their lives in new ways (reframe), ways that would have seemed foreign to them before they began to make significant changes.

Carl's Road to Better Health

Carl was eventually able to change and sustain a new behavioral lifestyle. Looking back, it seems that at least three contextual influences may have set him on a path to better health. Upon closer examination, each of these influences corresponds directly to Deutschman's agents of change.

1. Relate = Safety Nets; Connecting with Those Who Legitimize Rather than Stigmatize

Carl's safety net reappeared soon after he fell back into his old habits. His closest friend, whose similarly unhealthy behaviors placed him at risk for later medical problems, made a commitment to follow Carl's new routines. They exercised together three or four days a week. Recall from our earlier discussion that Kathy and others at the office replaced the pastries available during their morning meetings with fresh fruit and began taking walks after lunch, accompanied by Carl whenever time allowed.

2. Repeat = Personal Pathways to a Sense of Mastery

Carl enrolled in a health maintenance program at the request of his doctor. The program provided the structure and coaching he needed to consistently execute new habits. It also provided an ongoing support system that helped him and other participants to translate mistakes and setbacks into learning experiences. In addition, the program's behavioral model focused on mastery-building activities, with built-in procedures to combat common barriers to successful behavior change (Jeffrey Penner, personal communication, March 9, 2009). One common barrier was a sense of futility many participants experienced when new routines were disrupted. Another barrier pertained to what participants believed to be their need to diet, which they associated with discomfort. Carl learned that he wouldn't have to eat less, but actually would be encouraged to eat more. The only difference was that "more" came to mean more fruits and vegetables.

3. Reframe = Seeing Strengths, Challenges, and Experiences in a New Light; Seeing Abilities as Malleable

Carl eventually learned to see previous barriers to successful behavioral change in a new light. Prior to his heart attack, he lacked energy and felt out of shape. Well into his new behavioral lifestyle, he felt better physically and psychologically. Successful behavioral routines led to mastery of new behavioral skills. New mastery led to new meaning. New meaning reinforced his new lifestyle.

Agents of change appear to correspond to other contextual influences as well. In exploring change agents among parolees with lengthy criminal histories (discussed in the following chapter), Deutschman observed that relationships inspiring change formed with a community of people rather than with a single individual (relate). A community of individuals who instill a sense of hope in others can also serve as a buffer in the face of risk exposure (social context). In addition, successfully changing one's behavioral lifestyle to overcome illness or improve one's health may symbolize a turning point for some people. In this respect, any or all of Deutschman's three agents of change can correspond to contextual influences that speak to turning point experiences. See Table 8.1 for how contextual influences correspond to Deutschman's three agents of change.

Table 8.1. Deutschman's Three Agents of Change and Corresponding Contextual Influences

Three Agents of Change	Contextual Influences
Relate	Safety nets Connecting with those who legitimize rather than stigmatize Social context
Repeat	Personal pathways to a sense of mastery
Reframe	Seeing strengths, challenges, and adverse life experiences in a new light Seeing abilities as malleable, not fixed
Relate, Repeat, Reframe	Our greatest source of strength: each other; turning points

THE IMPACT OF NEW PERCEPTIONS REGARDING BEHAVIORAL RISKS ON LATER LIFE HEALTH OUTCOMES

Why was sustaining behavioral change so difficult for Carl? Upon closer examination, the culprit may have been our five erroneous perceptions, which can lead to ineffective remedies (facts, fear, and force), resulting in disappointing results. New perceptions, on the other hand, may lead to new possibilities, not the least of which is greater access to contextual influences (agents of change) that can help us rise above life's challenges. For those trying hard but unsuccessfully to engage in healthier behaviors, the new perceptions seem to capture views held by experts who specialize in helping people adopt healthier behavioral routines.

1. Some people who perform exceptionally well on intellectual, creative, artistic, or complex behavioral tasks that most others find difficult are not necessarily as capable of performing equally well or better on behavioral tasks that most find easy, for reasons having nothing to do with being lazy or lacking moral character.

Experts in health maintenance know how damaging it can be when those struggling to master new behavioral routines view setbacks in personally harsh and devaluing ways. Routines are more likely to be mastered when they are associated with positive emotions. When Carl first set out to change, he did so entirely out of fear. Setbacks soon led to feelings of defeat, which eventually led to a return to old, unhealthy routines. He was on the road to behavioral mastery once he learned to associate new behavioral routines with feeling better rather than feeling worse.

2. To know how to live a healthier behavioral lifestyle and to want to live this behavioral lifestyle may not be enough to consistently, predictably and independently engage in a healthy behavioral lifestyle. What's more, it's possible that no amount of "facts, fear, or force" will remedy this. The remedy instead may come in the form of "relate, repeat, and reframe."

Experts know how to prepare us for the inevitable setbacks that occur when trying to learn new routines and habits. Thanks to coaching from a health maintenance program, Carl learned that inconsistency is to be expected. All is not lost. The program taught him strategies for preventing feelings of defeat when daily routines were interrupted. The program's support system, composed of others susceptible to similar patterns of inconsistency, helped greatly in this regard.

3. When it comes to changing our unhealthy ways, a strong desire to change may not be enough. We may also need a new set of skills.

Obesity rates continue to climb, particularly for children. According to Jeffrey Penner of the Institute for Health Maintenance in San Diego, the reason for this is directly related to two factors, both contextual: easy access to inexpensive, calorie-dense foods, and a daily lifestyle with no requirement for significant physical activity. Eating fewer calories and doing more physical activity in an environment promoting just the opposite requires the acquisition of specific skills (Jeffrey Penner, personal communication, April 5, 2014). Greater appreciation of contextual influences facilitates acquisition of these skills.

4. Unhealthy behaviors are more likely to occur within certain situations. To sustain a healthy lifestyle, context counts, more so than we may realize.

Penner and other experts know that context counts a great deal when it comes to losing weight, avoiding unhealthy habits, and engaging in new routines. Recall how Kathy and others at Carl's office kept healthy food around for snacking and began taking exercise breaks after lunch. Recall also that Carl's closest friend began exercising with him three or four times a week. These examples represent contextual changes that increased the likelihood of engaging in new routines and decreased the likelihood of reverting to old ones.

5. For resilient individuals of strong character, these contextual influences can still determine whether we change our ways or whether our efforts end in failure.

Experts recognize how important it is for us to believe that behavioral change is possible, especially when previous attempts were unsuccessful. When Carl initially attributed failed attempts at change to a lack of resilience or personal resolve, he grew increasingly discouraged. When he learned ways to alter his environment and other contextual influences, he grew hopeful. He eventually realized that behavioral setbacks were temporary, limited, and not the result of a lack of strength or moral character (not permanent, pervasive, and personal). He and others involved in the health maintenance program began to see the process of successful behavioral change in a new light, and saw their struggle to sustain new routines as a testament to their resilience in the face of challenge.

FINAL THOUGHTS

Many of us thought that protective processes observed in the lives of children who beat the odds protected them from later health problems. As noted earlier, results from the Kauai Longitudinal Study suggest otherwise. These children were actually at greater risk decades later than were those who succumbed. When it comes to improving later health outcomes among school-age children, it's best that we extend our safety net to include all children, especially those beginning to evidence known behavioral risks, among them smoking, overeating, consuming unhealthy foods, and failing to exercise regularly. While changing an unhealthy habit may not be easy, Deutschman observed that it will occur more frequently if we think in terms of relate, repeat, and reframe. Each of these agents of change corresponds to one or more contextual influences that can change the odds for children at risk for a range of negative outcomes. Unfortunately, five familiar erroneous perceptions can prevent us from accessing our contextual influences. New perceptions, on the other hand, can allow access to these influences, thus offering the possibility of improved health, mental health, and quality of life outcomes down the road.

In Carl's case, it took a heart attack to realize this. What we suspect is that the same contextual influences (agents of change) that helped save his life could have prevented his heart attack had he enjoyed access to them during his school years, when behavioral risk factors first appeared. While it's too late for Carl, it's not too late for other children who find themselves on a similar unhealthy behavioral trajectory.

SUMMARY

- According to journalist and writer Alan Deutschman, a number of people who have undergone major heart surgery know their disease can grow worse if they don't change, know it's within their power and control to change, and know they may die if they don't change, but seem to find dying easier than changing.

- To convince people to change so they won't die, Deutschman says that we typically rely on three approaches, each of which fails more than we realize: facts, fear, and force. Instead, we need to focus on the three R's: relate (forming a bond with individuals or a community that inspires hope), repeat (practicing and ultimately mastering new behavioral skills necessary for effective behavior change), and reframe (learning to view one's life in a new way that would have seemed foreign prior to successfully changing.

- These three agents of change correspond directly to contextual influences previously discussed. "Relate" corresponds to relational influences (safety nets, connecting with those who legitimize rather than stigmatize), "repeat" corresponds to contextual influences that assist in developing a sense of mastery (personal pathways to a sense of mastery), and "reframe" corresponds to contextual influences that assist us in viewing strengths, challenges, and adverse life experiences in a new light (seeing abilities as malleable, not fixed).

- As is the case with paradoxically uneven learning and behavioral profiles, unhealthy behavioral habits can be paradoxical as well, resulting in similar erroneous perceptions. New perceptions, on the other hand, can pave the way for new agents of change.

- When it comes to improving later life health outcomes, it's best that we extend our safety net to include all children, especially those beginning to evidence known behavioral risks.

Chapter 9

~~~~~~~~~~

PREVENTING AND REDUCING YOUTH VIOLENCE, YOUTH CRIME, AND FUTURE RISK OF INCARCERATION, ONE SCHOOL DAY AT A TIME

As well as studying agents of change among coronary bypass patients, Alan Deutschman also studied prison inmates following parole. He focused particularly on parolees with long criminal histories that resulted in lengthy prison terms. A number of experts in the criminal justice system question whether the population of parolees he chose to study were truly capable of change. This pessimistic outlook was supported by a 2002 study conducted by the U.S. Department of Justice that tracked over 200,000 inmates after their release from 15 different state prisons in 1994. Results showed that 67.5 percent were arrested again within three years (Langan and Levin, 2002).

Probabilities, however, should not be confused with possibilities. Not all prisoners returned to prison following their release. Some changed their ways. Those who did, according to Deutschman, again seemed to rely on three agents of change: relate, repeat, and reframe. He arrived at this observation after studying a group of parolees residing at the Delancey Street Foundation, a live-in program in the San Francisco Bay Area known for its success in reintegrating former prisoners back into society. Roughly 500 former prisoners with lengthy criminal histories live there, along with one professional staff member, Mimi Silbert, who cofounded the program decades ago. Delancey Street residents are required to practice living like law-abiding citizens who don't use drugs, don't resort to threats and violence, and who dress, walk, and talk like law-abiding citizens do. Residents also must learn three or more marketable skills. Residents of Delancey Street currently run a successful moving company, print shop, a bookstore/café, and a restaurant. The program supports itself with profits from these businesses. According to Deutschman, most residents graduate after about four years, then live on their own. Estimates are that nearly 60 percent of those who make it through the program are able to sustain productive lives. This was not supposed to be possible given their criminal histories.

Residents are drawn together by a common culture (relate). According to Deutschman, emotional connections can occur not only with a person who inspires hope but also with a culture that inspires hope. Residents learn self-respect through the concept "each one, teach one." If one resident has a skill that another resident lacks, he helps the other resident develop the skill. A resident who doesn't know how to read can learn to read with the help of a resident who reads well. As mentioned, residents must also practice living each day as a law-abiding citizen who doesn't use drugs, doesn't resort to threats and violence, and dresses, walks, and talks in a certain way (repeat). According to Deutschman, the opportunity to engage in constant, repetitive successful behaviors produces clear and immediate feelings of success, and more important, a feeling of hope. By acting this way, in time some come to see themselves this way (reframe). It's an illustration of learning by doing, the connection of mastery to meaning. Delancey Street has shown that a larger than expected percentage of unskilled people with long and serious criminal records can eventually become sober, law-abiding, skilled workers (Deutschman, 2007).

As noted in the previous chapter, Deutschman's three agents of change correspond directly to one or more contextual influences that can change the odds.

PREVENTING AND REDUCING YOUTH VIOLENCE, YOUTH CRIME, AND FUTURE RISK OF INCARCERATION

Thanks to these three agents of change, at least some criminal offenders appeared to change their ways and thus avoided further incarceration. Question: How, if possible, might their incarceration have been prevented in the first place? One possible way would have been to provide them access to the three agents of change during their school years, which could have offset risk factors associated with future incarceration. The following discussion illustrates the potential benefits that can accrue when we do so. We begin the discussion with a brief introduction to what some in the field of prevention refer to as the "school-to-prison pipeline."

School-to-Prison Pipeline

Studies show that nearly 80 percent of those serving time in prison never earned their high school diploma (Lehr et al., 2004; Office of Juvenile Justice and Delinquency Prevention, 1995). Studies such as these are often cited to increase public awareness of the school-to-prison pipeline (Advancement Project, 2005). Many believe that future rates of incarceration can be reduced by preventing students from dropping out of school. Many also believe that effective practices for achieving this currently exist. Longitudinal research studies show that academically successful children who bond with school and their teachers are significantly less likely to drop out (Cook, Gottfredson, and Na, 2009; Evelo et al., 1996; Gottfredson, Wilson, and Najaka, 2002; Sprague et al., 2008). And the same is true for students participating in school-based mentoring programs that closely monitor school attendance, performance, and behavior (Cook, Gottfredson, and Na, 2009; Sinclair et al., 1998).

Carl never dropped out of school, but he did consider suicide. Javier had thought about dropping out, but didn't. His foster parents, his social worker, and others in his circle of support were able to convince him otherwise. Bill, on the other hand, did drop out. Soon after, he had a brief encounter with the juvenile justice system, the result of chronic truancy. Fortunately for him, there were no other contacts with legal authorities. Had he not joined the army, he might not have been so fortunate.

Zero Tolerance: Facts, Fear, and Force?

In an effort to better understand factors contributing to the school-to-prison pipeline, some experts in the field of prevention cite "zero tolerance" policies as a contributing cause. Zero tolerance policies bear some similarity to the "broken windows" theory of crime prevention (Gladwell, 1999; Kelling and Coles, 1996). The theory maintains that something as minor as a broken window in a building may actually communicate something important to those passing by. Among other things, it can look as though no one cares about the building, and no one is in control of its appearance. As a result, acts of vandalism can be expected to increase. The broken windows theory maintains that by paying attention to the small signs and signals (broken windows, graffiti, etc.), we can alter the social climate in ways that prevent and reduce crime. In the early 1990's, when the crime level in New York City was very high, the theory was put to a test. Subway trains were scrubbed clean. People entering subway stations without paying were apprehended by the police. Other minor infractions were treated with similarly harsh consequences. In light of the far more serious crimes occurring in the city daily, some felt that it made little sense to assume such a tough stance toward these less serious infractions. Yet crime in the city decreased. Although other factors likely played a part, some attributed the decrease to changes inspired by the broken windows theory.

Zero tolerance policies rely on somewhat similar logic. By responding to offenses at school with strict, predetermined punishments such as suspension and expulsion, zero tolerance policies are intended to reduce serious behavioral incidents at school. This logic was likely the basis of a decision on the part of school administrators at an Oregon middle school. School administrators had learned that a handful of students were responsible for generating the vast majority of school discipline referrals for student misbehavior. Having exhausted all available resources, the school administrators expelled the students. To their surprise, a new handful of students were soon generating the majority of school discipline referrals (Jeffrey Sprague, personal communication, September 24, 2015).

Hypothetically, imagine the same handful of expelled students in first grade. Might any of them have been exhibiting paradoxically uneven learning and behavioral profiles? Though we can never know for sure, it's certainly possible. I recently reviewed the school histories of several high school students who were either suspended or expelled. The majority evidenced uneven profiles.

What's more, their school histories revealed that this trend went as far back as the first grade. Most exhibited long-standing problems in regulating their emotions and behavior. Problems in this regard also appeared related to executive function weaknesses. Co-occurring learning disabilities were also common. In a few instances, interpersonal trauma was also suspected.

Some of these histories were similar to Carl's, others were similar to Javier's. Others seemed similar to Bill's. All of these students received multiple and ongoing interventions in hopes of improving their behavior. The interventions, however, proved ineffective, and problems grew increasingly more serious over the years. In each case, the last of these interventions was suspension or expulsion.

As we know, when remedies for learning, behavioral, or other challenges are based on erroneous perceptions, disappointing outcomes can result. Such may have been the case for these suspended or expelled students. Conversations with school study team members who knew them well and were aware of their multiple emotional and behavioral challenges reveal that their years of school failure and frustration were influenced by the same five misperceptions discussed in part I of this book.

New perceptions, on the other hand, lead to new possibilities, among them easier access to contextual influences (three agents of change) that can offset childhood risks associated with negative later life outcomes. With respect to the hypothetical first-graders, consider the possibilities if experiences and interventions had instead been guided by the new perceptions discussed in previous chapters.

Final Thoughts

Studies suggest that a number of risk factors contribute to youth violence, youth crime, and future incarceration (Wasserman et al., 2003). Peer influences have to be considered, as do family and neighborhood influences, among other factors. Specific skill sets have to be kept in mind as well, including skills in regulating emotions and controlling behavior. (We covered strategies for building these skill sets in Chapter 7.) Studies also suggest that certain risk combinations pose more serious problems than others. One particularly worrisome combination appears to be neurological vulnerability co-occurring with exposure to severe abuse. Studies conducted by Dorothy Lewis, M.D. showed the highest rates of criminal activity occurring among youth whose histories revealed both risks in combination (Gladwell, 1997; Lewis, 1998). Lewis drew further attention to this worrisome combination in a study she conducted involving children on the inpatient unit of Bellevue Hospital in New York. Of the 55 children in the study, 21 had engaged in some form of homicidal behavior. What distinguished these 21 children from the others were signs of neurological vulnerability and exposure to abusive and violent experiences.

Still, there's reason to believe that certain protective processes can offset multiple risks. Results from the Kauai Longitudinal Study, for example, revealed that some youth who were in trouble with the law were actually managing their lives well at age 40.

A Word of Caution

Here is where I add a word of caution. Not everyone in the Kauai Longitudinal Study rebounded from a troubled past. About one in six of the original sample was having difficulty at age 40. Included among them were also a small number of chronic criminal offenders. By age 18, these chronic offenders had been arrested at least four times.

A Ray of Hope

We know that by age 10, these chronic offenders from the Kauai Longitudinal Study had already been identified as having serious school-related problems and being in need of remedial help. We also know they attended school at a time when learning, behavioral, emotional, and other challenges were viewed very differently than they are today. Much less was known about neurodevelopmental challenges or the impact of environmental influences on how children learn, behave, and express their emotions. Today it's far more possible to provide these children the benefits of a meaningful and rewarding school day, much like Steven enjoyed when he was a child. If you recall, Steven's developmental trajectory resembled trajectories of those in the Kauai Longitudinal Study who beat the odds and didn't succumb to the effects of multiple risk exposure. Steven will attest to the important role that school played in his eventual life success. The first day of first grade was a turning point in his life. School provided access to contextual influences that allowed him to succeed in spite of risk exposure. Herein lies a ray of hope. Weaving these contextual influences in and around a school day may well do the same for at least some children who struggle much like Werner and Smith's chronic criminal offender's did when they were 10, as it also may for some, if not all, of our hypothetical first graders.

Positive Pipelines to Positive Life Outcomes

Eliminating the school-to-prison pipeline isn't only about eliminating a path leading to negative life outcomes. It's about providing new pathways to positive life outcomes. Creating a meaningful and rewarding school day for children exposed to multiple risks can help accomplish this. It provides opportunities for them to learn something about life that those who failed at school never had the opportunity to learn: our actions control our destiny. Experiences that teach us this in one life area can often help us endure challenges we experience in other life areas. Just ask Steven.

Finally, in the spirit of new, positive pipelines leading to better life outcomes, here is a brief update on the middle school that expelled a handful of students responsible for the majority of the school's serious behavioral incident reports. Recall that administrators soon realized that in the months that followed, a different handful of students were again responsible for the vast majority of school discipline referrals. School administrators eventually embarked upon an entirely new school-wide approach toward preventing and reducing similarly serious behavioral incidents. With the help of Jeffrey Sprague and colleagues at the University of Oregon's Institute on Violence and Destructive Behavior, school staff received training in School-wide Positive Behavior Intervention and Supports (SWPBIS). At the start of the academic year, school staff incorporated tertiary (targeted) prevention practices that served as an alternative to suspension or expulsion. Universal (primary) prevention practices were also introduced in an effort to create a social climate where all students felt they belonged, including students with learning, behavioral, social, and other differences. Secondary (selected) prevention practices were introduced as well, which provided supports to students showing early signs of developing more serious problems down the road.

These efforts proved successful. School discipline referrals decreased dramatically school-wide, and the majority of discipline referrals were no longer being generated by a small number of students. Sprague and colleagues proved what a number of prevention scientists have been thinking for some time now. It's indeed possible to prevent and reduce youth violence, youth crime, and future risk of incarceration, one school day at a time.

SUMMARY

- Deutschman studied agents of change among prison inmates following parole, focusing on parolees with long criminal histories that resulted in lengthy prison terms. Recidivism rates in these instances are known to be very high.
- Some parolees changed their ways. Those who did seemed to rely on the same three agents of change: relate, repeat, reframe.
- The opportunity to engage in constant, repetitive successful behaviors produced clear and immediate feelings of success, and more important, a feeling of hope in parolees. By acting this way, some came to see themselves this way (reframe).
- Researchers who study the school-to-prison pipeline note that 80 percent of prison inmates never earned their high school diploma. Helping students succeed at school and helping them stay in school can reduce future rates of incarceration.
- Years of school failure and frustration can arise as a result of the five erroneous perceptions.
- New perceptions can lead to new possibilities, among them easier access to agents of change (contextual influences) that can offset childhood risks associated with negative later life outcomes.

Chapter 10

PREVENTING CHILD
ABUSE AND NEGLECT,
ONE SCHOOL DAY AT A TIME

With funding from the Doris Duke Charitable Foundation, the Center for the Study of Social Policy launched the Strengthening Families Initiative, a broad strategy for preventing child abuse and neglect. Unlike previous approaches to prevention that concentrated on identifying family risks and deficits, this new program focuses on five protective factors. Each factor promotes family strengths and resilience in the face of adversity. Each has also been linked through research to reduced incidents of child abuse and neglect. The five protective factors are (1) parental resilience, (2) social connections, (3) knowledge of parenting and child development, (4) concrete support in times of need (including access to mental health and other services, and (5) healthy social and emotional development. The first four protective factors buffer families and promote strength and resilience, while the fifth promotes healthy child development (Center for the Study of Social Policy, 2007).

1. Parent Resilience: The ability to bounce back from challenges. While studies show that the majority of maltreating parents were themselves subjected to abusive and/or neglectful experiences as children, research also shows that the majority of parents who were maltreated as children do not go on to

217

be maltreating parents (Egeland, Bosquet, and Levy-Chung, 2002). Among the reasons, according to some experts, is their ability to "love well," derived in part by their exposure to supportive and caring relationships (Higgins, 1994).

2. Social Connections: The family's circle of support, including other family members, friends, neighbors, and others in the community. Studies show a link between social isolation and child maltreatment (Center for the Study of Social Policy, 2007). Conversely, social connections and social safety nets can serve to buffer parents from risks associated with child maltreatment.

3. Knowledge of Parenting and Child Development: Access to information and knowledge necessary to raise children, including information that helps families understand appropriate expectations for behavior. Experts have found a link between child maltreatment and a parent's lack of understanding of normal child development. In instances where parents lack this understanding, common stresses of childrearing can trigger harsh and punitive reactions (Rappucci, Britner, and Woolard, 1997).

4. Concrete Supports in Times of Need: Access to financial resources to cover day-to-day expenses, including unexpected costs. This also includes access to health care resources (Medicaid or insurance), and access to informal support from social networks in times of need. Parents susceptible to maltreating their children are often exposed to multiple sources of stress in the absence of resources that would allow them to cope more successfully.

5. Social and Emotional Competence: A child's ability to interact positively with others and express emotions effectively. Children's misbehavior can result from a number of different sources, and may not be the result of willfulness or manipulation. Knowledge of effective practices for increasing children's social and emotional skills reduces the likelihood of harsh and punitive reactions to behaviors that may be beyond a child's ability to control.

More than 30 states currently embrace the five protective factor model. These states are actively engaged in training professionals and caregivers to help families access these factors and in the process, grow stronger and more resilient in the face of challenging life circumstances (Center for the Study of Social Policy, 2009, 2011).

But for even the strongest and most resilient of families, there are limits to emotional endurance. And among the most potent forces capable of driving families toward these limits is human misunderstanding.

Our five understandable yet erroneous perceptions about the paradoxically uneven learning and behavioral profiles of otherwise resilient children can lead to entirely understandable yet ineffective remedies, which unfortunately may lead to disappointing results. And this can even be the case for families with access to the five evidence based protective factors just described. It can be the case for (1) parents who, in spite of their resilient ways, are emotionally depleted, having exhausted every resource they know in an effort to help their child, to no avail; (2) families that enjoy a wide circle of support that includes social connections with other family members, friends, and others in the community, all of whom may be equally depleted by a child's uneven ways; (3) parents who are knowledgeable about parenting and child development as it pertains to children not given to these uneven profiles and who, as a result, fully expect logical consequences for behavioral errors to result in better results; (4) parents who have access to concrete supports in times of need, including access to financial resources to cover day-to-day expenses and access to health care resources, none of which may lead to greater understanding of a child's uneven ways; and (5) parents who are knowledgeable about social and emotional competencies in childhood, again as these competencies pertain to children not given to paradoxically uneven learning and behavioral profiles. Fifteen-minute homework assignments that take three hours to complete and then are not turned in the following day can be as mystifying to experts in child development as to nonexperts.

But if human misunderstanding can serve to weaken the protective properties of the five protective factor model, then human understanding can strengthen them—human understanding, that is, of our context-sensitive ways. Proponents of the five-factor model can thus immunize strong and resilient families by helping them replace misperceptions with empirically validated ones.

SUMMARY

- The Strengthening Families Initiative, a broad based strategy for preventing child abuse and neglect, focuses on five protective factors: (1) parental resilience, (2) social connections, (3) knowledge of parenting and child development, (4) concrete support in times of need (including access to mental health and other services), and (5) healthy social and emotional development.
- Even families with access to these protective factors can fall prey to the misperceptions outlined in Chapter 1.

Chapter 11

WHAT CAN BE:
THE ADULT YEARS

REPAIRING AND STRENGTHENING OUR CLOSEST PERSONAL AND PROFESSIONAL RELATIONSHIPS

It can bring promising careers to a screeching halt, bring loving marriages to a bitter end, pit caring parents against talented teachers, and as we've already seen, transform otherwise resilient young children into demoralized young adults.

CAREER DAMAGE

Up until his early 30s, John worked as a real estate agent for a company in Southern California and was making enough money to put a down payment on a new home, send his two children to private school, and get out from under years of debt. What's more, he was very good at what he did. Company executives would tell you he was among the highest income-generating agents they had. But then the unthinkable occurred: John was fired. Why? Although executives didn't come out and say it in these exact words, they felt that the company cared more about John than he did about the company. Why else would he be late for important meetings, not get his paperwork in on time, forget to return phone calls, or forget to follow directions from his supervisor? Why would he continue to make these same mistakes despite constant reminders—reminders that eventually turned into warnings? There was only one logical explanation. The company cared more about John than he cared about the company, and that's not the culture that executives wanted to promote. So they fired him.

Company executives had no way of knowing it at the time, but they were completely wrong about John. He cared very much about the company. But he was paying the price for a problem he's had for as long as he could remember. Despite knowing what he's supposed to do, he has a difficult time consistently, predictably, and independently doing what he knows. And not only did it cost him the best job he ever had, it was about to cost him his marriage as well.

ENDING MARRIAGES

John's 12-year marriage was in jeopardy because, his wife says, "It's obvious that he cares a lot less about me than I care about him. Why else would he say he's going to do one thing, then completely do another? It's like he doesn't listen to a word I say. Just yesterday, all he had to do was be back home by 5:00 PM so we could make it to our child's play at school on time. He promised me he would get back here by five. I was counting on him. Our son was counting on him. He lied to us. I've put up with this for years, and I'm sick of it. I'm already raising two kids. I don't have time to raise a third. Enough. It's over." It's easy to understand why she feels the way she does, and she's right about John's irresponsible behavior. But she's wrong about John caring less about her than she cares about him. It appears that way, logically speaking. But nothing could be further from the truth.

PARENTS VS. TEACHERS

It had been a long time since John and his wife had a full week of calm, relaxing, and enjoyable evenings at home. That's because at least once or twice a week during the school year, for as long as they could remember, they would argue and fight over the same thing: how to get their son, now 10, to complete a 15-minute homework assignment in less than three hours! The stress this was adding to their already strained relationship was actually contributing to their possible breakup. John and his wife blamed their son's teacher, who, by the way, blamed them: "He can do it in 15 minutes if he wants to. Be more consistent. Set limits. I think he's manipulating you." Differences of opinion grew into a war of words, hurt feelings, and angry threats.

For John, a few of the classic misperceptions were taking their toll on virtually every aspect of his life. Things went from bad to worse. He grew increasingly depressed and began drinking heavily. When intoxicated, he would become enraged and lash out violently at his wife and children. One of his two kids bore the greatest brunt of his enraged episodes, the ten-year-old.

Years have passed since these tumultuous times, and the news is good. John, now retired, went on to start his own business. He and his wife are still married, now happily. Their son made it through school and eventually started his own successful business. And John and his wife developed a deep respect for teachers of students who learn and behave in uneven ways.

John, by the way, is someone we've already met. He's Carl's father. And the 10-year-old who took three hours to complete a 15-minute homework assignment? That was Carl. As it turns out, misperceptions can be passed down from parent to child.

At first I feared that I might be overstating the impact that a few erroneous perceptions can have on our lives. But as I thought more about it, I began to realize that I may have actually been understating their effect. Over the years, I've had the opportunity to get to know a number of people who rebounded from a difficult past, including those whose school and adult life experiences resembled Carl's. I've had the opportunity to get to know their spouses and partners, on occasion their parents and siblings, on other occasions even their co-workers and employers. Story after story, the underlying message is clear. These misperceptions don't disappear once we're done with school. In some instances, they affect us throughout our entire lives, and in the process do serious harm. The preceding description of John's earlier plight was not an exaggeration.

The good news is that in many cases these damaging outcomes can be prevented and damaged relationships not only repaired but strengthened. These and many other positive outcomes are all achievable, given greater awareness of the often inconspicuous effects that contextual influences can have on virtually every aspect of our lives. In the sections that follow, we continue our earlier discussion, with particular attention to how contextual blind spots can affect our closest relationships. We begin by revisiting the effects of cognitive dissonance, this time from a relational point of view. We then move on to two new blind spots.

COGNITIVE DISSONANCE REVISITED

Cognitive dissonance, it turns out, can play a significant role in how we relate to others and in how others relate to us. Furthermore, it can do so without us being aware of it. Start with a very common and admirable personal belief: I am a good and caring person, for example. Now imagine yourself in a situation where you act in an entirely contradictory way to this belief. Say you do something to hurt someone, and you can't attribute this action to any reason. No one asked you to do it. You weren't coerced. It wasn't part of your job. You have no ready explanation for why you did what you did. Based on cognitive dissonance theory, you convince yourself the person deserved it. Cognitive dissonance theory says that to preserve our self-view as a good and caring person, we can change how we feel about the person we hurt. Studies by social psychologist Elliot Aronson (1995, 2010) showed cases in which this is exactly what occurred. We're used to believing that how we view a person influences how we act toward them. Aronson's research says something very different: that how we act toward the person can influence how we view the person.

Recall the three common interventions that Alan Deutschman identified, the ones we often rely on to motivate people having difficulty changing their behavior: facts, fear, and force. When they don't work as well as we might hope, we can feel hurt and angry. And being human, we say things we may not really mean. Cognitive dissonance theory shows that we can convince ourselves we did mean it. People of high integrity don't say mean and nasty things about other people for no reason, unless of course, those things are true.

Being more alert to the dynamics of cognitive dissonance theory can prevent us from believing the things we say out of hurt and anger. This awareness can also be very important to people who struggle with various life challenges or differences. People of strong character, for example, don't go around saying unkind things about other people, their teachers and former employers included, unless of course they manage to convince themselves that what they say is true. These dynamics affect us all—the misperceivers and the misperceived alike.

When allowed to operate under our radar, cognitive dissonance theory appears capable of convincing us that the things we may have said out of hurt and anger, things we really didn't mean, we really did mean after all. As an aside, cognitive dissonance can also work in reverse. When we do something nice for someone, or when we do a favor for someone we don't know, we may actually come to like that person more. "We do not love people so much for the good they have done us," wrote Tolstoy, "but for the good we have done them" (quoted in Aronson, 1995).

TWO MORE BARRIERS

As a result of misperceptions, we said things we didn't mean and hurt the people we care the most about. We held on to entrenched, erroneous beliefs and discarded more enlightened ones. We are far more understanding now than we were in the past, and we're truly sorry. Forgive and forget. Let bygones be bygones.

Understanding the dynamics underlying cognitive dissonance puts us on a new and hopeful path for this to occur. Unfortunately though, two other potential barriers may lie ahead that can prevent us from repairing and strengthening our most important personal and professional relationships. Researchers refer to the first one as "relational devaluation" and to the second one as "the magnitude gap."

Relational Devaluation

"He's doing it on purpose. He knows what he's supposed to do. He just doesn't want to." In the heat of the moment, it can feel as though there's only one plausible explanation for why someone would be so inconsistent and unpredictable in keeping their word and handling their responsibilities: The person must not care as much about us as we care about them. Researchers refer to this perception as "relational devaluation" (Leary and Springer, 2001). Someone we are close to said or did something that got us believing that they don't feel as close to us as we feel toward them. It doesn't mean the person doesn't love us, and it doesn't mean the person doesn't value the relationship. It's more a matter of degree.

How common is this? When Leary and Springer (2001) reviewed narratives of events that people wrote describing incidents of hurt feelings—118 people's experiences were reviewed in all—they found evidence of relational devaluation in all narratives. Hurt feelings also linger. In one of the reviewed studies, 90 percent of participants reported that when they think about past events that caused hurt feelings—events that happened between 1 and 10 years ago—they continue to evoke hurt feelings. Furthermore, we seem to cause the greatest hurt to the people we care the most about. Participants in another of the studies attributed only 2 percent of hurtful experiences to strangers. On the other hand, roughly 70 percent were attributable to close friends and romantic or dating partners and roughly 26 percent to family members, acquaintances, teachers, and coaches. The more we want someone to value our relationship, the more we risk feeling devalued, and the more likely we are to experience hurt feelings as a result.

John's wife says, "It's obvious he cares a lot less about me than I care about him." According to John's boss, "The company cares more about John than he cares about the company. That's not the culture that executives wanted to promote." The Williams' to their son Carl: "We know you can finish your work if you really want to. We've seen you do it. Why won't you just do it?" From spouses, to partners, to employers, to co-workers, to parents, to teachers, we can find story after story of caring individuals reaching out to lend a helping hand and who, in return, feel devalued by those they seek to help or better understand. Left unattended, relational devaluation can do serious harm to our closest personal and professional relationships.

Although the people closest to John misunderstood some of the reasons underlying his uneven ways, did he also misunderstand the actions and reactions of some of these people? Yes he did. In fact, when we delve deeper into the nature of human perception and our meaning-making ways, we find that we're all susceptible to misunderstanding others, and we are all, at one time or another, misunderstood. As we're about to see, this may help explain why in some instances it can be so hard to forgive.

The Magnitude Gap

Letting go of a hurt we've been carrying around too long is a gift to ourselves, with documented health benefits, both physical and emotional. But if it's such a gift, why is it so hard to do? Roy Baumeister (1999) has a theory, beautifully borne out in a study. Volunteers were asked to write about something they did that made another person very angry, then write about something someone else did that made them very angry. Thus they produced two narratives, one as victimizer, the other as victim. The stories were as different as night and day. As victimizer, subjects usually saw their actions as unintentional, the result of extraneous circumstances beyond their control. And they believed the person they angered was overreacting. "Why can't they let bygones be bygones?" On the receiving end, perceptions were entirely different. "The S.O.B. did it on purpose." "He knew what he was doing." "She knew how I would feel." "How could anyone be so insensitive?"

As victim, volunteers were more likely to perceive deliberate intent. It's about character, not context. They remembered the smallest details. Let bygones be bygones? Not according to those victimized. According to Baumeister, it's "never forget."

At some point, we're all perpetrators of hurtful experiences in the eyes of others. At some point, we're also on the receiving end. And there appear to be predictable differences in how we perceive events based on which of these two roles we occupy at any given moment. Baumeister refers to these differences in perception as "the magnitude gap." The magnitude gap helps explain why it's sometimes so hard to forgive. Victimizers and victims can view the same event or experience very differently, each convinced their perceptions are accurate and based on fact, each truly believing they're right. As victimizer then, are we supposed to feel remorseful and apologize? For what? If we do apologize, are we sincere about it? Do we really understand how our actions registered in the mind of whomever we hurt or angered? As victim, our wounds may run deep, possibly the result of a perception of events quite different than that of our victimizer. For the victim, though, there's one important difference. The victim may feel there's a debt to be paid. Someone did something perceived to be intentionally harmful, and that's not fair.

Here's where the magnitude gap comes into play. Victims are likely to calibrate their retaliatory strikes based on the degree of hurt they feel. Remember, victims often interpreted deliberate intent into the hurtful actions of others. They remember what happened to them for longer periods of time and in greater detail than did the person who hurt them. Retaliatory behaviors—direct or indirect—are calibrated according to how badly we were hurt. On the receiving end of these retaliatory strikes, victimizers might find themselves confused or in a state of disbelief. "Why are you reacting this way? Can't you see that I didn't mean to hurt you? Don't you see the reasons that I did what I did?" Hurt and angry for reasons that are unclear or that are felt to be unjustified, the victimizer's perception can change to one of victim, and as victim there may be a debt to pay. Baumeister's simple experiment shows how grievances between people can spiral completely out of control as a result of the magnitude gap.

Unfortunately for John, the last thing his employer was about to do was forgive him. Nor was John's wife in a forgiving frame of mind. John was saying one thing but doing another. He and his wife were hardly forgiving of Carl's work habits. Fifteen-minute assignments shouldn't take three hours.

Forgiving those we care about is what we do to repair our most important personal and professional relationships. It allows us to put value back in a relationship we perceived as devalued. But forgiving others is not something we're inclined to do when we're convinced our perceptions are accurate and our actions are justified. We are all susceptible to misperceptions and we are all likely to be misinterpreted from time to time. Fortunately, as we become more aware of how common it is for us to view things differently depending on which end of a misunderstanding we find ourselves, we're more likely to find it easier to let go of hurt and anger and allow ourselves the gift of forgiveness.

WHAT CAN BE

By way of review, misperceptions need not damage people's careers, cause irreparable harm to relationships, pit caring parents against caring teachers, caring employers against equally caring employees, or transform resilient children into demoralized young adults. In many cases, these damaging outcomes can be prevented and our damaged relationships not only repaired but strengthened. All of these outcomes are achievable, given greater human understanding. And greater human understanding is achievable given greater awareness of the often inconspicuous role that contextual influences play in the meaning we attach to the events, conditions, and experiences occurring in our lives. But achieving this awareness is often easier said than done. We suffer from contextual blind spots that override our best intentions. The good news is that these blind spots can be removed. Hopefully, the discussion here has helped to do this.

SUMMARY

- Misperceptions don't disappear once we're done with school. In some instances they can affect us throughout our entire lives, and do serious harm to relationships.
- In many cases damaging outcomes can be prevented and damaged relationships repaired and strengthened with a greater awareness of contextual influences.
- Cognitive dissonance appears capable of convincing us that we really did mean the things we may have said out of hurt and anger, things we really didn't mean.
- There is evidence of relational devaluation in most cases of hurt feelings. We seem to cause the greatest hurt to the people we care the most about.
- The magnitude gap explains why it's sometimes so hard to forgive. Victimizers and victims can view the same event or experience very differently, each convinced their perceptions are accurate and based on fact, and each truly believing they're right.

PART II SUMMARY

Prevention specialists are becoming increasingly aware of the impact of multiple childhood risk exposure on later life outcomes. We now know, for example, that as risk exposure increases, so does our vulnerability to a host of potential learning, behavioral, emotional, and later life medical problems, if these risks exist in the absence of protective mechanisms that can neutralize or outweigh their impact. In addition, recent studies have identified a link between exposure to multiple categories of adverse childhood experiences and behavioral and stress-related risk factors associated with early death (Felitti et al., 1998; http://www.acestudy.org). Exposure to multiple childhood risks and adversities can stretch even the most resilient among us beyond the limits of emotional endurance.

A number of childhood risks and adverse life experiences can also translate into learning and behavioral profiles typically perceived in entirely understandable yet erroneous ways. Case in point: chart reviews chosen randomly from a school serving children and youth with serious learning, behavioral, and emotional challenges revealed the presence of multiple childhood risk exposure on one hand, and the presence of uneven learning and behavioral profiles on the other. Perhaps this should come as no surprise, as almost all of these histories showed evidence of co-occurring executive function problems and learning disabilities. In addition, most students met diagnostic criteria for ADHD, and more than half were believed to be suffering from the effects of traumatic stress (interpersonal trauma).

Multiple childhood risk exposure seems in many cases to translate into uneven learning and behavioral profiles. These profiles can, in turn, translate into misperceptions on the part of loving parents, caring teachers, and expert health care professionals. This can result in understandable interventions that can unfortunately lead to disappointing results.

Lessons learned from those who overcame exposure to adverse childhood experiences, among them those who failed at school but who succeed at life, show us that many people do eventually rise above their difficult past. In doing so, several contextual influences seem to play an important role in helping them create a pathway to a better quality of life. Why were they unable to access these contextual influences decades earlier? The reason can be traced back to a few entirely understandable yet erroneous perceptions.

Human misunderstanding, it turns out, may be our most powerful risk mechanism for prolonging a difficult past. The good news is that human understanding may turn out to be our most powerful protective mechanism for rising above one, human understanding that is, of our context-sensitive ways.

Chapter 12

~~~~~≈≈≈≫

ARE THERE THINGS THAT COUNT THAT CAN'T BE COUNTED? AND DO THE THINGS WE COUNT, COUNT?

It's high noon on the savanna. You and two fellow behavioral biologists huddle together behind a bush, peering through your binoculars at what must be hundreds of zebras, each one looking more or less identical. Your job: observe just one. Observe everything it does, everywhere it goes. It seems impossible. They all look so alike. Here's your solution. Tiptoe up to the closest one in the herd and, marker in hand, place a tiny little spot slightly to the side of its rump, high enough to be visible through the thick brush. "Great idea," say your colleagues. Thanks to this ingenious solution, it's easy to distinguish your zebra from the others.

You leave your hiding post to attend to other business and return the next day to start your work. But there's a problem. You can't find your zebra. Having never read anything by Robert Sapolsky (1998), you're sure it's roaming around out there behind the herd, never to be seen again. "Wait," you say. "There are hundreds of zebras out there. We'll just do it again." So you do, again successfully. It's time for another break. A few hours pass, and it's back to work. But once more, the new zebra is nowhere to be found. Frustrated, you place a mark on the rump of a third zebra, this time not letting it out of your sight. For hours you and your fellow researchers observe its every move. Then you notice something ominous. About a quarter of a mile away, a pride of lions are gathered, their eyes fixed on the herd of zebras. With no warning, they attack your zebra! The one with the spot on its rump! To your horror, they catch it, and have it for dinner. Your stomach churns. Now you know what happened to the two other zebras.

As your shock subsides, you realize that a couple of important lessons were learned on the savanna. First, in a world perceived as threatening and dangerous, appearing conspicuously different from a survival point of view can make things a lot worse than they already are. Second, no matter how much you want to help zebras, if you're unaware of the real dangers they have to contend with every day, inadvertently, you may do more harm than good.

≫

It was a very special place. Or an awful place. A place where you learned about your greatest gifts and talents or your worst short-comings. Where you came to see yourself as smarter than most or not very smart at all. Where you found the confidence you needed to succeed in the world or learned that you'll never amount to much. It was a place where you saw firsthand the value of persever-ance or the futility of perseverance. It was a very warm and friendly place or a very mean and nasty place The place? School.

A number of people currently enjoy meaningful and success-ful lives, thanks largely to their earlier school experiences. And a number of others enjoy meaningful and successful lives *in spite of* their school experiences. Up until recently, not much attention was paid to successful people who did poorly in school. One reason was that few among us probably realized how many of these people are actually out there. But another and even bigger reason might be that many of us doubted it was actually possible. Those doubts are understandable. After all, think of the thousands of hours people spent trying their hardest to help these failing children turn things around in school, sometimes with little or nothing to show for it. And if these children continued to struggle and fail in school with all this help and support, how could they ever succeed in the real world without it?

What did we miss? Why were we so wrong about them? Remem-ber the zebra—the one with that inconspicuous spot on its rump. That dot may be inconspicuous to us maybe, but not to a zebra trying to survive in a threatening and dangerous environment. To a zebra, being conspicuously different in places where difference signals threat and danger can make things a lot more threatening and dangerous than they already are. What we missed was that humans are inclined to feel the same way. We forgot that in a world we perceive as threatening and dangerous, appearing conspicuously different can make things a lot worse than they already are. And no matter how much we might want to reach out and help others, struggling school-age children included, if we can't take the danger out of difference, we may do more harm than good.

So to all those zebras out there—who by the end of first grade were already convinced beyond a shadow of a doubt that they were dumb, stupid, or bad, who would get physically sick before tests or the day report cards came out, who would tremble in fear as the school bully drew near and feel angry and alone when others stood by and did nothing, who were mercilessly stigmatized and ridiculed daily for the problems they experienced, then stigmatized and ridiculed even more for seeing doctors, therapists, learning specialists, or others simply trying to help them overcome or navigate around these problems, who felt terrible about not being able to be the person those they loved the most wanted them to be, and who ultimately came to see school as one shameful and humiliating experience after another—know that your strength and courage under very difficult circumstances did not go unnoticed. On the contrary, your experiences provide important lessons that can be used to improve the lives of countless others. These lessons are many, too many to cover in a single book. Still, it seems important that we highlight at least some of them.

First, thank you for helping us appreciate the important role that human understanding plays in overcoming a difficult past, not to mention the role that misunderstanding plays in prolonging one. Your experiences have shown us that the meaning we attach to life's adversities, past and present, can determine whether we come to see ourselves as resilient and courageous on one hand or helpless and hopeless on the other. They also show us that the meaning others attach to our adversities past or present can influence the meaning we ourselves attach to those same adversities. It takes a lot of strength and courage to see life's adversities in a new light. But for even the most resilient among us, it may not always be possible when too many others can only see them in a very old light. Thanks to you we also know that a few seemingly logical yet erroneous perceptions about the uneven ways some of us respond to our day-to-day lives can lead to very unfortunate outcomes for a number of otherwise resilient children. What's more, we also now know that these same erroneous perceptions decades later can cause great harm to our most cherished personal and professional relationships.

Thanks to you, we can now see that resilient people sometimes think and act differently within social contexts that are warm and friendly rather than mean and nasty. When it comes to understanding human resilience, in other words, context counts—more so than most of us realize. And you show us how adept people can be at raising personal expectations while simultaneously leveling their playing field. The creative ways you use tools, technologies, strategies, and available resources to navigate learning, behavioral, and other challenges is a testament to your resilient spirit.

Through your many years of trial and error, you also show us that it's not always trying harder that allows people to master the simple things. Sometimes it's trying differently. You teach us as well that it's entirely possible to know what to do yet have difficulty consistently, predictably, and independently doing what we know, in part because they call into play different skills. Improving the ability to consistently execute sometimes requires learning a new set of strategies related specifically to these functions. Thank you for helping us appreciate this.

What's more, you prove that rarely is there anything so wrong with us that what's right with us can't fix. You're living proof that our strengths are more than capable of overriding whatever weaknesses we might be struggling with. It all depends on what we choose to focus on.

You show us the many different ways of being smart, different ways that can't be measured by how well one does in school. Based on your life experiences, there's good reason to believe that knowing this and truly believing this can often outweigh the emotional effects of a lifetime of stigmatizing and devaluing judgments about our abilities and future capabilities.

Through your life experiences you help us see that no matter how smart one might be in whatever areas, it does not make them wise. To be wise is to know how to use our strengths and our successful life experiences to serve not only our own personal needs but the needs of others as well.

Furthermore, you show that overcoming life's hardships may sometimes have less to do with the strength that lies within us and more to do with the strength that lies between us. Our greatest source of resilience may actually be each other.

You're also helping solve a mystery that's plagued a lot of people for a long time—teachers, employers, health care providers, mental health professionals, spouses, partners, and family members included. The mystery of why talented people of all ages can be so productive when it comes to doing interesting and intellectually challenging things, but far less productive when it comes to doing things that seem so simple. The problem is what to call it. The reality is that we may never find one name or label that fully captures this mysterious human phenomenon. That's been frustrating to a lot of people, so much so that some have stopped searching. The result? Entirely understandable yet erroneous perceptions: it's a matter of character, a lack of emotional strength, or a lack of resilience. To the contrary, you're some of the most hard-working, resourceful, and resilient people one would ever want to meet. And many of you always have been, from the first day of school through today.

Thanks to you, we know more than ever before about how to legitimize and validate human differences so that those fighting to succeed in spite of these differences see themselves as resilient and courageous, rather than helpless and hopeless. When we put our minds to it, we also know how to create conditions that highlight personal strengths in ways that help us see our weaknesses in the context of these strengths. We even know how to create conditions that value what we have to contribute and motivate us to contribute even more, when we put our minds to it. In other words, we know exactly how to take the danger out of difference. The problem is that we usually forget to do it, which can help explain why those thousands of hours of help, year after year, by dedicated and caring people trying to change troubled lives might not have produced the results that were hoped for. They were provided in places where feeling different felt very dangerous.

Thanks to you, we know now that children who succumb to adversity can eventually rise above a difficult past and go on to lead successful lives. What's more, this can be the case for children who succumb to a range of different adverse childhood experiences, beyond those leading to school failure.

Finally, you prove that it's impossible to predict with absolute certainty any person's life course. It's among the mysteries in life that makes one a believer in turning point experiences; in second-, third-, and fourth-chance opportunities; in knowing that lives can change for the better at any point in time, sometimes in response to completely unanticipated and unpredictable events. It goes to prove that when it comes to overcoming life's adversities, there are things that count that can't be counted, and not everything we count, counts.

ACKNOWLEDGMENTS

It's really true. Our greatest source of strength is each other. This book would never have been completed had Terri and I not enjoyed the unwavering support of a number of people. We wish to acknowledge some of them below. Others we will be visiting soon, and delivering them this book, with a personalized inscription recognizing how much we cherish their friendship and support.

Thank you Ken Heying, Roland Rotz, Amy Ellis, Gretchen Gillingham, Jeff Rowe, Meg Lawrence and Danielle Miller. Thank you not only for your friendship, but for the way you touch so many people's lives, personally and professionally. A special thanks to you, Gretchen, for how you help people—children and adults—see life's challenges in a hopeful new light. Who would have thought that a simple gift bag symbolizing unique strengths and talents could have meant so much to so many for so long. A special thanks to you too, Ken. It's no coincidence that you were the first to read a draft of this book.

On the first Friday after the publication of this book, I'll be personally delivering a copy to Jeff Penner. With a few exceptions (the result of unforeseen circumstances), Jeff and I have been having lunch together every Friday for over 30 years. He's a very close friend and also a very skilled health care professional. He specializes in helping people learn how to lead healthier, more active lives. Jeff will be seeing his name in print here for the first time, and reading about how much I value his friendship, and the work he does to help others avoid serious health-related illnesses.

To Hill Walker and Jeff Sprague, a special thank you to the two of you as well. Your work has touched so many lives for so many years, mine included.

To my dear friend Sharon Weiss, thank you for your support and encouragement. I'm so excited at the thought of personally delivering to you a copy of this book. Expect a visit soon after the book is published. Marie Paxson, Kristin Stanberry, and Stephanie Miyaki, you'll be receiving a personal copy as well. It's the least I can do to express my gratitude for your help, support, and encouragement.

To my friends at CHADD, thank you for helping make this nation more aware of the trials and tribulations of those impacted by ADHD, executive function challenges, and other learning differences. For those who share an interest in these areas of challenge, let me personally extend an invitation to you to attend a National CHADD Conference. You'll meet some of the top professionals in diverse fields of study, including education, psychology, psychiatry, and neuroscience, among others. More important perhaps, you'll also meet people from all walks of life who've journeyed a long way to educate themselves on the latest tools, technologies, and resources for helping those impacted by these and other challenges lead more successful lives. You'll also have the pleasure of meeting many of their loved ones as well.

My book has cited a number of trailblazers from wide ranging professional fields, each of whom has contributed significantly to our understanding of various risk factors (and/or other challenges) as well as ways to overcome them. I've included their websites or e-mail addresses on the book's web page so that you can contact them personally and learn more about their important work. I'd like to also mention a few here by name, and extend my sincere thanks: Vince Felitti, MD, Dennis Embry, PhD, Christian Moore, LCSW, Robert Brooks, PhD, Sam Goldstein, PhD, Michelle Garcia Winner, MA, SLP, and Leah Kuypers, MA Ed, OTR/L. And while on the topic of trailblazers, let me not forget to include some names already mentioned, Hill Walker, PhD, Jeff Sprague, PhD, and Jeff Rowe, MD in particular.

To the amazing teachers and other school staff at the High Tech Schools in San Diego, thank you for proving that schools can inspire students to dream big and to work hard in pursuit of those dreams. And to the teachers and other school staff at Health Sciences High and Middle College, you too are amazing. Never have I witnessed a school so adept at removing perceptions of threat and danger from difference. Where else do high school students put on a yearly conference for other local high school students focusing on ways to stamp out stigma?

To Lindsay Jones, daughter of the late Clare Jones, oh, how I miss your mother. I still think of her often and am so grateful to have had the opportunity to know her, to learn from her, and to be her friend.

I am deeply grateful to our team at W.W. Norton and Company for their guidance, expert feedback, and unwavering support. Thank you Deborah Malmud, Director of Professional Books, Elizabeth Baird, Project Editor, Ben Yarling, Associate Editor, Alison Lewis, Editorial Assistant, Kevin Olsen, Marketing and Publicity Director, and Natasha Senn, Marketing and Publicity Assistant. I feel so fortunate to have had the opportunity to work with you. A special thanks to you, Deborah, for making this book possible.

Finally, to all of those who have participated in our Monday evening meetings over the last 20 plus years, we hope that you have learned as much from us as we have from you. Here's wishing you a happy and healthy year. We hope to see you next Monday.

REFERENCES

ABC News. (Producer). (1993, January 23). *Common miracles: The new American revolution in learning* [video]. New York, NY: ABC News Store.

Abikoff, H., Nissley-Tsiopinis, J., Gallagher, R., Zambenedetti, M., Seyffert, M., Boorady, R., & McCarthy, J. (2009). Effects of MPH-OROS on the organizational, time management, and planning behaviors of children with ADHD. *Journal of the American Academy of Child and Adolescent Psychiatry, 48,* 166–75.

Advancement Project. (2005, March 24). *Education on lockdown: The schoolhouse to jailhouse track.* Washington, DC: Advancement Project. Retrieved from www.advancementproject.org.

American Psychiatric Association. (2013). *Diagnostic and statistical manual of mental disorders* (5th ed.). Arlington, VA: APA.

Anda, R. F. (2011). *The health and social impact of growing up with adverse childhood experiences: The human and economic cost of the status quo.* Retrieved from www.acestudy.org

Aronson, E. (1995). *The social animal* (7th ed.). New York, NY: Freeman.

Aronson, E., & Patnoe, S. (1997). *The jigsaw classroom.* New York, NY: Longman.

Aronson, E. (2000). *Nobody left to hate: Teaching compassion after Columbine.* New York, NY: Freeman.

Aronson, E. (2010). *Not by chance alone: My life as a social psychologist.* New York, NY: Basic Books.

Barkley, R. A. (2002, October). *Mental and medical outcomes of AD/HD.* Presented at the 14th Annual CHADD International Conference, Miami Beach, FL.

Barkley, R. A. (2010a). *Taking charge of adult ADHD.* New York, NY: Guilford Press.

Barkley, R. A. (2010b, November). *The role of emotion in understanding and managing ADHD.* Presented at the 22nd Annual CHADD International Conference, Atlanta, GA.

Barkley, R. A. (2011a). *Barkley Adult ADHD Rating Scale—IV.* New York, NY: Guilford Press.

Barkley, R. A. (2011b). *Barkley Deficits in Executive Functioning Scale (BDEFS).* New York, NY: Guilford Press.

Barkley, R. A. (2011c). *Barkley Functional Impairment Scale (BFIS).* New York, NY: Guilford Press.

Barkley, R. A. (2013*). Taking charge of ADHD,* 3rd ed.: *The complete authoritative guide for parents. New York,* NY: Guilford Press.

Barron, B. J., Schwartz, D. L., Vie, N. J., Moore, A., Petrosino, A., Zech, L., . . . Cognition and Technology Group at Vanderbilt. (1998). Doing with understanding: Lessons from research on problem and project-based learning. *Journal of Learning Sciences, 7*(3,4), 271–312.

Baumeister, R. (1999). *Evil: Inside human violence and cruelty.* New York, NY: Freeman.

Baumeister, R. F., & Tierney, J. (2011). *Willpower: Rediscovering the greatest human strength.* New York, NY: Penguin Press.

Baumeister, R. F., Twenge, J. M., & Nuss, C. K. (2002). Effects of social exclusion on cognitive processes: Anticipated aloneness reduces intelligent thought. *Journal of Personality and Social Psychology, 83,* 817–27.

Baumeister, R. F., Vohs, K. D., & Tice, D. M. (2007). The strength model of self-control. *Current Directions in Psychological Science, 16,* 396–403.

Beardslee, W., & Podorefsky, D. (1988). Resilient adolescents whose parents have serious affective and other psychiatric disorders:

Importance of self understanding and relationships. *American Journal of Psychiatry, 145,* 63–68.

Blackwell, L. S., Trzesniewski, K. H., & Dweck, C. S. (2007). Implicit theories of intelligence predict achievement across an adolescent transition: A longitudinal study and intervention. *Child Development, 78,* 246–63.

Blair, C., & Razza, R. P. (2007). Relating effortful control, executive function, and false belief understanding to emerging math and literacy ability in kindergarten. *Child Development, 78,* 647–63.

Boedrova, E., & Leong, D. (2007). *Tools of the mind: The Vygotskian approach to early childhood education* (2nd ed.). New York, NY: Prentice Hall.

Bowers, B. (2007, December 6). Tracing business acumen to dyslexia. *New York Times.* Retrieved from www.nytimes.com

Bransford, J. D., Brown, A. L., & Cocking, R. R. (Eds.). (2000). *How people learn: Brain, mind, experience, and school.* Washington, DC: Committee on Developments in the Science of Learning, National Academy Press.

Bremner, J. D. (2001). *Does stress damage the brain?* New York, NY: Norton.

Bremner, J. D., Southwick, S. M., Darnell, A., & Charney, D. S. (1993). Chronic PTSD in Vietnam combat veterans: Course of illness and substance abuse. *American Journal of Psychiatry, 153,* 369–75.

Brooks, R. (2013, November). *The power of the mindsets: Nurturing motivation and resilience in children with ADHD and ourselves.* Presented at the 25th Annual CHADD International Conference, Washington, DC.

Brown, T. E. (2014). *Smart but stuck: Emotions in teens and adults with ADHD.* San Francisco, CA: Jossey-Bass.

Brown, T. E., & Quinlan, D. M. (1999). *Executive function impairments in high I.Q. individuals with ADHD.* Presented at the International Society for Research on Child and Adolescent Psychopathology, Barcelona, Spain.

Bryant-Davis, T. (2003, April). *The path to wholeness: African American adult survivors of childhood violence.* Presented at Children and Trauma: Coping in the Aftermath, Children's Institute International's National Forum, Los Angeles, CA.

Burton, R. A. (2008). *On being certain: Believing you are right even when you're wrong.* New York, NY: St. Martin's Press.

Cacioppo, J. T., & Patrick, W. (2008). *Loneliness: Human nature and the need for social connection.* New York, NY: Norton.

California Work Group. (1995). *Watching "Not in Our Town" together: A guide to promoting thoughtful viewing in the classroom.* Oakland, CA: California Working Group.

CBBC Newsround. (2008). *Hero boy saved friends from quake.* Retrieved from http://news.bbc.co.uk/go/pr/fr//cbbcnews/hi/newsid_7410000/newsid_7410800/7410881.stm.

Center for the Study of Social Policy. (2007, July). *Strengthening families: A guidebook for early childhood programs* (2nd ed., rev.). Washington, DC: Center for the Study of Social Policy. Retrieved from www.cssp.org

Center for the Study of Social Policy. (2009, October). *A look at strengthening families in the states.* Washington, DC: Center for the Study of Social Policy. Retrieved from www.cssp.org.

Center for the Study of Social Policy. (2011). *Mapping a course to child, family and community well-being: Annual report.* Washington, DC: Center for the Study of Social Policy. Retrieved from www.cssp.org

Chapman, D. P., Dube, S. R., & Anda, R. F. (2007). Adverse childhood events as risk factors for negative mental health outcomes. *Psychiatric Annals, 37,* 359–64.

Chess, S., & Thomas, A. (1987). *Know your child: An authoritative guide for today's parents.* New York, NY: Basic Books.

Chess, S., & Thomas, A. (1999). *Goodness of fit: Clinical applications for infancy through adult life.* Philadelphia, PA: Bruner/Mazel.

Cook, P. J., Gottfredson, D. C., & Na, C. (2009, March 9). *School crime control and prevention.* Retrieved from http://ssrn.com/abstract=1368292.

Deutschman, A. (2007). *Change or die. The three keys to change at work and in life.* New York, NY: Regan/Harper Collins.

Deutschman, A. (2005, May). Change or die. *Fast Company Magazine,* (94), 53.

Diamond, A., Barnett, W. S., Thomas, J., & Munro, S. (2007, November 30). Preschool program improves cognitive control. *Science, 318*(5855), 1387–88.

Dosier, R. (2002). *Why we hate: Understanding, curbing, and eliminating hate in ourselves and our world.* New York, NY: Contemporary Books.

Dowell, B. (2003, October 5). Secrets of the super successful . . . they're dyslexic. *Times Online.* Retrieved from http//:www.the-times.co.uk/tto/health/article1880462.ece.

Dube, S. R., Felitti, V. J., Dong, M., Giles, W. H., & Anda, R. F. (2003). The impact of adverse childhood experiences on health problems: Evidence from four birth cohorts dating back to 1900. *Preventive Medicine, 37,* 268–77.

Dweck, C. S. (2006). *Mindset: The new psychology of success.* New York, NY: Random House.

Eber, L. (2003). *The art and science of wraparound.* Presented at the Forum on Education, Indiana University, Bloomington, IN.

Eber, L. (2006, October). *School-wide systems of positive behavior interventions and supports (PBIS): Creating environments that promote success for students with emotional/behavioral challenges.* Presented at the 18th Annual CHADD International Conference, Chicago, IL.

Egeland, B., Bosquet, M., & Levy-Chung, A. (2002). Continuities and discontinuities in the intergenerational transmission of child maltreatment: Implications of breaking the cycle of abuse. In K. Browne, H. Hanks, & P. Stratton (Eds.), *Early prediction and prevention of child abuse. A handbook* (pp. 217–32). Chichester, UK: Wiley.

Erdley, C. A., Nangle, D. W., Newman, J. E., & Carpenter, E. M. (2001). Children's friendship experiences and psychological adjustment: Theory and research. *New Directions for Children and Adolescent Development, 2001*(91), 5-24.

Evelo, D., Sinclair, M., Hurley, C., Christenson, S., & Thurlow, M. (1996). *Keeping kids in school: Using check and connect for dropout prevention.* Minneapolis: University of Minnesota, College of Education and Human Development, Institute on Community Integration.

Felitti, V., Anda, R. F., Nordenberg, D., Williamson, D. F., Spitz, A. M., Edwards, V., . . . Marks, J. S. (1998). Relationship of childhood abuse and household dysfunction to many of the leading causes of death in adults: The Adverse Childhood Experiences Study. (1998). *American Journal of Preventive Medicine, 14*(4), 245–57.

Festinger, L. (1957). A *theory of cognitive dissonance.* Stanford, CA: Stanford University Press.

Figley, R. F. (1995). *Compassion fatigue.* New York, NY: Brunner/Mazel.

Fisher, J. (2000). In B. A. van der Kolk & F. Deidre (Producers), *Treating complex PTSD II: Stabilization techniques, therapeutic modalities* [video]. Nevada City, CA: Calvalcade Productions.

Forsyth, D. R., Kerr, N. A., Burnette, J. L., & Baumeister, R. F. (2007). Attempting to improve the academic performance of struggling college students by bolstering their self-esteem: An intervention that backfired. *Journal of Social and Clinical Psychology, 26,* 447–59.

Frankl, V. (1963). *Man's search for meaning: An introduction to logotherapy.* New York, NY: Washington Square.

Fredrickson, B. (2000, March 3). Cultivating positive emotions to optimize health and well-being. *Prevention and Treatment,* 0001a.

Fredrickson, B. L. (2001). The role of positive emotions in positive psychology. *American Psychologist, 56,* 218–26.

Fredrickson, B. L., & Losada, M. F. (2005). Positive affect and the complex dynamics of human flourishing. *American Psychologist, 60,* 678–86.

Gallagher, R., Abikoff, H. B., & Spira, E. G. (2014). *Organizational skills training for children with ADHD. An empirically supported treatment.* New York, NY: Guilford Press.

Gardner, H. (1993). *Multiple intelligences: The theory in practice.* New York, NY: Basic Books.

Gardner, H. (1999). *Intelligence reframed.* New York, NY: Basic Books.

Gerber, P. (2001). Employment of adults with learning disabilities and ADHD: Reasons for success and implications for resilience. *ADHD Report, 9*(4), 1–5.

Gerber, P. J., Ginsberg, R. J., & Reiff, H. B. (1990). *Identifying alterable patterns of employment success for highly successful adults with learning disabilities* (Final Report H133G80500). Washington, DC: National Institute on Disability Research and Rehabilitation, Department of Education.

Gladwell, M. (1997, February 24.). Crime and science. Damaged: Why do some people turn into violent criminals? New evidence suggests that it may all be in the brain. *New Yorker.* Retrieved from http://gladwell.com/damaged/.

Gladwell, M. (1999). *The tipping point: How little things can make a big difference.* Boston, MA: Little, Brown.

Gladwell, M. (2000, August 21 & 28). Performance studies. The art of failure: Why some people choke and others panic. *New Yorker.* Retrieved from http://www.newyorker.com/archive/2000/08/21/2000_08_21_084_TNY_LIBRY_000021523.

Glueck, S., & Glueck, E. (1968). *Delinquents and nondelinquents in perspective.* Cambridge, MA: Harvard University Press.

Goldstein, S. (2001, October). *Good days are when bad things don't happen. Rethinking the care and treatment of children with ADHD.* Presented at the 13th Annual CHADD International Conference, Anaheim, CA.

Golly, A. (2002). *Training for professional staff.* San Diego, CA: San Diego Center for Children.

Gottfredson, D. C., Wilson, D. B., & Najaka, S. S. (2002). School-based crime prevention. In L. W. Sherman, D. P. Farrington, B. C. Welsh, & D. L. MacKenzie (Eds.), *Evidence-based crime prevention* (pp. 56–164). London, UK: Routledge.

Gould, S. J. (2001, September 26). The time of gifts. *New York Times.* Retrieved from http://www.nytimes.com/2001/09/26/opinion/a-time-of-gifts.html

Gross, J. J. (1998). The emerging field of emotion regulation: An integrative review. *Review of General Psychology, 2,* 271–99.

Gross, J. J., & Thompson, R. A. (2009). Emotion regulation: Conceptual foundations. In J. J. Gross (Ed.), *Handbook of emotion regulation* (pp. 3–26). New York, NY: Guilford Press.

Hale, J. B., & Fiorello, C. A. (2004). *School neuropsychology: A practitioner's handbook.* New York, NY: Guilford Press.

Hart, B., & Risley, T. R. (1995). *Meaningful differences in everyday experiences of young American children.* Baltimore, MD: Brookes-Cole.

Hechtman, L. (1991). Resilience and vulnerability in long-term outcome of attention deficit/hyperactivity disorder. *Canadian Journal of Psychiatry, 36,* 415–21.

Higgins, G. O. (1994). *Resilient adults: Overcoming a cruel past.* San Francisco, CA: Jossey-Bass.

Hinshaw, S. P., & Stier, A. (2008). Stigma as related to mental disorders. *Annual Review of Clinical Psychology, 4,* 367–93.

Hinshaw, S. P. (2007). *The mark of shame. Stigma of mental illness and an agenda for change.* New York, NY: Oxford University Press.

Hopkins, G. (2000). An Education World e-interview with Carol Dweck: How can teachers develop students' motivation—and success? *Education World.* Retrieved from http://www.education-world.com/a-curr/curr197.shtml

Jones, C. (2002). *Practical strategies for helping children with ADHD at home and at school: What works.* Parent and Professional Ongoing Lecture Series, Learning Development Services, San Diego, CA.

Kamen, L., & Seligman, M. E. P. (1986). *Explanatory style predicts college grade point average.* Unpublished manuscript, University of Pennsylvania, Philadelphia.

Kassarjian, H., & Cohen, J. (1965). Cognitive dissonance and consumer behavior. *California Management Review, 8,* 55–64.

Katz, M. (1997). *On playing a poor hand well: Insights from the lives of those who have overcome childhood risks and adversities.* New York, NY: Norton.

Katz, M. (2002a, June). B.E.S.T.—Building effective schools together. *Attention Magazine,* 12–13.

Katz, M. (2002b, October). The jigsaw classroom. *Attention Magazine,* 12–13.

Katz, M. (2004a, October). The good behavior game. *Attention Magazine,* 10–11.

Katz, M. (2004b, December). An update on BEST behavior. *Attention Magazine,* 8–9.

Katz, M. (2006, April). The WhyTry program. *Attention Magazine,* 10.

Katz, M. (2007, August). Wraparound in schools. *Attention Magazine,* 6–7.

Katz, M. (2008a, April). Promoting six universal principles of behavior: An update on PeaceBuilders. *Attention Magazine,* 8–11.

Katz, M. (2008b, October). Brainology: Using lessons from basic neuroscience. *Attention Magazine,* 8–9.

Katz, M. (2009a, April). Tools of the mind. *Attention Magazine,* 7–8.

Katz, M. (2009b, June). Response to intervention (RtI) for behavior and academics. *Attention Magazine,* 6–7.

Katz, M. (2009c, October). Getting beyond the labels: Project Eye-to-Eye. *Attention Magazine,* 8–9.

Katz, M. (2009d, December). Bullying prevention and intervention. *Attention Magazine,* 6–8.

Katz, M. (2010a, February). The movement of imperfection. A celebration of human differences. *Attention Magazine*, 9–10.

Katz, M. (2010b, April). KIPP: An innovative network of college-preparatory charter schools. *Attention Magazine*, 8–9.

Katz, M. (2010c, December). The jigsaw classroom. *Attention Magazine*, 6–7.

Katz, M. (2011a, April). Seeing behavior challenges as lagging skills: An update on Collaborative Problem Solving. *Attention Magazine*, 6–7.

Katz, M. (2011b, June). Transforming compassion into action: The Heroic Imagination Project. *Attention Magazine*, 6–7.

Katz, M. (2011c, August). Learning to think socially: The ILAUGH model of social thinking. *Attention Magazine*, 6–7.

Katz, M. (2011d, December). Active minds: Changing the conversation about mental health. *Attention Magazine*, 6–7.

Katz, M. (2012a, August). Succeeding in the face of challenges. *Attention Magazine*, 7–8.

Katz, M. (2012b, October). The Zones of Regulation: A curriculum designed to foster self-regulation and emotional control. *Attention Magazine*, 7–8.

Katz, M. (2012c, December). Celebrating human differences. *Attention Magazine*, 7–8.

Katz, M. (2013a, February). LETS erase the stigma. *Attention Magazine*, 7–8.

Katz, M. (2013b, April). The Irvine Paraprofessional Program: A vision for the future. *Attention Magazine*, 7–8.

Katz, M. (2013c, June). The Specialisterne story. *Attention Magazine*, 32.

Katz, M. (2013d, December). Eye to eye. *Attention Magazine*, 6–7.

Katz, M. (2014a, April). "Me Want Cookie," "Me Can Wait": Sesame Street's vision for helping preschool-age children improve self-control and other executive functions. *Attention Magazine*, 6–7.

Katz, M. (2014b, Summer). Executive function: What does it mean? Why is it important? How can we help? *Special Edge*, 8–10.

Katz, M. (2014c, August). PAX Good Behavior game: An update. *Attention Magazine*, 6–7.

Katz, M. (2015a, June). Restorative practices. *Attention Magazine*, 4–5.

Katz, M. (2015b, August). Mindset works: Tools and resources for transforming "fixed mindsets" into "growth mindsets." *Attention Magazine*, 4–5.

Kellam, S. G. (1999, December). The influence of the first-grade classroom on the development of aggressive behavior. *Phi Delta Kappa Center for Evaluation, Development, and Research, 25*.

Kellam, S. G., & Chinnia, L. (2003, September 24). *Baltimore Whole Day First Grade Program: Testing effectiveness, sustainability, and a base for going to scale*. Washington, DC: National Research Council Committee on Research in Education Randomized Field Trials in Education: Implementation and Implications, Baltimore City Public School System and AIR's Center for Integrating Education & Prevention Research in Schools.

Kelling, G. L., & Coles, C. M. (1996). *Fixing broken windows*. New York, NY: Touchstone.

Keogh, B. (2003). *Temperament in the classroom: Understanding individual differences*. Baltimore, MD: Paul H. Brookes.

Kim, J., & Cicchetti, D. (2010). Longitudinal pathways linking child maltreatment, emotion regulation, peer relations, and psychopathology. *Journal of Child Psychology and Psychiatry, 51*, 706–16.

Kirk, J. (1992, September, October). Ivory tower meets the elementary school classroom: University and district combine efforts to serve children with ADD. *Special Edge*, 8–11.

Klingberg, T. (2009). *The overflowing brain: Information overload and the limits of working memory*. New York, NY: Oxford University Press.

Kotkin, R. (1999, October). *The Irvine Paraprofessional Model: Innovative programs serving the needs of children, youth, families and adults with ADHD*. Presented at the 11th Annual CHADD International Conference, Washington, DC.

Langan, P. A., & Levin, D. J. (2002). *Recidivism of prisoners released in 1994*. Washington, DC: Bureau of Justice Statistics.

Langer, E. J., & Chanowitz, B. (1988). Mindfulness/mindlessness: A new perspective for the study of disability. In H. E. Yuker (Ed.), *Attitudes toward persons with disabilities* (pp. 68–81). New York, NY: Springer.

Langer, E. (1989). *Mindfulness*. Cambridge, MA: Perseus Books.

Laub, J. H., & Sampson, R. J. (2006). *Shared beginnings, divergent lives:*

Delinquent boys to age 70. Cambridge, MA: Harvard University Press.

Lavie, N., Hirst, A., de Fockert, J. W., & Viding, E. (2004). Load theory of selective attention and cognitive control. *Journal of Experimental Psychology, 133,* 339–54. doi:10.1037/0096-3445.3.339

Lavoie, R. (2007). *The motivation breakthrough: 6 secrets to turning on the tuned-out child.* New York, NY: Touchstone.

Leahy, R. L., Tirch, D. D., & Napolitano, L. A. (2011). *Emotion regulation in psychotherapy.* New York, NY: Guilford Press.

Leahy, R. L. (2002). A model of emotional schemas. *Cognitive and Behavioral Practice, 9,* 177–90.

Leary, M. R., & Springer, C. A. (2001). Hurt feelings: The neglected emotion. In R. M. Kowalski (Ed.), *Behaving badly: Aversive behaviors in interpersonal relationships* (pp. 151–75). Washington, DC: American Psychological Association Press.

LeDoux, J. (1998). *The emotional brain: The mysterious underpinnings of emotional life.* New York, NY: Simon and Schuster.

Lee, J., Semple, R.J., Rosa, D., & Miller, L. (2008). Mindfulness-based cognitive therapy for children: Results of a pilot study. *Journal of Cognitive Psychotherapy: An International Quartely, 2*(1), 15-28.

Lehr, C. A., Johnson, D. R., Bremer, C. D., Cosio, A., & Thompson, M. (2004). *Essential tools: Increasing rates of school completion: Moving from policy and research to practice.* Minneapolis, MN: National Center on Secondary Education and Transition, University of Minnesota.

Lehrer, J. (2009, May 18). Don't! The secret of self-control. *New Yorker,* 26–32.

Lewis, D. O. (1998). *Guilty by reason of insanity.* New York, NY: Ivy Books.

Luthar, S. S., Cicchetti, D., & Becker, B. (2000). The construct of resilience: A critical evaluation and guidelines for future work. *Child Development, 71,* 543–62.

Maran, M. (2009, June). The activism cure. *Greater Good Magazine.* Retrieved from http://greatergood.berkeley.edu.article/item.the_activism_cure/.

Marsh, H. W., & Craven, R. G. (2002a, February). *The pivotal role of frames of reference in academic self-concept formulation: The big fish little pond effect.* Sydney, Australia: Self-Concept Enhancement and Learning Facilitation (SELF) Research Centre, University of Western Sydney.

Marsh, H. W., & Craven, R. G. (2002b, April 2). *Big fish little pond effect: New theory, research and application.* Presented at the annual meeting of the American Educational Research Association, New Orleans, LA.

Marshall, J. (1997, August 28). Best crime-fighting tactic: Host a neighborhood barbeque. *Christian Science Monitor.* Retrieved from http://www.csmonitor.com/1997/0828/082897.us.us.4.html

Masten, A. S. (2001). Ordinary magic: Resilience processes in development. *American Psychologist, 56,* 227–38.

Masten, A. S. (2014). *Ordinary magic: Resilience in development.* New York, NY: Guilford Press.

Masten, A. S., & Reed, M. J. (2005). Resilience in development. In C. R. Snyder & S. J. Lopez (Eds.), *Handbook of positive psychology* (pp. 74–88). New York, NY: Oxford University Press.

Mathews, J. (2009). *Work hard. Be nice.* Chapel Hill, NC: Algonquin Books.

McFarlane, A. C., & van der Kolk, B. A. (1996). Trauma and its challenge to society. In B. A. van der Kolk, A. C. McFarlane, & L. Weisaerth (Eds.), *Traumatic stress: The effects of overwhelming experience on mind, body, and society* (pp. 24–46). New York, NY: Guilford Press.

Mirsky, L. (2014, Summer). The power of the circle. *Educational Leadership,* 51–55.

Mischel, W., Ayduk, O., Berman, M., Casey, B. J., Gotlib, I., Jonides, J., . . . Shoda, Y. (2011). "Willpower" over the life span: Decomposing self-regulation. *Social Cognitive and Affective Neuroscience, 6,* 252–56.

Moffitt, T. E., Arseneault, L., Belsky, D., Dickson, N., Hancox, R. J., Harrington, H., . . . Caspi, A. (2011). A gradient of childhood self-control predicts health, wealth, and public safety. *Proceedings of the National Academy of Sciences, USA, 108,* 2693–98. doi:10.1073/pnas.1010076108.

Moffitt, T. E. (2012, July 3). *Children's self-control and the health and wealth of their nation: Tracking 1000 children from birth to maturity* [Transcript of public lecture at Gresham College]. Retrieved from http://www.gresham.ac.uk/lectures-and-events/childrens-self

-control-and-the-health-and-wealth-of-their-nation-tracking -1000.

Mooney, J., & Cole, D. (2000). *Learning outside the lines: Two Ivy League students with learning disabilities and ADHD give you the tools for academic success and educational revolution.* New York, NY: Touchstone.

Mooney, J. (2008). *The short bus: A journey beyond normal.* New York, NY: Holt.

Murrell, A.R., & Scherbarth, A.J. (2006). State of the research & literature address: ACT with children, adolescents and parents. *International Journal of Behavioral Consultation and Therapy, 2,* 531-543.

Myers, D. G. (2000). *Exploring social psychology* (2nd ed.). New York, NY: McGraw-Hill.

Ochberg, F. M. (2001). When helping hurts: Sustaining trauma workers. On *Gift from Within* [DVD]. Camden, ME.

Ochberg, F. M., Figley, C. R., Dyregroy, A., Wilson, J. P., & Panos, A. (2006). Preventing and treating compassion fatigue. On *Gift from Within* [DVD]. Camden, ME.

Office of Juvenile Justice and Delinquency Prevention. (1995). *Juvenile offenders and victims: A national report.* Pittsburgh, PA: National Center for Juvenile Justice.

Overmier, J. B., & Seligman, M. E. P. (1967). Effects of inescapable shock upon subsequent escape and avoidance learning. *Journal of Comparative and Physiological Psychology, 63,* 23–33.

Perepletchikova, F., Axelrod, S. R., Kaufman, J., Rounsaville, B. J., Douglas-Palumberi, H., & Miller, A. L. (2011). Adapting dialectical behaviour therapy for children: Towards a new research agenda for paediatric suicidal and non-suicidal self-injurious behaviours. *Child and Adolescent Mental Health, 16*(2), 116–21.

Perry, B. (2002). *Understanding psychological trauma* [video series]. Crystal Lake, IL: Magna Systems [distr.].

Pescosolido, B. (2010, February). *The stigma of mental illness: Data & directions from a decade of research & theory.* Keynote address, Annual Conference on Improving Services for Children and Families, San Diego, CA.

Post, S. G., & Neimark, J. (2007). *Why good things happen to good people: How to live a longer, healthier life by the simple act of giving.* New York, NY: Broadway Books.

Prochaska, J. O., Norcross, J. C., & DiClemente, C. C. (2002). *Changing for good:* New York, NY: William Morrow.

Quartz, S. R., & Sejnowski, T. J. (2002). *Liars, lovers, and heroes: What the new brain science reveals about how we become who we are.* New York, NY: HarperCollins.

Rachman, S. (1979). The concept of required helpfulness. *Behavior Research and Therapy, 17,* 1–6.

Rappucci, N. D., Britner, A., & Woolard, J. L. (1997). *Preventing child abuse and neglect through parent education.* Baltimore, MD: Paul H. Brookes.

Rauch, S. L., van der Kolk, B. A., Fisler, R. E., Alpert, N. M., Orr, S.P., Savage, C. R., . . . Pittman, R. K. (1996). A symptom provocation study of posttraumatic stress disorder using positron emission tomography and script-driven imagery. *Archives of General Psychiatry, 53,* 380–87.

Rosenthal, R. (2002, October 18). Experimenter and clinician effects in scientific inquiry and clinical practice. *Prevention and Treatment, 5,* 38.

Rosenthal, R., & Jacobson, L. (1992). *Pygmalion in the classroom: Teacher expectation and pupils' intellectual development.* Bethel, CT: Crown House.

Ross, L., & Nisbett, R. E. (1991). *The person and the situation: Perspectives of social psychology.* New York, NY: McGraw-Hill.

Rotz, R. & Wright, S. D. (2005). *Fidget to focus: Outwit your boredom: Sensory strategies for living with ADD.* New York, NY: iUniverse.

Rutter, M. (1979a). *Fifteen thousand hours: Secondary schools and their effects on children.* Cambridge, MA: Harvard University Press.

Rutter, M. (1979b). Protective factors in children's response to stress and disadvantage. In M. W. Kent & J. E. Rolf (Eds.), *Primary prevention of psychopathology* (vol. 3, pp. 49–74). Hanover, NH: University Press of New England.

Rutter, M. (1990). Psychosocial resilience and protective mechanisms. In J. Rolf, A. S. Masten, D. Chicchetti, K. H. Nuechterlein, & S. Weintraub (Eds.), *Risk and protective factors in the development of psychopathology* (pp. 181–214). New York, NY: Cambridge University Press.

Sapolsky, R. M. (1998). *Why zebras don't get ulcers: An updated guide to stress, stress-related diseases, and coping.* New York, NY: Freeman.

Seligman, M. E. P. (1992). *Helplessness: On development, depression and death.* New York, NY: Freeman.

Seligman, M. E. P. (1998a). *Learned optimism.* New York, NY: Pocket Books.

Seligman, M. E. P. (1998b, September 3). *Depression and violence.* Presentation by the American Psychological Association National Press Club, Morning Newsmaker, 9:00 AM, Washington, DC. Retrieved from http://www.nonopp.com/ar/Psicolo gia/00/epidemic_depression.htm.

Seligman, M. E. P. (2002). *Authentic happiness.* New York, NY: Free Press.

Seligman, M. E. P. (2011). *Flourish: A visionary new understanding of happiness and well-being.* New York, NY: Free Press.

Seligman, M. E. P., & Maier, S. F. (1967). Failure to escape traumatic shock. *Journal of Experimental Psychology, 74,* 1–9.

Seligman, M. E. P., & Schulman, P. (1986). Explanatory style as a predictor of performance as a life insurance agent. *Journal of Personality and Social Psychology, 50,* 832–38.

Sesame Street Workshop. (2013). *Cookie's crumby pictures* [series featured segment]. Retrieved from http://www.sesameworkshop .org/season44/about-the-show/cookies-crumby-pictures/.

Shaywitz, S. E., Shaywitz, B. A., Pugh, K. R., Fulbright, R. K., Constable, R. T., Mencl, W. E., . . . Gore, J. C. (1998). Functional disruption in the organization of the brain for reading in dyslexia. *Proceedings of the National Academy of Sciences of the United States of America, USA, 95,* 2636–41.

Shaywitz, S. E., Fletcher, J. M., Holahan, J. M., Schneider, A. E., Marchione, K. E., Stuebing, K. K., . . . Shaywitz, B. A. (1999). Persistence of dyslexia: The Connecticut longitudinal study at adolescence. *Pediatrics, 104,* 1351–59.

Shearer, B. (2004). Multiple intelligences theory after 20 years. *Teachers College Record, 106,* 2–16. Retrieved from http://www .tcrecord.org.

Siegel, D. (1999). *The developing mind: Toward a neurobiology of interpersonal experience.* New York, NY: Guilford Press.

Simmons, R. (2002). *Odd girl out: The hidden culture of aggression in girls.* New York, NY: Harcourt.

Sinclair, M. F., Christenson, S. L., Evelo, D. L., & Hurley, M. M.

(1998). Dropout prevention for youth with disabilities: Efficacy of a sustained school engagement procedure. *Exceptional Children, 65,* 7–21.

Southham-Genow, M. A. (2013). *Emotion regulation in children and adolescents.* New York, NY: Guilford Press.

Sparrow, B., Liu, J., & Wegner, D. M. (2011). Google effects on memory: Cognitive consequences of having information at our fingertips. *Science, 333,* 776–78.

Spekman, N. J., Goldberg, R. J., & Herman, K .L. (1992). Learning disabled children grown up: A search for factors related to success in the young adult years. *Learning Disabilities Research and Practice, 7,* 161–70.

Sprague, J., Cook, C. R., Browning-Wright, D., & Sadler, S. (2008). *RtI and behavior: A guide to integrating behavioral and academic supports.* Horsham, PA: LRP Publications.

Sprague, J., & Golly, A. (2004). *Best behavior: Building positive behavior supports in school.* Longmont, CO: Sopris West Educational Services.

Sternberg, R. J. (1997). The concept of intelligence and its role in lifelong learning and success. *American Psychologist, 52,* 1030–37.

Sternberg, R. J. (2003). *Wisdom, intelligence and creativity synthesized.* New York, NY: Cambridge University Press.

Swann, W. B., Jr. (1996). *Self-traps: The illusive quest for higher self-esteem.* New York, NY: Freeman.

Tavris, C., & Aronson, E. (2007). *Mistakes were made but not by me.* Orlando, FL: Harcourt.

Tedeschi, R. G., & Calhoun, A. G. (2004a). Posttraumatic growth: Conceptual foundations and empirical evidence. *Psychological Inquiry, 15*(1), 1–18.

Tedeschi, R. G., & Calhoun, A. G. (2004b). Posttraumatic growth: New considerations. *Psychological Inquiry, 15*(1), 93–102.

Tedeschi, R. G., & Calhoun, A. G. (2012). *Posttraumatic growth research group.* University of North Carolina, Charlotte, NC. Retrieved from PosttraumaticGrowth@uncc.edu

Terr, L. C. (2003). "Wild child": How three principles of healing organized 12 years of psychotherapy. *Journal of the American Academy of Child and Adolescent Psychiatry, 42,* 1401–9.

Terr, L. C. (2009). Using context to treat traumatized children. In

R. A. King, S. Abrams, A. S. Dowling, & P. M. Brinich (Eds.), *The psychoanalytic study of the child* (pp. 275–97). New Haven, CT: Yale University Press.

Terr, L. C. (2013, February 8). *Three principles of trauma intervention and treatment.* Presentation at the Sacramento-Area Regional Training on Early Childhood Trauma Prevention, Intervention and Treatment, Roseville, CA.

U.S. Department of Health and Human Services. (1999). Mental health: *A report of the Surgeon General.* Rockville, MD: Author.

Vaillant, G. E., & Davis, T. J. (2000). Social/emotional intelligence and midlife resilience in schoolboys with low tested intelligence. *American Journal of Orthopsychology, 70,* 215–22.

Van der Kolk, B. A. (2000, February 13). *The black hole of trauma: Diagnosis and treatment of complex PTSD.* Presented at Los Angeles Center for Traumatic Stress and Sudden Bereavement. Los Angeles, CA.

Van der Kolk, B. A. (2001, January 20). *The body keeps the score: Memory and the evolving psychobiology of posttraumatic stress.* Presented at Los Angeles Center for Traumatic Stress and Sudden Bereavement. Los Angeles, CA.

Van der Kolk, B. A. (2002, June). *Trauma, violence and the physical experience of oneself.* Presented at the Safe Schools for the 21st Century Conference, Monterey, CA.

Van der Kolk, B. A. (2006). Clinical implications of neuroscience research in PTSD. *Annals of the New York Academy of Sciences, 30,* 1–17.

Van der Kolk, B. A., & Pynoos, R. S. (2009). *Proposal to include a developmental trauma disorder diagnosis for children and adolescents in DSM-V.* Retrieved from http://www.traumacenter.org/announcements/DTD_NCTSN_official_submission_to_DSM_V_Final_Version.pdf.

Vogel, E. K., McCollough, A. W., & Machizawa, M. G. (2005). Neural measures reveal individual differences in controlling access to working memory. *Nature, 438,* 500-503.

Walker, H. M. (2001). *Training for professional staff.* San Diego, CA: San Diego Center for Children.

Wasserman, G. A., Keenan, K., Tremblay, R. E., Coie, J. D., Herrenkohl, T. I., Loeber, R., & Petechuk, D. (2003, April). *Risk and protective factors of child delinquency.* Rockville, MD: Child Delinquency Bulletin Series, Office of Juvenile Justice and Delinquency Prevention.

Wegner, D. M., Erber, R., & Raymond, P. (1991). Transactive memory in close relationships. *Journal of Personality and Social Psychology, 61,* 923–29.

Werner, E. (1993, February). *A longitudinal perspective on risk for learning disabilities.* Presentation at the international conference of the Learning Disability Association of America, San Francisco, CA.

Werner, E. (2005, Summer). Resilience and recovery: Findings from the Kauai Longitudinal Study. *Focal Point: Portland Research and Training Center on Family Support and Children's Mental Health, 19*(1), 11–14.

Werner, E., & Smith, R. (1992). *Overcoming the odds: High risk children from birth to adulthood.* Ithaca, NY: Cornell University Press.

Werner, E., & Smith, R. (2001). *Journeys from childhood to midlife: Risk, resilience, and recovery.* Ithaca, NY: Cornell University Press.

Werner, K., & Gross, J. J. (2009). Emotion regulation and psychopathology. In A. M. Kring & D. M. Sloan (Eds.), *Emotional regulation and psychopathology: A transdiagnostic approach* (pp. 13–37). New York, NY: Guilford Press.

Wright, M. O., Masten, A. S., & Narayan, A. J. (2013). Resilience processes in development: Four waves of research on positive adaptation in the context of adversity. In S. Goldstein & R. B. Brooks (Eds.) *Handbook of resilience in children* (2nd ed., pp. 15–37). New York, NY: Springer.

Wrzesniewski, A., McCauley, C. R., Rozin, P., & Schwartz, B. (1997). Jobs, careers, and callings: People's relations to their work. *Journal of Research in Personality, 31,* 21–33.

Zimbardo, P. G. (2011). *The heroic imagination project.* Retrieved from http://www.Heroicimagination.org.

Zimrin, H. (1986). A profile of survival. *Child Abuse and Neglect, 10,* 339–49.

Zylowska, L. (2012). *The mindfulness prescription for adult ADHD: An 8-step program for strengthening attention, managing emotions, and achieving your goals.* Boston, MA: Trumpeter Books.

INDEX

Note: Italicized page locators indicate figures; tables are noted with *t*.

Index

African American children in inner-city, traumatic stress exposure, behavior problems, and, 92
agents of change. *see* change; relate, repeat, reframe approach
aggressive students, social climate of classroom and, 144
alcoholism, adverse childhood experiences and risk for, 39
animals, learned helplessness in, 20–21
antisocial personality disorder, 144–45
anxiety attacks, successful school-based treatment for, 142
appraisal, in emotional response, 181
Aronson, E., 138, 139, 224
artists, school or class, 136
Asperger's syndrome, 164
assessments
    personal strengths and talents, 160–62
    trauma-informed, 162–63
assistant resource specialists, 136
attachments, fostering, protective processes and, 31
attention
    in emotional response, 181
    mindful deployment of, 186–87
    working memory and strategic allocation of, 186
attention deficit hyperactivity disorder (ADHD), xxi, 180, 195, 231
    emotional self-regulation problems and, 181
    executive function challenges and, 13–14, 25
    genetic component in, 71
    sources of resilience for youth with, 85
    Specialisterne employees with, 139
    understanding, then and now, 69–72
attention deployment, 181, 182, 184–87, 193, 197
auditory dyslexia, 6–7
autism, high-functioning, Specialisterne and, 139
autism spectrum, 168–69

background knowledge, reading comprehension and, 94
Barkley, R., 70, 71, 144, 191
Baumeister, R., 60, 112, 190, 227, 228

Beardslee, W., 85
beating the odds
    thanks to those who changed the odds, 77–78, 100–101, 108–9, 171–73
    universal needs and, 129
    see also protective processes; safety nets
behavior
    cognitive dissonance and, 123
    fundamental attribution error and, 121–22
behavioral challenges, special jobs for students with, 137–38
behavioral change, misperceptions related to, 199–201. *see also* change; health outcomes later in life
behavioral profiles, executive function challenges and, 10–16. *see also* paradoxically uneven learning and behavior profiles
behavioral self-control, preschool children and, 194. *see also* self-control
behavioral vaccines, PAX Good Behavior Game and, 146–47
Beijing Olympics (2008), school hall monitor honored at, 137
beliefs, cognitive dissonance and, 123
BEST Behavior, 150
Bill (portrait of resilience--in context), xx, 112–15, 213
    grandson's transformed mind-set, 174–75
    IQ score and mid-life success, 114
    manual dexterity skills, 115
    struggles in school, 113, 211
    turning points, 113
bipolar disorder, 164
Boedrova, E., 194, 195
boredom, executive function challenges and, 12
boring tasks, successful completion of, 56–57, 97
Brainology, 158–59, 168
Branson, R., 8
Broca's area, speechless terror and, 189
"broken windows" theory, zero tolerance policies and, 212
Brooks, R., 138
Brown, T., 12

Index

children
   teacher perceptions and learning rate
      of, 41–42
   temperament categories in, 148
   traumatized, failure to meet PTSD
      diagnostic criteria and, 92
Children's Mental Health Ontario
      (CMHO), 164, 165
Chinese Olympic Team, 137
circles, restorative practices, 153
class artist, 136
classrooms
   changing social climate of, 144–49
   jigsaw, 138–39, 184
closeness to key people, traumatic life
      events and, 79, 101, 174–76
CMHO. *see* Children's Mental Health
      Ontario (CMHO)
cognitive change or appraisal, 181, 182,
      188–89, 193, 197
cognitive dissonance
   in action, 123–25
   erroneous perceptions and, 122–23,
      130
   relationship dynamics and, 224–25
   working in reverse, 225
cognitive tasks, social disconnection
      and, 111–12
Collaborative and Proactive Solutions
      (CPS), 163, 166–67, 184, 188
college success, explanatory style and,
      32–33
communications specialist, school job
      as, 136
compassion, 99, 102, 154
compassion fatigue
   erroneous perceptions and, 81
   impact of, 80–81
computer specialist, school job as,
      136
Concentration Game, 147
context deficit disorder, 120, 121–22,
      130
context-sensitive ways
   human strength and, 46, 47, 86
   resilience and, 58
contextual blind spots, 127
   best intentions overridden with,
      229
   closest relationships and, 224
   overcoming, 116, 117, 120, 129

contextual influences, 122, 196, 223,
      232
   aggressive first-graders and, 144
   bundling practices and, 135
   cascading effect of, 65–66
   context-sensitive ways and, 51
   as contextually expressed protective
      processes, 49, 51–52
   Deutschman's agents of change cor-
      responded with, 202–4, 204t, 207,
      208
   five new perceptions and, 133–34,
      178
   greater awareness of, 129
   growth mind-set and, 52
   healthy lifestyle and, 206–7
   human resilience and, 127
   mastery and, 52
   odds changed by, 117
   prevention of later health-related
      problems and, 132
   prolonged traumatic stress and, 93
   protective processes and, 30, 51, 86,
      133
   resilience and, 24, 26, 46
   that can change odds, levels of, 134,
      178
   transportability of, to child's school
      day, 52, 116
   types of, 49
   see also emotional self-regulation
      skills; life experiences--in context;
      relationships--in context; school
      failure, preventing; social context
contextual thinking, meaning attached
      to challenges through, 47, 86
Cookie Monster, behavior changes in,
      193–94
coronary bypass patients, Deutschman's
      agents of change study, 202–4,
      204t, 207, 208
CPS. *see* Collaborative and Proactive
      Solutions (CPS)
crime prevention, "broken windows"
      theory of, 212
criminal activity, neurological vulner-
      ability co-occurring with severe
      abuse and, 40
criminal behavior, turning points and,
      83. *see also* youth crime; youth
      violence

ABOUT THE AUTHOR

Mark Katz, PhD, is a clinical and consulting psychologist and the author of *On Playing a Poor Hand Well: Insights from the Lives of Those Who Have Overcome Childhood Risks and Adversities*. For over 30 years, he has been the Director of Learning Development Services, an educational, psychological, and neuropsychological center in San Diego, California. He is a recipient of the Rosenberry Award, a national award given yearly by Children's Hospital in Denver, Colorado, in recognition of an individual's contribution to the field of behavioral science, and also a recipient of the CHADD (Children and Adults With Attention Deficit Disorder) Hall of Fame Award. Katz is a contributing editor for *Attention Magazine*, and also writes the magazine's "Promising Practices" column. He has been a keynote presenter at a number of national conferences, and has conducted numerous trainings for schools, health care organizations, and community groups working to improve educational and mental health systems of care. He has been interviewed by *O, The Oprah Magazine*, *TIME*, *Men's Health*, CNN, and others in the media on topics pertaining to resilience and overcoming adversity.